Counseling the Aging

An Integrative Approach

Edmund A. Sherman

THE FREE PRESS
A Division of Macmillan Publishing Co., Inc.
NEW YORK

Collier Macmillan Publishers
LONDON

Copyright © 1981 by The Free Press
A Division of Macmillan Publishing Co., Inc.

The Free Press
A Division of Macmillan Publishing Co., Inc.
866 Third Avenue, New York, N.Y. 10022

Collier Macmillan Canada, Ltd.

Library of Congress Catalog Card Number: 81-66329

Printed in the United States of America

printing number
1   2   3   4   5   6   7   8   9   10

Library of Congress Cataloging in Publication Data

Sherman, Edmund A.
   Counseling the aging.

   1. Aged--Counseling of--United States.   2. Aged--Psy-
chology.   I. Title.   [DNLM: 1. Counseling--In old age.
2. Mental disorders--In old age.   WT 150 S553c]
HV1461.S52   362.6'6   81-66329
ISBN 0-02-928810-X   AACR2

Contents

Contents

Preface and Acknowledgments

A GREAT DEAL has been written of late about the plight of the elderly in our youth-oriented society. There have been telling and poignant portrayals of their circumstances in America (for example, Butler, 1975b) and there has been exhaustive documentation of the fact that indifference toward and even discrimination against the old are by no means restricted to America or to Western society (de Beauvoir, 1972). There has also been concern about the elderly as particular targets of exploitation and crime. To have to contend with the fear of crime along with the physical, economic, and social losses that go with aging is indeed a heavy burden to bear.

The physical and economic problems of older persons are well-known and well-documented. They will not be dealt with extensively in this book, but they will be specifically and systematically taken into account in the counseling model proposed here. This book is geared much more to dealing with problems such as depression, anxiety, and lowered self-esteem, problems which so often accompany the physical, material, and social losses of aging. The extent of these emotional conditions among our older citizens is expressed in the grim fact that the suicide rate for those 65 and older is more than three times that for the general population (Pfeiffer, 1977). Yet, despite the fact that they constitute over 11 percent of the population, only 2 or 3 percent of all persons seen at community mental health centers are over age 65 (Butler, 1975b). There is good evidence that the attitudes of mental health professionals and the manifestation of these attitudes in practice settings and programs are largely responsible for the underuse of mental health services by the aged (Lowy, 1979). Essentially, professionals have tended toward pessimism about the capacity for change in older persons. One major purpose of this book is to propose a way of providing mental health counseling that is based on a more optimistic—and still realistic—perspective.

The counseling approach outlined in this book is an outgrowth of my own experience as a practicing counselor working directly with older persons in individual and group treatment and also on my experience as a researcher and teacher in the field of social gerontology. The treatment theory—the principles and techniques involved in this approach—then, is derived essentially from the empirical findings of gerontological research and practice. It is a developmental approach in the sense that it looks on old age as a stage in its own right, with its own dynamics, tasks, problems, and perspectives, and not as an afterthought or appendage in the life cycle.

Unfortunately, the personality and treatment theories that have been applied in much work with the elderly have not been derived from any significant or systematic study of human development in the later years of adulthood. Consequently, there is a tendency to superimpose upon the later years conceptions based upon pre-adult development. Too frequently, this means that the older person is viewed as an individual who has regressed psychologically and is caught up in reawakened infantile, pregenital conflicts.

Even where such assumptions are not made, most treatment approaches are based implicitly or explicitly on theories of personality that are concerned with and derived from younger populations and do not generally address themselves to the particular circumstances, problems, and personality dynamics of the aged. Some of their concepts and techniques might prove to be applicable and beneficial in working with the elderly, but many are not. In contrast to these approaches, the one proposed here integrates a number of salient findings from gerontological research into its treatment methodology, hence the use of the term "integrative" to describe it. It is the intent of this book, with its developmental approach, to provide the knowledge and methods to deal with emotional problems encountered in practically all counseling work with the aged in settings as diverse as senior citizen centers, local offices for aging, churches and synagogues, nursing homes, hospitals, family agencies, and community mental health centers. The content of the book should be helpful to the range of students and professional practitioners who provide or intend to provide counseling services to the elderly in these various settings: social workers, geriatric and psychiatric nurses, physicians, psychologists, psychiatrists, and others.

It should be noted that the methods proposed here may not be applicable for counseling aging persons with severe and chronic organic brain disorder and perhaps some individuals with severe physical impairments. These would tend to be among the institutionalized elderly, but they comprise only a small portion of the total aged population. Therefore, it is safe to say that the subject matter of this book applies to the vast majority of adults over 60 in our society.

Plan of the Book

Chapter 1 begins with a description of the integrative approach to counseling and then goes on to deal with the meaning of the concepts of "aging" and "old." Particular attention is given to the useful distinction between the young-old and old-old and how the integrative approach addresses this. The epigenetic model of human development proposed by Erikson (1963) is then delineated with special emphasis on the developmental tasks of late adulthood. This model is then illustrated by two cases of older men who received counseling services under similar circumstances; one represents a process of unsuccessful aging eventuating in an emotional state of despair and the other represents a process of successful resolution of the tasks of aging and a state of ego integrity rather than despair. These cases also serve to illustrate some of the counseling issues which will be addressed by the integrative model of practice as it is delineated in later chapters. Finally, a model for assessing social breakdown in older persons is applied to the two case illustrations in conjunction with the epigenetic model outlined earlier in the chapter.

Chapter 2 provides background information from gerontological theory and research that should help to explain the differences in morale and life views among aged persons who encounter essentially the same life crises and traumas. The various personality and social factors that enter into different lifestyles and patterns of aging are also explored to identify the elements that appear to be related to successful aging and the achievement of ego integrity. The central importance of the life review process in resolving the issue of integrity versus despair is also highlighted in this chapter.

Chapter 3 outlines the requirements of an integrative approach to counseling the elderly and then incorporates a number of the insights gained from the theoretical and empirical work reviewed in Chapter 2 into the emerging practice model. The importance of client perception—the unique personal meaning of events to individual clients—is developed here as a central element in the integrative approach. Because of the centrality of client perception, cognitive techniques of counseling are seen as particularly appropriate for integrative practice, and the contribution of these techniques is delineated in this chapter. The contribution of other treatment approaches is then described. The social reconstruction syndrome from gerontological theory is presented in terms of its contribution to the development of the integrative model of practice. Then the components of the integrative model are presented together with assessment instruments and procedures for each component. The chapter ends with a summary of the principles of integrative practice.

Chapter 4 outlines the treatment continuum of the integrative model and then goes on to describe the differential objectives and methods of the model based on variations in types of problems and time factors. Referral activities and supportive approaches are seen as crucial for short-term practice and they are presented first. The family as a source of both problems and support is presented next, followed by consideration of the use of self-help and other informal resources. Case illustrations of referral, supportive, family, and self-help activities are provided, and the last part of the chapter outlines and illustrates a number of techniques of integrative practice. The chapter ends with a discussion of integrative group methods.

Chapter 5 is devoted entirely to an illustration of the application of integrative principles, objectives, and methods to a specific group from its beginnings to the outcome of treatment.

Chapter 6 presents material on integrative practice of a more extended nature. After some consideration of the different goals, objectives, and treatment emphases in extended as opposed to short-term counseling, the chapter provides two comprehensive case illustrations that demonstrate these differences.

The seventh and final chapter draws conclusions from gerontological theory and research, as well as from practice applications of the integrative model, and offers proposals for further development of the model. Finally, there is an exploration of the possible implications of the principles and concepts underlying the integrative approach to counseling for the subject of aging and the problems of aging in general.

I have been aided greatly by a number of individuals and organizations in the course of completing this work. My greatest debt is to the clients I have worked with as a counselor in various senior centers and in the Albany Center for Psychotherapy. Without them I would not have been able to verify personally and practically the value and applicability of integrative practice principles and procedures.

Students I have taught in social gerontology and social work practice classes, as well as those who have assisted me in gerontological research projects, have been particularly helpful with their challenging observations and questions, but none has been more helpful than Dorothy Dow Crane, an exceptional research assistant who has gone on to become an accomplished practitioner.

A number of my colleagues in the School of Social Welfare of the State University of New York at Albany have also been helpful. Special thanks go to Dr. Max Siporin who not only encouraged me to undertake and complete the book but provided constructive suggestions and help at critical junctures along the way.

The Institute of Gerontology at SUNY, Albany, has been the source of continuous support and encouragement of my gerontological interests and activities. Dr. Susan R. Sherman and Evelyn S. Newman, director and associate directors respectively of the Institute, deserve particular mention in this regard.

Gladys Topkis, senior editor at The Free Press, contributed greatly to the completion of this book. Her apt suggestions redirecting me toward the central purposes of the book helped to give it cohesion. My thanks also go to Ann Patterson, not only for her care and efficiency in the typing of the manuscript, but for her unfailing responsiveness to the time pressures involved.

Finally, special gratitude to my family for their patience and forbearance in the face of the time and effort I put into the book. The support and encouragement of my wife, Arleen, were crucial to its completion.

CHAPTER ONE

Integrative Counseling and the Problems of Aging

THE CENTRAL PURPOSE of this book is to provide students and practitioners in various helping disciplines with the principles, techniques, and intervention tools to deal with the recurrent problems encountered by aging persons in our society. A model of social breakdown in older persons which has wide practical application and permits an understanding of the onset and development of these problems is presented later in this chapter. This model, in conjunction with a developmental model based on Erikson's (1963) epigenetic paradigm, will serve as a framework for assessment of aging clients and their problems. This framework is not based upon the usual type of psychiatric diagnostic system or nosology. Although such a medical model has some value for conceptualizing some common psychiatric problems of the aging, such as brain disorders that involve structural damage or physiological disturbances to the brain, it is inadequate for conceptualizing the psychological problems emanating from the many internal and external stresses and strains experienced by older persons (Zarit, 1980). The integrative approach to assessment attempts, rather, to take into account the unique configuration of person, problem, and situation in each case so as to permit treatment planning as well as problem specification on an individual basis.

Further, the book provides a framework for the development of differential treatment objectives and approaches based upon the types and dimensions of the identified problem and the time factors involved in each case situation.

Specific approaches for short-term counseling, characterized by supportive techniques and referral activities, are offered along with case illustrations. Specific approaches for long-term or extended counseling using more cognitive, insight-oriented techniques are also described and illustrated with case materials. The use of these approaches in work with groups is also described and illustrated in a separate chapter on that subject. Thus the book presents a set of basic guidelines for assessment and treatment planning as well as a repertoire of techniques for application in short-term and long-term counseling in both individual and group situations.

What Is Integrative Counseling?

Integrative counseling can be defined as an eclectic counseling approach designed specifically for work with older adults. It includes a method of assessment, a differential treatment model based on type of problem and time factors, and a repertoire of techniques consistent with its treatment model. It is eclectic in that it does not draw entirely upon any one theory of personality or of aging, and its techniques are not derived from any one treatment theory. The central focus of the approach is to identify, use, and enhance the _normal_ development of personality functioning in the later years of adulthood as the basis for counseling older persons. The underlying theme of the approach is that certain capacities and strengths are normally developed in the course of aging which enable older persons to overcome the demoralization attendant upon the losses and problems of aging. When these capacities have not become operative because of circumstances or events, they should be uncovered, strengthened, and developed in the counseling process. Therefore, the integrative approach draws most heavily upon those theories of personality, aging, and treatment that are consistent with identified strengths and capacities of aging, hence the eclectic nature of the approach and its essential optimism. It is not optimistic in the naïve sense of denying the inevitability of the real losses and traumas of aging, but it is optimistic about the innate capacity of older persons to prevent or overcome the demoralization that results from these losses and traumas.

The integrative approach begins with the process of problem identification and specification for the purposes of treatment planning; in short, the process of assessment. The amount of background information to be obtained for assessment purposes will depend very much on the nature of the problem, the person, and the situation. Short-term counseling does not generally require an exhaustive history-taking. By definition, short-term integrative counseling consists of six to twenty-five sessions, but will most often involve only six to fifteen sessions within a few weeks. In these instances, the problem is usually quite obvious and quite pressing, such as need for medical, housing, or financial assistance in crisis situations, so there is neither time nor need to engage in a lengthy information-gathering process. It is clear, on the other hand, that in longer-term cases or in extended counseling, which might run from six months to one or two years or more, extensive background information will be required to deal with more chronic or larger, unresolved issues from the past and present. In such cases, the ongoing assessment will incorporate information according to the social breakdown/developmental framework to be presented later in this chapter. Although that framework will be presented to illustrate the salient problems, issues, and tasks of aging, it also serves as a guide to understanding, to assessment, of the older person and his or her problem in a developmental context. These uses will be illustrated by its application to the cases of the two men presented later in the chapter. Because of these very great variations in need for background information in the assessment process, no exhaustive, rigid outline or form for taking a history or anamnesis will be presented here. The breakdown and developmental models and the case illustrations to be presented will sensitize the reader to the kinds and extent of information required in varying problem, person, and time situations.

However, some data-gathering instruments will be presented here which can serve as assessment or diagnostic tools as well as devices for evaluation of extent of change in older clients in the course of counseling. These instruments come largely from the gerontological research literature and some were developed more specifically for integrative counseling purposes. Whether or not the reader chooses to use any of these instruments, they will provide very clear, operational definitions of the concepts that are central to assessment and treatment in integrative counseling, concepts such as self-esteem, locus of control, and life satisfaction. Consequently, when these concepts or terms are applied in case illustrations in the book or in the reader's own practice, their meanings will be much less ambiguous, more explicit, and more related to established gerontological concepts and measures, thereby reinforcing the relevance of the treatment approach to the field from which it was derived and to which it is being applied.

The integrative model of practice also includes a treatment continuum or guide for the selection of appropriate, differential goals and objectives for intervention and counseling in different types of identified problem situations. This model will be spelled out in much more detail in Chapter 4, but it will be described briefly at this point to attune the reader to the range and dimensions of its application. First of all, the integrative model recognizes the overwhelming importance of material needs in the lives of so many older persons. In fact, it is recognized that most of the problem situations that bring older persons to our attention involve needs for material services in the areas of health, housing, and physical and financial security. Furthermore, these material needs have to be handled first because they generally come to our attention in crisis or near-crisis situations, and one is not likely to deal effectively with the client's emotional problems without first meeting these critical and stressful material needs either directly or by referral to another agency. The counseling that goes with the material service has to be handled in a particular way. That is, the counselor has to provide emotional support and encouragement, as well as practical guidance in obtaining and using the hard services, without incurring undue dependency in helping the older client through the crisis.

Consequently, the integrative model's treatment continuum begins with a recognition of the need to provide hard services, particularly in the initial phases of counseling or in very short-term, crisis-oriented cases. The first phase of the four-phase continuum calls for the provision of maintenance conditions and services to meet the immediate situation or crisis. The objectives of this phase are to: (1) reduce the stress due to the situational crisis or problem; (2) remove the impediments to re-establishing the personal and situational equilibrium of the client; and (3) reduce dependence of the client on emergency supports or see to it that the client's physical and financial needs are met or that needed services are provided on an ongoing rather than an emergency basis. Methods for meeting these objectives, such as how to make effective referrals and the use of service inventories, are spelled out here along with the appropriate counseling approach, largely supportive and directive, in this phase of treatment.

The second phase calls for the provision of support and coping strategies in order to stabilize the self-esteem, sustain the morale, and sustain the coping efforts of the clients. The counseling objectives of this phase tend to be more psychological or personal than material or situational in nature. However, they are still short-term and geared toward the immediate or crisis situation as were the services of the first phase. The counseling approaches used in this second phase are still quite supportive and geared toward stabilizing the person's psychosocial functioning rather than toward attempting to bring about any significant changes in behavioral, emotional, or cognitive functioning. These latter changes are more in line with the third and fourth phases of the continuum, which are geared more toward obtaining increments in client functioning than toward making up for deficits.

The third phase calls for the counselor to encourage and help bring about a more internal locus of control in the client, that is, to enable the client to be and to feel more in control of his or her current life situation. The objectives in this phase are to enhance the client's coping skills, increase the problem-solving capacity, and increase the client's cognitive mastery of the problem situation. The counseling techniques proposed for this phase tend to come largely from the cognitive and cognitive-behavioral schools of psychotherapy. The term "coping skills" suggests the need for skills training, a behavioral approach. "Cognitive mastery" and "problem-solving capacity" suggest the need for largely cognitive techniques.

The fourth phase of counseling calls for positive changes in self-concept, self-esteem, and the evolution of alternate self-evaluations. The objectives here are to reduce "functionalistic" self-evaluations, clarify alternative self-evaluations, and increase the life satisfaction and ego integrity of the client. The word "functionalistic" comes from the term "functionalistic ethic," as it is used in the gerontological literature (Kuypers and Bengtson, 1973; Bengtson, 1973), and it will be spelled out in much more detail later. For the moment it can be said that the functionalistic ethic is one by which the person evaluates his or her own self-worth in terms of his or her functional value in society, which tends to be the person's productive functioning or monetary value in the economy. This is not seen as a valid or an emotionally sound standard for self-evaluation, in particular by older persons. At any rate, the objectives of this phase of treatment involve changes in basic attitudes toward self and toward one's life. Consequently, the techniques which are proposed and illustrated for this phase are much more cognitive and insight-oriented in nature than the techniques of the earlier phases. It should also be clear that the counseling involved in this phase represents long-term or extended counseling, which generally takes a minimum of six months but which can last as long as two years or more.

The client–counselor relationship is of course a central factor in the integrative approach. The use of cognitive or cognitive-behavioral approaches form only part of the treatment repertoire of the integrative approach. Accurate empathy, warmth, and genuineness (Truax and Carkhuff, 1967) on the part of the counselor are seen as essential factors in the conduct and effectiveness of integrative counseling. In addition, the use of natural helping networks—family, friends, and neighbors—and the use of age peers in mutual support groups and in therapeutic groups are often part and parcel of the integrative approach. These uses are described and illustrated in the text.

One final observation should be made in this brief overview of the integrative treatment model. The four phases that are outlined should not be viewed as invariable. It is entirely possible that there is no pressing material need and that the older person is in need of help with a problem of emotional or interpersonal functioning. In such a case it is possible to begin with the methods and objectives of the second phase.

What Is Aging and Who Is Old?

Since repeated references will be made to gerontological research and literature in this text, there should be at least some brief discussion of the field of gerontology and what aspects of it have the most relevance for integrative practice.

First, it should be said that gerontology is a very broad field of study that incorporates knowledge from the biological, behavioral, and social sciences and even the humanities. It includes the study of the human aging process as well as the problems of old age. This term "aging" refers simply to the process of growing older, and gerontology therefore includes the study of the entire aging process (Hendricks and Hendricks, 1979), not just old age itself. The importance of this lies in the fact that study of the total aging process can provide us not only with knowledge of how old age comes about under varying circumstances, but also with how this knowledge might help us to deal with the problems of old age. This is the area of applied gerontology and it is the premise upon which the integrative approach was developed.

Now, what is meant by the terms "old age," "aged," or just plain "old"? We can consider this question from the biological perspective, from the psychological, or from the social or cultural. No matter which we choose, we will find great variations according to the physical condition of the person considered, the attitudes and behaviors of that person, and the expectations or norms of the society or culture in which he or she lives. The most commonly used perspective is probably the biological, since biological changes may be more readily identified in terms of physical appearances, such as baldness, stooped posture, and skin changes. However, it is immediately evident that individuals of the same chronological age—say, 70—can vary immensely not only in their physical appearance but in their actual physiological functioning. It is also evident that presumed old age is very much in the mind of the beholder; the age at which a 5-year-old is apt to define another person as old is quite likely to be different from the definition of a 50-year-old. Furthermore, the presumed old person might or might not define himself or herself as old. This self-identified or perceived age is extremely significant in work with older persons, for it has important prognostic and treatment implications, as we shall see.

It has been somewhat convenient and therefore conventional to speak of 65 as the beginning of old age because that is the age of eligibility for full Social Security or other retirement benefits. This implies that the state of retirement might be indicative of old age, but many people are now retiring at age 55 and even 50, while others in their eighties are still working quite productively. Consequently, we have persons in their fifties facing the issue of a status passage from work to retirement, presumably an issue of old age, and 80-year-olds who have continued to work and do not face this issue.

We could go on indefinitely with examples of the absurdities involved in arbitrarily identifying a particular chronological age as old, but it is probably more relevant and fruitful to take a look at the gerontological research and literature to see what chronological criteria have been used for what purposes. It is indeed apparent that different gerontological investigators use different chronological ages to define old and elderly. They are aware of the ambiguous and somewhat arbitrary nature of the terms, but their definitions are determined by the purposes of their investigations. Thus, for example, a gerontologist who is an economist might well select the age of 65 as defining the beginning of old age for the purposes of an economic investigation or analysis because of the extreme importance of Social Security benefits as transfer payments in our economy. On the other hand, another investigator, say a psychologist, might select a different beginning age because of the known implications of that age for certain behaviors or other aspects of personality functioning. For example, Maddox (1968) conducted a now classic study of the persistence of lifestyle among the elderly in which "elderly" was operationally defined as 60 years of age or older for the purposes of that particular study. One could go through the literature and find old age or elderly defined as beginning at 55, 60, 65, 70, and even 75, depending on the purposes and factors of the study.

One of the more fruitful definitions or categorizations of age among older adults to come out of the gerontological literature in recent years is Neugarten's (1975) distinction between the *young-old* (ages 55-75) and the *old-old* (over 75). She made this distinction because factors such as earlier retirements and better health care have made for a category of older persons who are vigorous, active, and considerably better off physically and economically as a group than the over-75 group, which has significantly more chronic illness, poorer economic conditions, a lower educational level, and significantly more decrements generally than the young-old group. In fact, the old-old group look much more like the former popular stereotype of the elderly as frail, poor, isolated, and dependent than do the young-old. However, even this distinction has to be viewed cautiously, for there are many individuals over 75 who have relatively good health and economic resources and who are socially involved and active, just as there are those under 75 who are just the opposite. Nevertheless, the cutoff point of 75 years has shown up repeatedly in various studies to be statistically significant for a greater incidence of problems generally associated with "old age."

This has clear implications for an integrative practice, for it is clear that clients who fall into the old-old category are more apt to be those requiring the maintenance conditions and hard services in the first phase of the integrative treatment continuum. Of course, each case has to be assessed individually, but there is a greater likelihood of chronic ill health, poor circumstances, and need for protective services. Conversely, Neugarten's distinction has very important implications also for an integrative practice as far as the young-old are concerned. She notes in her influential article about the young-old (Neugarten, 1975) that they are not only more active and vigorous than the old-old, but they are better educated and more articulate. They will also be more apt to feel that they are entitled to health and welfare services and that these services should be of decent quality. Historically, they have lived through and participated in the emergence of broad-scale social services from the beginnings of the New Deal and beyond. Hence, they are more apt to feel entitled to social services rather than to feel ashamed of using them; such services are not equated in their minds with "the dole" or "welfare," as the old-old might feel according to an older, rugged-individualist ethic. Furthermore, because they are generally better educated and better informed, the young-old are apt to view certain of the new human services such as counseling, group therapy, and psychotherapy, as potentially helpful to them and may even actively seek them out. The old-old are more apt to view such services as stigmatizing, as indicating that they must be "touched," "crazy," or senile.

This text includes a number of case illustrations involving the young-old, several of them under 65. This is no accident; it is reflective of the actual use of programs and services for the so-called elderly by the young-old. In a survey I am currently conducting in senior centers in the Albany, New York, area, I have found that people under 65 who regularly participate in senior center activities make up from 8 to 21 percent of the clientele in the various centers. This averages out to about one out of every seven senior center participants. When the remaining young-olds (65–75) are included, the proportion goes to 76 percent. The executive directors and the program directors of the centers are well aware of the impact of the younger young-old on the milieu, activities, and programming of the centers. These younger members are more apt to participate in and to request more current affairs discussion groups, book discussion groups, new sorts of physical programs and activities (for example, yoga and other relaxation and fitness exercises), assertiveness and other human relations training, and so on. These directors indicate that there are no special centers for those older adults who straddle the late middle age and early old age category, that is, 55 to 65. These people are therefore becoming active in the existing senior centers.

These demographic facts should have a marked impact on the counseling of older adults in the present and in the future. In addition to the problems of depression, anxiety, and despair over losses of loved ones, over physical losses, over increased dependency on family and others, which are more characteristic of the old-old, the transitional problems of late middle to early old age will have to be taken into account as well, Thus, counselors may have to deal with marital and separation problems, with family problems involving the client's adolescent children and "old-old" parents, and with a number of problems of adjustment to early old age which include unresolved residues of middle age issues and conflicts.

This clearly requires a wider repertoire of counseling skills and knowledge than would be true if one were dealing with a much older and more frail group. Yet, although there may be some differences in the relative occurrence of certain kinds of problems between the young-old and the old-old, it is important to recognize that there are certain developmental issues and problems that are common to both age groups. When adults pass into late middle age, issues of achievement and power give way to issues of understanding and attempting to come to terms with their own mortality and the meaning of their lives. In describing the years from 50 until death, two prominent developmental psychologists have stated that "the primary integrating theme of this life stage no matter how long it lasts, is a search for personal meaning" (Hendricks & Hendricks 1979:126). The kinds of anxiety and potential for depression associated with concerns of mortality and the meaning of one's life and death become issues in counseling, particularly in more extended counseling. The integrative approach recognizes this developmental issue and specifically takes it into account. Therefore, because of the emerging importance and needs of the young-old and because of the commonality of certain problems between the young-old and the old-old, the integrative approach is intended for both groups, beginning at approximately age 60 and on. This is why the title of this book refers to counseling "the aging," rather than "the aged" or "the elderly."

The Developmental Model of Aging

The developmental model that will be referred to the most, but certainly not exclusively, in this text is Erikson's (1963) epigenetic theory of personality development. It has probably been more influential than any other recent developmental theory of aging, and even if other theorists disagree with this model, it generally serves as the model against which differences of opinion in the field are expressed. It is certainly a comprehensive theory, including the years of early infancy through old age, and it is delineated in terms of a set of easily identifiable stages. One particular value of Erikson's theory from a gerontological point of view is that it was one of the first to give serious attention to the developmental issues of later adulthood and old age.

Erikson's framework will be used here because of its relevance for the later years of life and because of its well-known and clearly delineated developmental stages. One may disagree with certain aspects of Erikson's view of personality functioning, as I do, but there is a general acceptance of the descriptive value of the nuclear conflicts and tasks he has identified for each of the eight stages in his model. Since Erikson's model is so well-known, the following description of it will be kept relatively brief.

Erikson has described the epigenetic principle that underlies his model in the following way: "this principle states that anything that grows has a ground plan, and that out of this ground plan the parts arise, each part having its time of special ascendancy, until all the parts have arisen to form a functioning whole" (1963:92). In addition to its being epigenetic, his theory is ego-psychological and concerned with the psychosocial development of the ego and its functioning in the person from infancy on. According to this epigenetic model, ego strengths develop beginning at birth through a process of maturation and experience and they accrue with rapid growth at critical junctures in the life cycle. The ego's ability to deal with a series of crises at each stage of life will have a great deal of bearing on how successfully the person can handle crises at later stages.

Each of the eight stages that Erikson posits represents a choice or crisis for the expanding ego. Although there is a different psychological issue involved in the nuclear conflict of each stage, the same issue is also present at other stages. Most important, a solution of the crisis at any stage of ego development has its effects on all subsequent stages. Without becoming enmeshed in the debate over whether there needs to be an almost completely successful resolution of each crisis, one can say that major unresolved residues of earlier crises can play a salient part in later crises. Thus, if a person has not "successfully" (that is, without major residues) resolved the issues of adolescence or any other earlier stage, he or she will not resolve the issues of late adulthood in the same way as one who has resolved the issues of the immediately preceding stages.

The nuclear psychosocial crises of the eight stages are: (1) in early infancy (0-18 months), the development of a sense of basic trust versus a sense of mistrust; (2) in early childhood (18 months-3 years), autonomy versus shame or doubt; (3) in childhood or play age (3-6 years), a sense of initiative versus a sense of guilt; (4) in middle childhood or school age (6-12 years), a sense of industry versus a sense of inferiority; (5) in adolescence (12-20), a sense of ego identity versus identity diffusion; (6) in early adulthood (21-34), the development of intimacy versus a sense of ego isolation; (7) in middle adulthood (35-60), the development of generativity versus a sense of stagnation; and (8) in late adulthood or old age (60 and over) ego integrity versus despair.

The eighth and last stage of development is of course the one that is of primary concern for integrative counseling, especially when one recognizes that in addition to the nuclear conflict of that stage there are apt to be some unresolved conflicts and transitional problems carried over from middle adulthood. The task of this last stage is to attain ego integrity, an assured sense of meaning and order in one's life and in the universe, as against despair and disgust, which may express itself in a feeling that one has failed and does not have the time to attempt another life or an alternative road to integrity. A successful resolution of this struggle and completion of this developmental task should include "acceptance of one's one and only life cycle as something that had to be and that, by necessity, permitted of no substitutions" (Erikson, 1963:268). The fruit of this struggle will be "wisdom," which Erikson defines as "the detached and yet active concern with life itself in the face of death itself, and one that maintains and conveys the integrity of experience, in spite of the decline of bodily and mental functions" (1976:23).

To what extent do people who reach old age achieve this integrity and wisdom? Some would say that very few do. Clayton (1975) did a cogent analysis of Erikson's theory of human development as it applies to the aged, and she came to the conclusion that "many people simply do not complete the life cycle. They die uncommitted, unresolved and frustrated, never having arrived at the stage where they could fully integrate and utilize their accumulated years of experience and knowledge" (Clayton, 1975:123). Using Erikson's model, in which personality change is centered on the struggle between the id and ego systems (individual versus societal conflicts), she concluded that most individuals seek foreclosure or enter prolonged moratoriums after adolescence. They most commonly and "realistically" opt for compromise rather than complete resolution between conflicting forces at each major life crisis, thereby failing to experience integrity (in Erikson's terms) in old age. However, she suggests that this ability to compromise may be one of the ego strengths or virtues necessary for individuals to attain integrity.

Erikson's emphasis on the need for resolution of the conflicting forces of each life stage has a rather categorical ring to it, but he qualifies his use of the term "resolution" when he writes, "We certainly do not postulate a total victory of Integrity over Despair and Disgust, but simply a dynamic balance in Integrity's favor" (1976:23). This sounds like a somewhat more attainable and therefore optimistic end stage. However, Erikson's insistence in his theory on the need for resolution at each life stage in order for the individual to move into and successfully complete the next stage significantly reduces the likelihood that anyone can attain true integrity, even if we allow for his moderating "dynamic balance" idea. Thus, if someone for whatever reason (for instance, death of mother, institutionalization) does not "resolve" the basic conflict of early infancy (trust versus mistrust), the likelihood of resolving the crisis of the next stage (autonomy versus shame and doubt) is markedly reduced, and the probability of failure is increased exponentially for every succeeding life stage.

Clearly, the probability of attaining ego integrity is extremely low for many adults, as Clayton contends, if we take a strict interpretation of Erikson's stage theory. The integrative approach does not subscribe to such a strict interpretation. In fact, it holds that there are alternative roads, even in late old age, to attain the kind of wisdom and acceptance that Erikson uses to describe the state of ego integrity.

Regardless of these different interpretations and reservations about his theory, Erikson seems to have captured and delineated the essential task of late adulthood with a richness and profundity that have not been equaled. For this reason, his conception of ego integrity is a central theme and a recurrent goal in the integrative approach to counseling the aging.

How does this desired end state manifest itself in an actual person's life? How does its opposite, a state of despair and disgust, manifest itself? Two actual case situations are presented here to illustrate successful and unsuccessful resolutions of the nuclear conflict of integrity versus despair. Both cases involve counseling by caseworkers from a family service agency, but the cases are not intended to depict the integrative approach to counseling. Rather, they are intended to illustrate how ego integrity and despair can manifest themselves in actual case situations. They can also serve to illustrate some of the factors counselors should take into account in the assessment process, and what indicators they should look for that might determine the extent and pervasiveness of despair and demoralization. Conversely, indicators of manifest and latent strengths which can be used to tip the balance in favor of ego integrity will also be illustrated. In addition to the diagnostic and prognostic aspects of assessment, the cases should serve to highlight some of the issues and considerations involved in differential treatment planning and approaches. Finally, the cases will be used to illustrate how the epigenetic model of human development can be applied in conjuction with the social breakdown syndrome or model (Kuypers and Bengtson, 1973) for the purposes of case assessment.

The first case is illustrative of an aging man for whom the dynamic balance between integrity and despair falls clearly in the negative direction. In the second case the dynamic balance is much less negative. In fact, it is clear in this case that with a little strategic help, using mostly the client's own intact strengths a balance is struck in favor of ego integrity. But, before these cases are presented the reader should be made aware of the fact that names and details in all the case illustrations in this book have been altered extensively to protect the anonymity of the clients.

A Case of Unsuccessful Aging

Martin Stern is a 75-year-old widower who is living with his 46-year-old daughter, her husband, and their 11-year-old daughter in their single-family home in the Queens section of New York City. His case came to the attention of a Jewish family service agency when his daughter called to request counseling help for her father, who she said was going to drive her and her family "crazy." She related the fact that her father had come to live with her six months before, just after his wife had died from a massive heart attack. He had been quite depressed as the result of his wife's death for the first four or five months, but he gradually regained more energy and involvement in former interests. His son-in-law took him to some major league baseball games to rekindle his interest in that sport, and it helped. He began attending some games on his own when his son-in-law was not available and resumed watching games on television. His daughter was sure he was back to his old self when he became more talkative and freely expressed his pet beliefs about the loose and profligate ways of the younger generation, the loss of old values and old-fashioned ways of having fun, the exorbitant prices of groceries, and everything else. She said he was just like this before her mother's death and that he had almost driven her mother crazy with run-on talk of this type, just as he would drive her crazy if he kept it up. His daughter was convinced he had completely gotten over her mother's death when he recently began criticizing the daughter's cooking and housekeeping in the same way he had criticized her mother's domestic activities and standards in the years before her death.

Although he would go to occasional ball games and sometimes take a trip by subway into Manhattan and walk around there, he spent most of his time at home and had not made any outside acquaintances. His daughter convinced him that he should go to a senior citizens' program at the local Jewish Community Center. He was not enthusiastic about the idea, but he had no rebuttal when his daughter told him he was too much under foot during the day and that he had to get out of the house and become engaged in something else. He attended the center for about six weeks, complaining much of the time about the "yentas" and the "phonies" who regularly attended the senior program. Finally, he came home one day and said he would never go there again because some men he had been playing cards with had accused him of cheating. His daughter could not convince him to overlook the incident or simply not to associate with those men any more, and to continue attending the center. He said that all the people at the center would know why he had left and that he had too much pride to go back there with "all those yentas" talking about him behind his back.

In desperation, the daughter called the director of the program to see what had happened and what could be done about getting her father back there. The director said that he would talk to the men who had been involved in the card game to see what had happened and what could be done about it. When he got back to the daughter, he explained that the men claimed not to have accused her father of cheating. They said that on that particular occasion he had had a run of good luck and that they had kidded him about his "slick" professional playing. They denied using the word "cheat" or "cheating" but admitted that they had the feeling he might be very sensitive about the kind of kidding they had engaged in. Although he was generally talkative and not standoffish, they had felt he was always somewhat guarded with them. However, they were willing to apologize about the kidding and make an effort to make him feel more at home at the center.

When his daughter told him about this, Mr. Stern said that he would not believe "those phonies if they swore on their mother's graves" and that they were only "putting on a show" for the director's benefit. He adamantly refused to return to the center, and his daughter called the director back to tell him of this and to ask where she could turn for help. She said she could not tolerate having him under foot all day long and that she was seriously thinking of sending him to a residential home for the aged, but that this would "kill him." The director suggested that she call Jewish Family Services, an agency which had been of help to a number of the participants in the senior program and their families in the recent past.

Shortly after the daughter applied to the agency, one of its caseworkers, Mrs. Meyers, contacted her to get more details about the problem. Among other things, Mrs. Meyers found out that the daughter and her husband were not willing to tolerate the situation much longer. There was only her 50-year-old brother in California who was divorced and recently remarried, this time to a 36-year-old divorcee who had three young children by her first marriage. There was no way the son could take his father under the circumstances. There were no other close relatives who could conceivably take him in. Mrs. Meyers also found out that the daughter had not even intimated to Mr. Stern that she might have to ask him to leave, for she was frightened about the effect the mere mention of it would have on him. He had often railed against young people in general who showed no loyalty and no sense of responsibility toward their elderly parents. He would say that it was truly a shame that these children would put their parents in nursing homes. He had always talked about how the family was everything; and if you did not have a family you had nothing, because you could not trust or depend on anyone else. She and her brother had heard this lecture repeatedly from their early childhood.

Mrs. Meyers agreed to visit Mr. Stern in the daughter's home to assess the situation, if he would be agreeable to such a visit. His daughter did broach the subject, and Mr. Stern said he was willing to talk to Mrs. Meyers since he had "nothing to hide." When she did visit him he seemed to welcome the chance to talk to someone new. Mrs. Meyers started by saying that she was there to discuss the situation involving his discontinuance at the center, his daughter's growing concern over the current situation, how he viewed it, and what could be done about it.

Mr. Stern reiterated his refusal to go back to the center, saying that the men had really implied that he was a cheater, even if they did not say it in so many words. As far as attending any other senior centers was concerned, he said most of the people who went to centers did so just to get a cheap meal under the Hot Meals Program, even though they could well afford to pay full price, and he reiterated his belief that they were mostly "phonies" and "yentas." He discussed these matters freely and he seemed to take a liking to Mrs. Meyers. He readily agreed to have a series of weekly sessions with her. She wished to establish a good working relationship with him to help him change his activity pattern and lifestyle enough to reduce the immediate pressure on the daughter. It might even enable him to stay in her home or take a place of his own and live independently.

In the following sessions Mr. Stern continued talking freely, reminiscing a great deal about his past. Mrs. Meyers was readily able to piece together the following background information from him, with some significant additions by his daughter. Mr. Stern said he was born and raised on the Lower East Side of Manhattan, the oldest of five children (three boys and two girls) born to immigrant parents from eastern Europe. He went to work before completing elementary school so that he could help contribute to the family income. He held a number of jobs as a delivery boy, first in the garment district pushing racks of clothes and then in distributing newspapers to stands from delivery trucks. He was later hired by a man who ran a busy newsstand in midtown Manhattan to handle the newsstand during the late afternoon and early evening hours. He came to know many people who worked in and frequented the area of the city surrounding Broadway and 42nd Street. There were men who ran different stands and concessions, the racing touts, the ticket hawkers, the police, the cabdrivers, and the myriad other persons who haunted that area, and he found them all fascinating. One of them offered him a job managing a cigar and magazine store in that area, which he did for over forty years right up to his retirement eight years ago. Throughout those years, he managed the store during the evening hours, generally from 4 P.M. to midnight; this was his preference because those were the hours that were the most active and interesting in many ways. There was no change in this, even after he was married at age 23, since his wife never insisted that he ask for different hours or that he change his job. She basically raised their two children single-handed. Mr. Stern was only involved with them on his days off or on extended holidays, and she seemed to prefer it that way. He brought home his pay, which she managed very well and very frugally, giving him an allowance she deemed appropriate. One of his biggest pleasures as a father was spending his pocket money on candy and amusements for his two children, but in many ways he was like the oldest child in the family instead of a father. His dependency on his wife and his willingness to let her take full responsibility for the care and disciplining of the children was something that was very clear to his daughter, to her brother, and to anyone else who knew the family well. His daughter said that Mr. Stern had not even learned to cook an egg before his retirement at age 67.

According to Mr. Stern, his retirement had come about as a result of a heart attack at that time. However, his daughter said that the heart condition was diagnosed as a mild infarction that had caused no appreciable damage, but that had caused Mr. Stern and his wife unwarranted grave concern about this condition from that time on. Despite the assurances by the doctors that he was able to carry on normally for a man his age, he not only quit his job but also gave up driving his car. In addition, Mr. Stern's enthusiasm for his job and his beloved Times Square area had begun to wane before the heart attack. He had been robbed in the store several times and the last time had been beaten, though not severely enough to cause any injuries beyond a few bruises. Therefore, his wife and children were relieved when he decided to retire. However, marital problems surfaced almost immediately upon his retirement. His wife found him to be under foot most of the time, whereas in the past he was asleep during most of the day and at work at night. Since he had never been involved or helpful domestically in the past, there was very little he seemed able to do now. When he would offer to help his wife to do some of the heavy housework, she would tell him it was not good for his heart. He would acquiesce in this, because he was becoming more preoccupied with his physical functioning, thinking he had developed a case of ulcers because of some heartburn he had experienced. His wife agreed with this self-diagnosis, since it reinforced the dependent nature of his relationship with her. She would fuss and worry over what food he ate and how it was prepared, and much of their time and energy was focused on food, meals, and how they were cooked.

The only valuable domestic function he had in the past was to drive Mrs. Stern to the stores for shopping, for she had never learned to drive. When he gave up his driving he came to feel totally useless at home. He had not developed any friendships in their neighborhood in Queens, because all of his prior associations had been on the job or at home with his family. He would make trips into Manhattan once or twice a week to visit some of his old haunts, but that became depressing because of the changes that had come about in the Times Square area over the years. Consequently, the trips became more infrequent and he began to spend more of his time at home. He was becoming openly critical of his wife's cooking and housekeeping, areas she felt to be her special preserve and strength. In addition, he began bringing up issues from the past with her. He took to blaming her for the fact that she had twenty years before talked him out of buying a newspaper stand in the Times Square area which he felt was a very lucrative one. He said that it was her stinginess and lack of imagination which had stopped them from making a great deal of money on the stand, which could have led to other investments. He did not recall that he had in fact acquiesced at that time without much of a fight when she pointed out that they could ill afford to risk what little savings they had, or to lose the regular job he had, since he had no other special skills to enable him to find another job. He nevertheless felt that he would have made "a killing" on the newsstand, and he felt that at his retirement he might even have been able to spend his time managing the investments of the money he would have made. The irritation and resentment between Mr. Stern and his wife had grown to a serious point at the time of her death. The ironic fact that she rather than Mr. Stern had died of a heart attack should not have come as a complete surprise to him, for she had suffered from a rather serious condition of high blood pressure for a number of years before it became markedly worse in the weeks just before her death.

Mr. Stern was badly shaken by his wife's death, despite the recent rancor between them, because of its suddenness and because of his dependence on her for everything from cooking and laundering to money management. Due to this dependence there was never any question of his remaining alone in their apartment or of finding a new one on his own. He simply went to live with his daughter, which was in accordance with his philosophy about filial responsibility, which his daughter accepted.

Given this history, the likelihood of Mr. Stern leaving his daughter's home and living independently was very slim, at least in the short run. The caseworker, Mrs. Meyers, continued to see Mr. Stern on a weekly basis, but he was not changing his behaviors or his attitude about becoming socially involved outside the daughter's home. Because of the growing tension in the home, Mrs. Meyers found it advisable to have sessions with the entire family, including Mr. Stern's son-in-law, granddaughter, and daughter, in order to negotiate the everyday matters of living together. Mr. Stern had to be confronted with the fact that his daughter and her family had reached the breaking point and that he would have to go into some kind of supervised residence for the aged if his behavior and attitudes did not change. He was shocked and deeply hurt by this, especially in the light of his beliefs about family loyalty. On the other hand, he was extremely frightened of the prospect of going to such a residence or of going out to live on his own. He therefore agreed to participate in the family sessions, but he has become rather morose, non-communicative and guarded with his daughter and her family. Although this has relieved the problem of his incessant and repetitious chatter, he now spends most of his time in his room watching television or taking solitary walks in the immediate neighborhood. He feels that his last remaining place of trust, his family, has failed him, and his sense of despair is deepening.

A Case of Successful Aging

Max Kaplan is a 76-year-old widower who lives alone in a one-bedroom apartment on the upper west side of Manhattan. As in the case of Martin Stern, his situation came to the attention of Jewish Family Services as a result of his dropping out of a senior service program at a local Jewish community center. However, in Mr. Kaplan's case the referral was made by the senior program director directly to the family agency rather than by a relative. The family agency, as a matter of policy, engages in a considerable amount of outreach. Its workers make special efforts to contact isolated or home-bound older persons who may not otherwise know about the agency's services. Referrals tend to come from other agencies or organizations, or friends and neighbors who know about the plight of these older individuals.

In this instance, the program director at the center had noted that Mr. Kaplan, who had regularly attended the center for the past six months, had not attended at all for the past ten days or so. None of the other program participants seemed to know why he had not been attending, so the program director, Mr. Burstein, had phoned Mr. Kaplan's apartment and found him at home. Mr. Kaplan said that he had not been in to the center because he had been mugged and injured a week and a half before, and although he was feeling much better physically he was still quite shaken by the whole experience. Mr. Burstein told him about the outreach services of the Jewish Family Services agency and asked him if he would be willing to have a social worker from the agency visit him. Mr. Kaplan said he would, and Mr. Burstein made the referral. The agency worker assigned to the case was Ms. Jacobi, who phoned Mr. Kaplan and arranged to visit him the very next day.

Ms. Jacobi found him to be a rather small but wiry man with a full head of gray hair who appeared to be in good health except for his left arm, which was in a cast and sling. He still had black marks under both eyes and a scab covering a cut on the bridge of his nose. He told Ms. Jacobi that he had been attacked from behind. Mr. Kaplan had been walking home at about 12:45 A.M. from a local movie house where he had just seen the last showing of a double feature. The mugging occurred on his own street, which was deserted at the time, but he made the mistake (he now feels) of not walking on the side of the street on which his apartment house is located and which is better lighted. His nose and arm were broken and cut and his eyes were blackened. He had blacked out after he hit the cement, so he was kept in a local hospital for two days for observation as well as for treatment for his broken arm and nose. It was found that he had suffered only a minor concussion and that there were no apparent aftereffects. However, he admitted to Ms. Jacobi that he was still very much shaken emotionally by the experience.

Mr. Kaplan clearly welcomed the opportunity to discuss his victimization and reaction to it. It was not as though he was morbidly preoccupied with the experience, but he felt that he needed to lay it out in all its inchoate, illogical, and emotional aspects and implications so that he could integrate it and come to terms with it and its meaning at this point in his life. As he related his reactions, it was clear that it was not so much the violence and physical injury that frightened him, but the suddenness and the lack of warning or any opportunity to prepare for it. There was also the rather eerie and disorienting fact that he had never seen his assailant because of his being hit from behind and his immediate unconsciousness. This all made him feel vulnerable, not just in terms of another attack, but more in terms of his general health and safety. It made him realize how quickly he could become incapacitated, whereas until now his health had been excellent for a person his age. He added that he was mending well and that he had no concerns about his current injuries and state of health, but that he was now worried about future disability. He said that he wanted not only to discuss his anxiety but also to actually make some plans for his future if and when he does become disabled, so that he will be prepared. He asked Ms. Jacobi whether she could give him some information about possible nursing homes or other health-related facilities he might consider going to in the event of a stroke or other disabling illness. He wondered whether there was the possibility of his getting to see some of these facilities so as to be prepared for what to expect, if she did not think this was premature or unrealistic.

Ms. Jacobi assured him that it was neither, that it was in fact quite sensible at least to visit nursing homes and learn about the quality and availability of such facilities. She said she could give him information about a number of facilities associated with the Jewish Federation of Agencies that were nonprofit organizations very much concerned about the welfare and morale of their residents. She added that she would be willing to show Mr. Kaplan some of these facilities if he wished. He said that he certainly would appreciate this. At this time, however, she inquired about his immediate welfare. She asked whether he was able to care for himself and whether he was eating properly, considering his arm was in a cast and sling. Also, she inquired about his financial circumstances in the light of the medical expenses he incurred as a result of the mugging. She indicated that there was a state agency, the Crime Victims Compensation Board, which might compensate him for some or all of his expenses. Mr. Kaplan said that Medicare was taking care of medical expenses, and he only had three dollars and some cents in his pockets when he was mugged, so he did not really need or qualify for compensation from any agency.

Mr. Kaplan did say, however, that he had not really been able to prepare himself a complete meal because of his broken arm and he missed the hot meals served at noon at the community center. It was almost time for lunch when the interview ended, so Ms. Jacobi offered to drive Mr. Kaplan to the center. At this point he said that he felt a little guilty about going back to the center for meals. When Ms. Jacobi asked why, he explained that when he first started attending the center about six months ago he participated in a number of the group programs, such as the current affairs group and the book discussion group. But he did not really enjoy any of these groups nor was he interested in other activities at the center, so he just started going there for the hot meals at lunch time. These he found to be nutritious and very economical, considering the modest 75¢ contribution for them. Now that Mr. Burstein was so thoughtful and kind toward him by calling him and then making the referral to the family service agency, Mr. Kaplan felt somewhat obliged to become more active at the center, if he intended to continue eating the noon meals there. Yet, he did not really care for the other activities of the center. Ms. Jacobi assured him that the hot meals program was an independent, federally funded program that he was entitled to regardless of whether or not he engaged in the social activities of the center. He rather sheepishly said that he guessed he knew that and that it was a little silly of him to feel guilty. He was going to make a special point to thank Mr. Burstein for his considerateness, and he would continue to have his meals there.

When Ms. Jacobi visited the following week, she indicated that arrangements had been made for the two of them to visit some health-related and skilled nursing facilities the following week. The discussion then turned to the current situation, with Ms. Jacobi asking whether living alone posed a problem for Mr. Kaplan in the light of his recent experience and his resulting anxiety and concern about the future. He replied that he honestly did not mind living alone, even now. Since his wife's death he had found that he was able to do so and that in fact he had come to appreciate the benefits of solitude, such as the opportunity for reading and simple contemplation. He first felt very lonely when his wife died, but when the worst grief over his loss was gone he began to adjust quite well. It was during that first spell of loneliness that he began participating in the activities of the center, about seven or eight weeks after his wife's death. At first these activities provided a

diversion and regular social interaction with others on a daily basis which met
his needs at the time. Now, he seemed content to visit with a couple of old
friends from the labor movement who still live on the Lower East Side of
Manhattan, where he was born and raised.

At the time of this second visit and in the course of four subsequent
contacts with Ms. Jacobi, Mr. Kaplan related the following facts about his
background. His parents were immigrants from eastern Europe, from what
was then the Russian part of Poland. His father was a tailor, and Mr. Kaplan
followed in his father's footsteps. However, it was not as a skilled craftsman
or master tailor that his father was able to work when he came to this country
as a young man. He had to go to work in the sweatshops of New York City,
where he did routine, stultifying work at the machines sewing together pre-
cut pieces of fabric in the production of cheap clothing. Mr. Kaplan, as well
as his older brother and two older sisters, worked in these shops after leaving
elementary school before graduation in order to work full time. Only one
child in the family of five children, Mr. Kaplan's younger sister, went on to
high school and did not have to work in the garment industry. She is still
alive and lives in Baltimore with her husband. They come up about once a
year to visit him and his 82-year-old sister who is widowed, quite senile, and
living in a nursing home in Brooklyn. The older brother and other older
sister are both dead, as are the parents.

Mr. Kaplan explained that the agony of working in the sweatshops led to
the two finest things in his life, his involvement in the labor movement and
the marriage to his wife. He said that as a young man he was quite angry
about the conditions his family and friends had to labor under in the garment
industry, and when still in his teens he joined and became active in the
Amalgamated Clothing Workers Union. He loved the good cause and com-
radeship of the movement, as well as the meaning it gave to his life, particularly to his early years. In addition, he feels that the labor movement provided him with an education he could not otherwise have obtained. He
participated in the Workmen's Circle right up into the 1930s. He noted that
the lectures, discussion groups, and seminars he attended over those years
allowed him to hear, read, and discuss not only the sweatshop writers like
David Edelstadt or Morris Rosenfeld, but figures like Marx, Engels, and
Bakhunin. He was exposed not only to the political writers but to the ideas
and writings of Spinoza and other major thinkers of a more philosophical
nature. He admitted to Ms. Jacobi that he still had a passion for Spinoza and
that he probably alienated some of the other older people at the community
centers by quoting from Spinoza's *Ethics* or by bringing up some other
writers the people were not interested in or were offended by. He added that
he still retained those secularist and somewhat socialist views of the Workmen's Circle. He observed that the community center, perhaps because it
was associated with a synogogue, seemed to attract Orthodox or at best
Conservative members, who held rather conventional views about life and

were not at all interested in intellectual matters. He indicated to Ms. Jacobi that he did not mean they were unintelligent or that he felt superior to them, but he found the current affairs discussion group and book discussion group to be shallow and unimaginative compared to what he had known in the Workmen's Circle or to what his conversations are like when he gets together with his few remaining friends from "the movement." He said he appreciated the social contact and even support that the people at the Community Center provided him in those lonely periods right after his wife's death.

His wife! She was the brightest thing in his life. He met her when he was 19 and involved in union organizing just as she was for the International Ladies Garment Workers Union. However, she was two years older than he and an established and highly effective organizer in her own right, so it was only natural that she at first paid him scant attention of any romantic sort. However, he was so taken by her and by the fire and spirit she exuded that he was determined to win her. His unremitting and single-minded pursuit of her finally did win her over and convinced her to marry him, although she was a truly liberated woman of those days who would have been willing to live out of wedlock with him as a matter of principle. He felt that she came to love him every bit as much as he did her, but their married life was not without some major disappointments. After the first few years of marriage they both felt a strong desire to have children, but they were unable to. They attempted to adopt a child, but there were extremely few Jewish children available for adoption, and according to the laws governing adoption in New York State at that time children could be adopted only by persons of the same religious affiliation.

The Kaplans finally decided that they would like to care for foster children if they could not adopt a child, so they applied to the Jewish Board of Guardians to become foster parents. Because they were now in their early thirties, they were first given boys in the 8-to-11-year age range. Mrs. Kaplan had to leave her work in a dress factory (neither she nor Mr. Kaplan had ever held any paid union positions in the course of their organizing activities) in order to care for the boys who were placed with them. The money they received for this did not match Mrs. Kaplan's former income, but Mr. Kaplan had by this time become a master tailor and was working for a clothing house that paid him comparatively well. Furthermore, the satisfaction they got out of caring for the boys was a much greater compensation as far as they were concerned.

They were never able to have more than one or two boys at any one time because they did not have enough bedrooms in their upper west side apartment. The Board of Guardians considered them excellent foster parents, and in later years the agency persuaded them to take in emotionally disturbed boys in the 12- to 16-year range because of the large numbers of such children coming into the foster care system. The Kaplans were given special additional training by the agency in how to handle the kinds of emotional problems presented by disturbed children. Mr. Kaplan told Ms. Jacobi with a chuckle that for all the training sessions, workshops, seminars, and consultation visits from the agency's social workers, he and his wife never honestly felt that they were really on top of the emotional problems presented in so many different ways by the boys. They came from such disturbed and deprived backgrounds that at times it seemed almost hopeless to keep trying to have an impact on their lives, but there were several boys from such backgrounds who came out of their care in a much better emotional condition than the Kaplans even hoped for. A number of the boys, who are for the most part well-established with families of their own and with regular employment, keep in contact from time to time by mail, by phone, and by an occasional visit. On the other hand, some of the children remained troubled and have gone on into an emotionally disturbed adulthood culminating in troubled marriages, institutionalization, imprisonment, and in one case suicide. He is grateful that he and his wife were able to help save some and he recognizes that not all could be saved, but at least it was not for the lack of trying on his or his wife's part.

The Kaplans stopped taking foster children when his wife was 57 and she had been warned by the doctors of her dangerously high blood pressure. Given the stress involved in handling disturbed teenagers it was clear that she could not continue in the role of foster parent. Five years later, she had a serious, incapacitating stroke and was paralyzed on the right side. After spending some time in a rehabilitation hospital, she became able to feed herself with her left hand, but she was basically confined to a wheelchair, except for some exercise on a walker going short distances across the room and back. Her speech was not seriously affected, but she could no longer read and write. Her cognitive functioning was clearly affected so that her basic activity was watching television or engaging in fairly simple conversations with Mr. Kaplan and any friends, relatives, or neighbors who might visit.

Mr. Kaplan gave up his job as a tailor with the clothing firm in order to care for his wife in the apartment. He was only 61 years old and therefore not entitled to any retirement benefits. He tried to take in tailoring that he could do in his apartment while caring for his wife, but that never provided anywhere near enough money to support him, much less the two of them. It was therefore necessary to apply for public assistance. He continued, however, doing whatever tailoring he could do and reporting regularly whatever small income he earned to the Department of Social Services so that it could be budgeted according to the Department's formula. When Mrs. Kaplan died eight months ago, he still found it necessary to receive Supplemental Security Income, because his need to retire early to care for his wife prevented him from receiving maximum Social Security benefits. He claimed that he had no regrets or any feeling of shame, for, as he half-jokingly said to Ms. Jacobi, "I really do believe in the rule 'to each according to his need and from each according to his ability.'" He feels that he has given according to his ability and therefore has no difficulty in accepting according to his need.

Ms. Jacobi had six contacts with Mr. Kaplan, three of which involved visits to health-related and nursing facilities. He found these visits very helpful and reassuring because he had the opportunity to see the kinds of facilities and quality of care involved. This was no longer an unknown. In addition, he found that he would be eligible for admission to facilities with varying levels of care, beginning with domiciliary arrangements that allowed a maximum of independent living within a secure setting as well as more extensive and skilled care if that became necessary. He told Ms. Jacobi during her last visit that even if he could not get into one of those fine facilities he felt quite good about his future, as well as his present. Just talking to her during these visits, having the chance "to think out loud," was very helpful. He was no longer shaken and anxious as a result of the mugging.

He observed that it was ironic that he was not really fearful of death at the time he was mugged. He had long before worked that through. What had thrown him about the experience was not just its suddenness, but the instantaneous *loss of control* over the nature and circumstances of his life. He said that as he absorbed the experience over the past several weeks he had learned something useful from it, namely, that although it is important to continue exercising control over the course and circumstances of your life to the extent you can, you are doomed to defeat and futility if you feel that you must exercise that control at all times and under all circumstances. To be able to let go of that "terrible need" for total control was the valuable lesson he learned from the experience. He said he should have learned that from his wife's life when she was struck down to a level of mental simplicity and physical dependency from the level of mental sharpness and physical vigor that were her characteristics. He had absorbed and integrated that lesson for her, but not for himself. His lesson had to be this last, first-hand experience.

As far as his present lifestyle is concerned, he is enjoying going out again and walking and visiting his favorite museums and parks. He still reads a great deal, both at home and in the public library, and continues his once or twice weekly visits with his two old friends from the labor movement. He will continue to take his full midday meal at the community center, but he will not be attending the other activities of the senior program.

The Social Breakdown Syndrome

When we compare the two men just described in terms of their backgrounds we find quite a few similarities, but when we look at their current lifestyles and attitudes we find some striking differences. Both are males who are alike in age, formal education, economic background, and the city in which they were raised and still live. Where the two men differ most is in the way they deal with the issue of integrity versus despair. What is it about Martin Stern and his circumstances that has led him to a state of imminent if not actual despair? What is it about Max Kaplan that enabled him to attain the ego integrity which is so evident in his current adjustment? Some explanations for Max Kaplan's adjustment will be offered here and in the next chapter. For the moment, however, particular attention will be paid to the factors and processes that led to Martin Stern's "demoralization," a term which Frank (1974) has aptly used to characterize psychological breakdown in its many forms and guises. Frank sees the state of demoralization as a form of hopelessness that is close to despair. This is indeed an all too familiar frame of mind among many elderly in our society.

One of the most useful models to describe this type of demoralization first appeared in the mental health literature in an article by Zusman (1966) describing a process of psychological breakdown brought about by a negative interaction of the social environment with the person's self-concept in a downward cycle of increasing incompetence. This is called the social breakdown syndrome, and it has been found to have much explanatory and descriptive value for the problems older persons face in our society (Kuypers and Bengtson, 1973). The essential steps are illustrated in Figure 1-1.

The cyclical nature of the syndrome is illustrated by the arrows. The breakdown process begins with some kind of event, usually traumatic, that activates the precondition or susceptibility and starts the cycle. The kinds of

FIGURE 1-1. *The Social Breakdown Syndrome: A Vicious Cycle of Increasing Incompetence.*

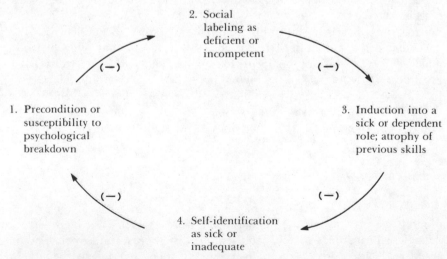

Source: V. L. Bengtson, *The Social Psychology of Aging* (Indianapolis: The Bobbs-Merrill Co., 1973). Copyright © 1973 by The Bobbs-Merrill Co. Reprinted by permission.

precipitating events that have most general application in the lives of older persons tend to be age-related crises: widowhood, the loss of a valued role as worker, the loss of substantial income because of retirement, the loss of role as parent when one's children leave home and often the area, the onset of painful, debilitating, or life-threatening illnesses. One of these events can combine with a susceptibility or pre-existing condition to start a downward cycle that next involves the labeling of the individual by others as deficient or incompetent. For example, someone with atherosclerosis (precondition) suffers a mild stroke and is apt to be subtly labeled by family, friends, and even helping professionals as deficient or incompetent. This labeling becomes something of a self-fulfilling prophecy in that the person is inducted into a sick and dependent role by others' expectations of low physical and mental functioning. Since the person is not encouraged or trained to redevelop temporarily impaired physical and mental capabilities, those capacities or skills are allowed to atrophy. Next, the person comes to believe that he or she is as inadequate or sick as identified by others and thereafter engages in a self-labeling process which feeds back into the precondition that precipitated the breakdown. This begins the second round of the cycle, with the person functioning at a lower level than when the process started. With each complete turn of the cycle, functioning and morale worsen.

Preconditions to Breakdown

There are some preconditions and a susceptibility to social breakdown that are more prevalent among older persons than among other age groups. Among the most obvious are physical ones. The biological processes of aging do take their toll in the form of lowered physical strength and stamina, greater vulnerability to orthopedic and vascular disorders and decreased resilience or recuperative powers. There are also environmental and social preconditions not necessarily related to age, such as poor housing or health care and low income. Although these preconditions are not restricted to older persons, they are more prevalent among the aged and they tend to interact with age-related problems in a way that exacerbates the impact on the older person.

There are psychological susceptibilities as well as physical, social, and environmental ones. One of the most useful ways of conceptualizing psychological preconditions for breakdown is by the developmental, ego-psychological framework which Erikson made so meaningful for our purposes in gerontology. Erikson held that unresolved issues from earlier developmental stages can serve to undermine or at least complicate efforts to deal with age-related problems at later stages of development. These unresolved issues represent psychological weaknesses, susceptibilities, or preconditions for potential breakdown in the process of dealing with the age-related crises of later life. For assessment purposes in our work with the aging it would, of course, be helpful to know the history of the person's developmental experiences at each stage of the life cycle to determine the presence of residual unresolved issues that might predispose the person toward the social breakdown syndrome and despair in late adulthood. However, we frequently do not have the luxury of obtaining an exhaustive psychosocial history in many of the settings and circumstances in which we work with the aging, and it is entirely possible that the process of obtaining such a history would be counterproductive for the rapport necessary in a counseling relationship. More important, to some degree we should be able to assess the presence of such problems and predispositions on the basis of current functioning as expressed in the thoughts, behaviors, and affects of the older person. Thus, although the issue of trust versus basic mistrust arises in the very earliest months of infancy in conjunction with the nurturing relationship between the mother and the infant, unsuccessful resolution of this issue can be assessed in adults of all ages in the absence of detailed knowledge of the mother/infant relationship in the first months of life. In fact, descriptive scales have been devised which measure the level of adult functioning on each of Erikson's modalities or stages (Prelinger and Zimet, 1964). The best way to illustrate this is to take a look at each of the issues of the psychosocial stages as currently expressed in the functioning of Martin Stern and Max Kaplan.

The first psychosocial issue of trust versus basic mistrust can be assessed by looking at the extent to which trust predominates in the thinking, behavior, and affects of the person or the extent to which mistrust predominates. A sense of trust would be expressed as a strong conviction that one's emotional and physical needs will be satisfied; that one is "all right" within one's self and within one's body; and that the frustrations as well as the demands coming from the outside generally make sense. It can be seen that such feelings tend to predominate in Max Kaplan. He is convinced that his needs will be met even if he has to go to a nursing home. One also gets the impression that he has accepted the demands, frustrations, and even major losses in his life as generally making some sense. There can be little doubt that mistrust predominates in Martin Stern, even though it is not complete. He mistrusts outsiders and refers to them as "phonies," although he does make concessions for some people, particularly his own family. He clearly does not feel all right within himself and within his body, about which he has hypochondriacal concerns.

The second psychosocial issue of autonomy versus shame and doubt would be regarded as successfully resolved if the person has a sense of being the originator of his own actions, of having a will of his own and being able to exercise it, of being largely in control of himself, of being independent. If doubt and shame predominate, there is an excessive concern with being exposed as weak, bad, powerless, or incompetent. This may include a wish to hide one's personal life from others, and there is often much doubt about the efficacy of one's own plans and actions.

There is some evidence that Max Kaplan had and has a sense of being the originator of his own actions, of being independent. It does seem that autonomy predominates in his current functioning. Martin Stern, on the other hand, gives evidence of feeling that he is not independent, that circumstances, bad luck, or his wife have prevented him from making plans, investing his money, and "making a killing." He was certainly concerned about being exposed as a card cheat at the senior center, even after he was assured that no such aspersions had been or would be cast on him.

The third issue, initiative versus guilt, is manifested either in ambition and pursuit of accomplishment and competitiveness or in guilt over the aggressive aspects of ambition and competition, expressed in self-restriction and paralysis or inhibition of action. As far as Martin Stern and Max Kaplan are concerned, there is not much evidence with regard to this issue. It is possible that it does not present a particular problem for either of them. To put this in terms of the social breakdown syndrome, there is no evidence of a predisposition for psychological breakdown based on the conflict between initiative and guilt.

The fourth psychosocial issue of industry versus inferiority refers to an active interest and involvement in the production and completion of things. There is an emphasis on development of skills and know-how for the purposes of achievement and recognition. The opposite feeling is that one's skills and aptitudes are found wanting, are not up to standard, that one is inferior, incapable, and isolated. This is an important theme that frequently reasserts itself in the later years with the approach of retirement. If a person has been skillful and productive and has obtained recognition for it, there may be satisfaction with a job well done and acceptance of retirement without demoralization in a well-integrated personality. If, however, there has always been a large residue of feelings of inferiority, retirement can pose a major threat to self-esteem. Losing the formal, paid role of worker and wage-earner may mean that the last institutional vestige of industry has been stripped away from a person who had a prior sense of inferiority.

It would seem that Max Kaplan did not suffer from any large residue of feelings of inferiority, for his retirement did not appear to represent an assault on his self-esteem. He probably was industrious in his trade of tailor, but he also had some feelings of competence and accomplishment from his labor organizing and foster parenting. Although Martin Stern seemed to enjoy his job and social contacts in the cigar store, we have no evidence that he had a sense of accomplishment about it. However, there is little doubt that the loss of his work role did lead to a marked loss of self-esteem.

The fifth issue of identity versus identity diffusion represents the primary issue of adolescence in Erikson's model, but it is easy to see that a reawakening of this issue is practically inevitable in old age. Identity has to do with a feeling of internal consistency and continuity, recognition by others of these qualities, and a sound integration of inner wishes and motivations with the social realities of work, sex, peer relationships, and the community. Identity diffusion, conversely, refers to a sense of inconsistency between one's drives and wishes and the social realities. There are apt to be conflicting interests and doubts about one's sexual identity, one's ability to relate to others, one's choice of vocation, and one's sense of purpose in life. Here, too, it is fairly evident that Max Kaplan has domonstrated a well-developed sense of identity and good social integration. Martin Stern's identity, however, is somewhat diffuse. He had wished to be an entrepreneur and to make a financial killing from the newsstand and subsequent investments. He also has no sense of assuredness in him that others recognize his identity. He certainly has doubts about his ability to relate to others, as evidenced by expressed attitudes toward the people at the community center.

This assessment of Martin Stern leads rather easily into the next stage and the issue of intimacy versus isolation. Although this modality concerns all potential continuing intimate relationships with others, it is primarily concerned with the depth and mutuality of relationship with a loved partner, usually the spouse. If this issue has been resolved in favor of intimacy, the partnership will be characterized by mutual trust and by mutual agreement on and engagement in major life endeavors such as work, recreation, and procreation. If resolution of the issue has been settled in favor of isolation, then the person has a sense of being or having to be alone and self-absorbed because of the fear of ego loss in a truly mutual, intimate relationship. Certainly, there is not much mutuality in the history of ongoing everyday regulation of work, recreation, and child-rearing in Martin Stern's marriage. During his working years, he was usually absent from home. Decision making about and ongoing care of the children were left entirely to his wife. After he retired and he and his wife were able to spend much of their time together, there was a marked lack of mutuality. With Max Kaplan, on the other hand, there appears to have been a good deal of mutuality with his wife, at least as far as major life decisions were concerned. First their mutual interests in the labor movement and later their decisions to have children, to adopt, and finally to become foster parents were all made with a great deal of mutuality.

The seventh psychosocial stage concerns the issue of generativity versus stagnation. Generativity is marked by a deep interest and involvement in establishing and guiding the next generation. Even if there are no actual parental responsibilities there should still be deep concerns and involvements of an altruistic and creative nature. Contrariwise, stagnation is an absence of generative involvement as well as a sense of creative impoverishment and lack of purpose. Here again, we find that Martin Stern is somewhat lacking and vulnerable in this dimension. He was never fully absorbed as a father in child care and rearing, and he was never able to develop a sense of cumulative, creative activity. There is definitely a feeling of stagnation on his part, a feeling that he should be investing in and building something.

At this point, it should be useful to recapitulate the information gained from using Erikson's schema for assessing the psychological preconditions for the social breakdown syndrome in Martin Stern. Comparatively, we can say that little or no evidence of psychological vulnerability or predispositions for breakdown came out of the analysis of Max Kaplan's situation using Erikson's psychosocial paradigm. In fact, there was considerable evidence of ego strength, adaptability, and creativity.

It is clear that Martin Stern did not handle certain modal conflicts well and thus had certain psychological preconditions for breakdown. First, he is somewhat lacking in basic trust. His mistrust of others outside his own family precludes his reaching out to or accepting from others the kinds of assistance or support that might prevent demoralization. Although he was willing to talk to the agency worker, Mrs. Meyers, this did not represent a peer relationship. Secondly, there is an imbalance in favor of shame and doubt over a sense of autonomy, which makes him somewhat secretive and circumspect, again constricting possibilities for outside contacts and supports. Although there is no clear evidence of lack of initiative in him, there appear to be some feelings of inferiority as contrasted with feelings of industry and accomplishment. There is also some identity diffusion, the belief that he is not what he wanted to be (an entrepreneur) and that he does not wish to appear to others as he appears to himself. His problems with intimacy, and particularly mutuality, in his marriage also leave him somewhat vulnerable, while his relative stagnation and lack of generative activities mean that he had entered late adulthood in an already somewhat demoralized state. He is therefore predisposed toward further breakdown.

Social Labeling and Induction into a Sick Role

Let us see now how these features or preconditions interact with other components of the breakdown syndrome in its downward cycle. To begin with, Martin Stern retired somewhat prematurely because of his reaction to the myocardial infarction (precondition). Retirement can be considered an age-related crisis that could set off a breakdown cycle in some people, and in Mr. Stern's case it was more damaging because it was not really a voluntary retirement. This unfortunately leads directly to point 2 in the breakdown syndrome: social labeling as deficient or incompetent. He had to retire because he felt no longer physically competent to manage the cigar store. He was told by his family that he was no longer able safely to continue his work. This social labeling began Martin Stern's induction into a sick or dependent role, point 3 in the syndrome. His tendency, reinforced by his wife, to stress his physical problems also plays into his predisposition toward dependency, as noted in his residual difficulties in the psychosocial modality concerning autonomy.

Self-Identification as Sick or Inadequate

Finally, some other preconditions make it more probable that he will identify himself as sick or inadequate, point 4 in the syndrome. His difficulty with the industry/inferiority issue inclines him toward accepting the notion that without employment he must be either sick or deficient (inferior), and it is much more acceptable to identify oneself as sick than as deficient with regard to industry or ambition. Further, his problem with identity diffusion together with the lack of formal identity as worker or breadwinner because of retirement make it even more likely that he will accept the label (identity) of sick. He does in fact see himself as being "a heart case" and of having an ulcer, even though there is no solid medical evidence of such a condition.

Martin Stern's self-labeling goes beyond his identification as sick; it goes to the extent of his identification as *inadequate* to care for himself. When he made one or two feeble attempts to learn some domestic skills after his retirement, his wife easily discouraged him. She made it known that he had to be cared for and, by implication, that he was incapable of real independence. He made no effort whatsoever to attempt to live independently after his wife's death and confirmed his self-labeling as inadequate by having his daughter care for him.

Mr. Stern has been in the downward cycle of the breakdown syndrome for more than one rotation. On the first cycle, his heart condition and subsequent retirement led to labeling of him by his wife and children as sick and as inadequate to care for himself. He was thus inducted into the sick and dependent role, and then he labeled himself as sick and inadequate. This process continued, and when his wife died it was repeated all over again with his move to his daughter's house. He was functioning at an even lower level on this rotation and his social skills atrophied even more than before, as evidenced by the problems he had at the senior center and the almost total isolation in his current situation.

The Eighth Stage

It is easy to see that there tend to be a number of significant preconditions for breakdown in the elderly, such as greater physical vulnerability and possible psychological vulnerability due to reactive depressions and other emotional problems brought on by the death or illness of significant others. The fact that these preconditions do not lead to more widespread social breakdown in older persons is in fact remarkable. It should also be clear that in our society there is a great deal of social labeling of the elderly, especially when they are no longer employed, as deficient or no longer competent. Further, the elderly are almost continually in jeopardy of being inducted into sick or dependent roles, with the attendant atrophying of previous skills. In fact, there is some evidence that some of our formal helping and treatment services encourage illness or dependency. For example, a study of older persons residing in their own homes in Cleveland showed a significantly higher rate of institutionalization among those receiving intensive protective services than in a control group of elderly who received no special services (Blenkner, Bloom, and Nielsen, 1971). The researchers theorized that the higher rate of institutionalization was indicative of greater acceptance of the dependent role, probably because of the implicit social labeling and induction into the role by those who were providing professional help. Finally, it should be noted that there is a tendency among many elderly to identify themselves as sick or inadequate. Butler and Lewis (1977) have commented that the elderly accept negative stereotypes of themselves and idealize youth to a greater extent than most people realize (1977:101). This is because they were reared in their youth with essentially the same stereotypical attitudes toward youth and old age as currently exist.

On the basis of these prevailing facts and attitudes we have reason to be concerned about the potential for despair among the elderly in our society. Unfortunately, Erikson himself has not addressed this question explicitly, and his writing, though rich and engaging, tends to be somewhat metaphorical and elusive. It is even difficult to determine the more specific meanings and elements of the global task he posits for old age. This is why the foregoing analysis of Martin Stern and Max Kaplan bypassed the eighth and last stage of the epigenetic model. As Peck (1968) has noted, "Erikson's eighth stage, Ego-Integrity vs. Despair, seems to be intended to represent in a global, nonspecific way all of the psychological crises and crisis-solutions of the last forty or fifty years of life" (1968:88). Peck delineated in more specific terms what is entailed in Erikson's eighth stage, and this delineation has received wide acceptance in the gerontological literature. Peck identifies three component tasks within Erikson's global task of that stage:

1. ego differentiation versus work-role preoccupation
2. body transcendence versus body preoccupation
3. ego transcendence versus ego preoccupation

The first task has to do with the impact of retirement on the individual's sense of self, whether the person has retired from his or her primary vocational pursuit or whether a person's self-identified primary role as parent has been removed by the departure of grown children. The more one's major identities and self-esteem are bound up in the primary vocational role, the greater is the work-role preoccupation and sense of worthlessness and self-devaluation when the work role is no more. Ego differentiation, on the other hand, means the successful establishment of a different and varied set of valued activites that would allow for a sense of satisfaction and self-worth.

The second issue deals with the impact of the physical decline of the body in terms of resistance to illness, recuperative powers, and an increase in aches and pains. For those who have placed primary value on physical pleasure and comfort in their lives, physical decline represents a grave insult to the sense of well-being, and the result is a pervasive preoccupation with their bodies. However, there are those who have developed social and mental sources of pleasure and self-respect that allow them to overlook and ignore physical deterioration and discomfort.

The third issue of ego transcendence versus ego preoccupation has to do with the certain prospect of personal death and the extinction of the ego or self. Inability to come to terms with this fact is reflected in a narcissistic self-concern, anxiety, and preoccupation. Ego transcendence, on the other hand, might be achieved by living generously and unselfishly so as to leave contributions to the culture that will last beyond one's personal death through one's children, friendships, and actions significant for others. There are other ways of achieving a more positive acceptance of the fact of death which Peck alludes to in mentioning Chinese and Hindu philosophers, but he does not elaborate on these. Erikson speaks of an assured sense of order and meaning in the universe and in one's life that allows for self-transcendence. Kohlberg (1973) has proposed a level of moral development, which he claims some persons achieve in late adulthood, that provides them with "the sense of being a part of the whole of life." At this level, "we identify with the cosmic or infinite perspective and value life from its standpoint" (1973:203).

Religion, of course, provides this perspective for some people, but not all. The values and identities even of those who have been actively religious have been shaped in a largely secular society, and we do see religious elderly persons who are characterized by despair and disgust rather than integrity. The point is that some people are able to go beyond ego preoccupation, with or without formal religion, and it is important to learn how they have done it and how their approaches might be used to help others to do the same. Max Kaplan, for example, would appear to be one who has gone beyond ego preoccupation without any vestige of formal religion.

At this point, it might be helpful to apply Peck's more detailed framework to the analysis of the eighth and last stage of life of the two men represented in the case illustrations.

There is no question that Martin Stern was unhappy with his retirement from work and the loss of self-esteem that his breadwinner role afforded him. He was not able to work out successfully an alternate set of valued activities that would be reflective of ego differentiation. His senior center experience and his failure to work out a set of activities independent of his family reflect lack of ego differentiation.

Max Kaplan, on the other hand, changed his work role without morbid preoccupation. His decision to leave his skilled trade as a master tailor to care for his wife was the right one from an emotional point of view and from a life-span perspective. Consequently, Mr. Kaplan felt no great regret about leaving his job or for having to accept public assistance in order to be with and care for his wife.

There is also evidence of greater body preoccupation rather than body transcendence in the case of Martin Stern. His reaction to the mild heart condition suggests this. His self-diagnosis of ulcers in the absence of a medical examination further attests to body preoccupation. This is in clear contrast to Max Kaplan, who really was not preoccupied with the physical injuries he sustained in the mugging. In fact, he saw these as much less important than the emotional implications of the experience. There is reason to believe that Max Kaplan has adjusted in the direction of body transcendence.

The task of ego transcendence versus ego preoccupation also appears to be more successfully handled by Mr. Kaplan than by Mr. Stern. Ego preoccupation in the form of obsessive self-concern is less evident in Max Kaplan. Martin Stern, on the other hand, tends to show a considerable amount of self-preoccupation, and he has developed no social, altruistic, religious, or philosophical activities or perspectives to attain ego transcendence. As a result of this, the prognosis for Mr. Stern is not good. He is becoming more depressed, self-preoccupied, and isolated, as well as more distrustful. Although he is not so grossly disturbed as to have apparent delusions or hallucinations, there is reason to be concerned about further depression, possibly a yearning for death, and perhaps a potential for suicide. Erikson (1976) has described a state of masked despair which is strongly suggestive of the course of social breakdown Martin Stern is experiencing: "Rationalized bitterness and disgust can mask that despair which in severe psychopathology aggravates a senile syndrome of depression, hypochondria, and paranoic hate" (1976:23).

Counseling Implications of the Two Cases

There will be occasion in later parts of this book to refer to the case situations of Martin Stern and Max Kaplan as they serve to illustrate points in the assessment and treatment process of integrative counseling. At this point, only a few points will be made about the counseling implications of these cases to illustrate the basic developmental issue of this book.

First, the reader is probably aware of the relative ease with which the counselors were able to obtain background information on these two men. Even Martin Stern, with his growing mistrust, seemed pleased to discuss his past as well as his present life. In fact, it is the exception rather than the rule that one finds an older person who does not care to review his or her past.

This tendency toward reminiscence in "the life review process" (Butler, 1963) will be treated in more detail later. It is worth noting at this point that this general tendency enhances the history-taking aspect of assessment not only in terms of counselor time and effort but also in terms of developing client–counselor relationships.

Another point worth making has to do with the complex issue of dependency in these two cases. As was noted earlier in regard to the Cleveland protective services study (Blenkner et al., 1971), we have to be careful of bringing about undue dependency in the very process of providing counseling. In the case of Martin Stern there was a sense of pervasive dependency in his background and current functioning. His worker, Mrs. Meyers, has not only to contend with this dependency as a major obstacle to Mr. Stern achieving a greater sense of competence and autonomy, but she has to be aware of his inclination to assume a dependent role relative to her and to hold her accountable (rather than himself) for future failures and frustrations, as he blamed his wife after his retirement.

Conversely, Mr. Kaplan's background is one which indicates a resolution of the autonomy versus shame and doubt issue in favor of autonomy. Nevertheless, he shows an appropriate type of dependency in accepting the brief supportive and informational counseling Ms. Jacobi had to offer. In fact, we can speak of a "healthy" kind of dependency in old age as distinct from the defensive show of independence, of denial of realistic needs, in some older persons. Such independence is not adaptive, whereas the appropriate type of dependency is. Mr. Kaplan did not let his dependency go beyond just what was needed to see him through the shaky period after he was mugged. Furthermore, Ms. Jacobi was aware of this and went no further than was desired or indicated by Mr. Kaplan. It is worth noting that she made no effort to try to encourage him to return to the social activities of the senior center. She did not make the all too common assumption that all older persons can and should benefit from such social activities. She knew her client, his essential strength and autonomy, and she respected these.

In addition to this "appropriate dependency," Mr. Kaplan demonstrates another strength that should come with normal aging and which the counselor should be aware of and prepared to draw upon. This is a capacity I have termed "cognitive mastery," and by this I do not mean simply intellectual mastery. Rather, it is the capacity to think through and work through the meaning and implications of occurrences in one's life within a larger (life-span) perspective than the immediate one surrounding the occurrences. Mr. Kaplan showed this in putting the occurrence of the mugging into a larger perspective and working it through until it was actually adaptive for him. By thinking and working it through, he came to realize that it was the total lack of preparedness and the sudden loss of control in his life that most upset him. He came to accept the fact that this happened and that it could happen again in some other form, (such as an accident or stroke). He did what he could about future preparedness, that is, he previewed some possible settings he might go to in the event he became debilitated. Beyond this he accepted and integrated the fact that such an event could occur and that he would live in the present rather than fearing the future. It is this dual feature of (1) doing what one can about a situation and (2) accepting what one cannot change which is the essence of cognitive mastery. Mr. Kaplan did not react to the mugging by engaging in an anxious search for physical safety measures or by restricting his life space by not going out of his apartment unless necessary. This latter type of adjustment has been called "passive mastery" in the gerontological literature (Neugarten, 1965). Cognitive mastery is of a different nature, and because of its importance for integrative counseling it will be explained in much more detail later. At this point, it should suffice to say that cognitive mastery is one of a number of strengths that should develop in the normal course of aging and that it is a capacity upon which the integrative approach draws.

CHAPTER TWO

Personality Development in Late Adulthood

THERE HAS BEEN a virtual explosion of empirical studies on aging in the past two decades ranging from personality development to social activities, lifestyle, patterns of successful and unsuccessful adjustment, and so on, but there has been very little systematic theory building to explain the multitude of facts that have come out of this spate of studies. The conceptual schemes that have been called theories of aging often seem to be derived more from ideological than empirical bases, and they therefore fail to explain many of the facts that have been discovered in research findings. It is the intent here not only to present the most prominent findings and theories in the gerontological literature but also to mine them for the purposes of practice: prevention, intervention, and rehabilitation. The objective is to find out more about the complicating and contingent factors in problems faced by the aged, factors to which the gerontological practitioner should be attuned in assessment or diagnosis. In addition, we want to identify certain positive factors in the aging process that can assist in the prevention and amelioration of many supposedly age-related problems. In fact, it is a major contention of this chapter that there are personality developments in later adulthood that point to the growth of compensating psychological strengths and resources in very many older persons, even as their physiological and environmental strengths and resources diminish. In other words, there are potential strengths to be drawn upon by the older persons themselves and by the practitioners who work with them when it comes to the goal of attaining ego integrity and meaning in their lives in the face of problematic circumstances.

Prominent Theories of Aging

Although the first few theories presented here are not quite so prominent as those presented later, they represent the kind of partial theory that helps to explain some salient facts but fails to explain many others. They also represent, together with the last three, a kind of continuum beginning with theories that view the older person largely as a product or victim of age-related crises, losses, or larger social forces to theories that view the person as more inner-directed and capable of change and adaptation.

The minority group theory (Streib, 1965) tends to view the elderly largely as victims, and with much factual justification. This theory essentially contends that the aged are discriminated against primarily because they share a common visible biological characteristic, much like blacks or other racial minorities. Given the negative stereotypes and attitudes toward old age in society and the identifiable physical characteristics, the aged become easy targets for discrimination. Many of the products of discrimination are certainly present among the aged, including low income, unequal opportunities, and generally low status. Groups such as the Gray Panthers are very aware of these facts and have organized themselves accordingly.

The major problem with this theory is that although it applies well to the situations of many elderly persons it does not apply at all to others. For example, the U.S. Senate and the Supreme Court have disproportionate numbers of septagenarians with a great deal of influence and power. Nevertheless, this is an important and factually based conception of aging in our society, even though it lacks the attributes and explanatory power of a full theory.

Another theory which draws upon the shared characteristics of the aged to explain their circumstances and living patterns is the subculture theory (A. Rose, 1962). A subculture is a group within the larger society that shares many of society's cultural characteristics but also exhibits characteristics that are unique to it and are not generally found in other segments of society. Because of society's negative attitudes toward old age, many of the elderly are forced to live with and interact with one another in various segregated social and housing arrangements. This segregation from the larger society and the consequent interaction with one another are therefore seen as the prerequisites for the development of a genuine subculture. Again, there are problems with this theory in that there are some very dramatic differences among elements in the aged population that challenge the idea of a single subculture. For example, a subculture formed by wealthy aged would be vastly different from one formed by the poor, for whom financial need would be a pervasive theme. There would also be little interaction between the wealthy and the poor. However, the theory does describe a great deal about the aged in our society, and "subculture" is less pejorative in connotation than "minority."

Another theoretical framework from which to view the psychological experience of aging might be called role theory. Again, this is not a fully developed theory and it is not necessarily associated with any one author, but it does have a common theme, which is that the loss of significant roles is the dominant factor in the psychological ills of the aged. Miller (1965) has noted that when older persons are forced to retire, a crisis in identity is generated because of the loss of role and its associated norms and expectations. Phillips (1957) found in his research that older persons who had undergone role changes brought about by retirement, death of spouse, and so on, tended to experience greater maladjustment than persons who had not. An interesting and important aspect of the relationship between role loss and poor adjustment was the discovery of a mediating factor—"age identification." It was found that such a role loss in conjunction with a self-identification as "old" was strongly associated with maladjustment. But if the person underwent one such role change and was not self-identified as "old," the relationship did not hold. This age identification factor has been found repeatedly to be associated with poor morale in the aged, and it is a valuable prognostic indicator and an important piece of information for assessment and intervention, as will be illustrated later.

However, there are several problems with the role theory approach to aging. First, loss of a significant role in and of itself is not associated with poor adjustment if the "old" age identification factor is not present. Second, the theory does not provide us with an explanation of the personality factors that lead to a self-designation as old. Third, the negative identity outcomes found to be associated with retirement apply only to forced retirement, but numerous empirical studies show that most retirements are in fact voluntary (Blau, 1981). Therefore, most situations are left unexplained by this theory.

Unlike the above theories, the so-called activity theory sees the older person more as the determiner of his or her own adjustment and morale in old age. It has the slightly evangelistic overtones of the "power of positive thinking" (actually, "positive acting") and it is the theory that seems to correspond most to popular, common-sense notions about successful aging. Basically, it holds that older persons should remain active, especially when their major life roles have been lost. These roles should be replaced by other useful activities, whether paid or volunteer, formal or informal. Actually, the theory indicates that the norms of activity for middle age should be continued into old age. As a matter of fact, activity theory speaks directly to the problematic issue of age identification noted above in the discussion of role theory. Those older persons who remain active according to middle age norms tend to identify themselves as middle-aged rather than old. Furthermore, it has been found that activity tends to be associated with positive life satisfaction in some studies (Riley and Foner, 1968). The major problem with activity theory is that it does not take into account the necessity for reduced activity among many aged, especially those markedly affected by declining health. Furthermore, there have been research findings to the effect that general activity level is not significantly associated with life satisfaction (Lemon, Bengtson, and Peterson, 1972; Maddox, 1970).

The disengagement theory of aging has an explanation for the finding that life satisfaction does not necessarily decrease as a result of decreased activity in old age. The meaning of "disengagement" here is the process by which the aged individual gradually relinquishes roles and activities in society. Cumming and Henry (1961) noted in the course of a study of older persons in Kansas City that quite a few of their subjects welcomed retirement and a reduction in activity. They also noticed that disengagement was generally initiated by the elderly persons themselves, who tended to see it as a release from the pressures of the workaday world and a chance to reflect about themselves and their lives. Cumming and Henry saw this disengagement as a natural process that seemed to occur mostly as a mutual withdrawal of the person from the larger social system and the system from the person. They reasoned from a macro social perspective that society requires that persons in key positions have the energy, skills, and life expectancy to carry out necessary functions. From this broad social perspective, then, disengagement becomes institutionalized so that there is a mechanism whereby the elderly, with diminished ego energy and life expectancy, as well as possibly obsolescent skills and knowledge, can be replaced by younger persons with the requisite attributes.

From the perspective of the individual, what appears to happen is that the reduced interaction with others as a result of major role loss gives the person more energy and time to spend on reflection and concerns about self. It has been found that older people do tend to become more introverted and less oriented toward achievement in the external world (Riley and Foner, 1968). Neugarten (1969) has called this phenomenon the "interiority" of personality in old age.

This conception of aging certainly does not view the older person as a victim of role loss. There are, however, certain problems with the disengagement theory. The most frequently cited is the fact that many people do not voluntarily disengage, and in those cases it appears that there is decreased morale and greater maladjustment. Cumming (1963) elaborated further on the theory to take this objection into account. She noted that there can be disequilibrium when society desires disengagement and the person does not. This she calls "forced disengagement." Also, the person might desire disengagement and society does not, which she calls "forced engagement." An example of this would be an elderly person who is forced to remain the leader of a group or organization because no other leader can be found. The forced engagement and the forced disengagement situation both lead to low morale;

when there is mutual withdrawal by person and society, better morale results.

Another argument against the disengagement theory is similar to the one used against the minority theory, namely, that many persons in their sixties and seventies remain active and influential, particularly in government and public affairs. There appears to be no disengagement mechanism in these cases. Finally, later research cast light on factors that had not been sufficiently taken into account by the theory and that more adequately explain the relationship between activity and morale in old age. In a follow-up of a number of the persons studied by Cumming and Henry (Neugarten, Havighurst, and Tobin, 1968), it was found that there are developmental factors in aging that make for a greater continuity in personality and lifestyle than is assumed in either the activity or the disengagement theory. These researchers noted that "those characteristics that have been central to the personality seem to become even more clearly delineated, and those values the individual has been cherishing become even more salient" (Neugarten, Havighurst, and Tobin, 1968:177).

Their study showed that a number of different patterns of aging emerged when the factor of personality was analyzed in conjunction with activity and life satisfaction. Given the continuity of personality found in this study, the theory developed from it came to be known as continuity theory. Unlike activity and disengagement theory, it does not predict a single direction in the person's adjustment to aging. It indicates that there are many possible directions a person's adjustment can take, given different factors and circumstances. It does not indicate that lost roles must be replaced, as is assumed by the activity theory, nor must disengagement follow role loss. Instead, the individual has certain options which are contingent upon biological, psychological, and situational factors and which can lead to many more outcomes than would be predicted by the other theories. For this reason, the continuity theory probably comes closest to explaining the complex varieties of aging seen by most helping professionals. The patterns of aging which the authors of this theory generated in their follow-up study are dealt with later in this chapter.

The last theory to be mentioned in this section is not as prominent in the gerontological literature as the last three. However, it is a promising one, and it is the one on which the integrative approach draws heavily. It is called phenomenological theory, and it has been described by Crandall (1980) as "perhaps the most comprehensive and complete theory" in the gerontological field. It is not a new theory and can be said to have been founded and developed before World War II in Germany by Edmund Husserl (1958, 1968, 1970) in his writings on philosophy and psychology. It has been viewed primarily as a European development from its origins in Germany to its later evolution in France by thinkers like Marcel Merleau-Ponty (1962, 1963, and 1964). However, it did make its appearance in the American behavioral science literature forty years ago (Snygg, 1941), and it has been further developed within the context of American behavioral science (Combs, 1949; Combs and Snygg, 1959; Combs, Richards, and Richards, 1976; Giorgi, 1970; Keen, 1975).

In essence, phenomenological theory says that to understand human behavior it is necessary to understand the person's perceptual (phenomenal) world. The basic idea is that we perceive and interpret the world selectively—different people perceive the same phenomena differently. This perceptual world has been widely recognized and variously described as the person's "assumptive world" (Frank, 1974), "personal construction" of the world (Kelly, 1955), or the person's "reality world" (Cantril, 1957). Whatever it is called, phenomenological theory holds that if you can understand the person's perceptual framework you can understand and predict the person's behavior. When this is applied to the field of aging, we recognize that different aged persons will react differently to events such as widowhood, retirement and health changes. In fact, the longer one works in the field of aging the more one is struck by the fact that the manner in which older persons adjust to these events is very much determined by the way they perceive them.

A number of studies which demonstrate this fact will be cited as we go along, and a more comprehensive discussion of the perceptual/phenomenological view of aging will be provided at the end of this chapter. For the moment, it should be noted that this theory has not gained more prominence in the gerontological literature largely because of the difficulty in conducting the sort of scientific research deemed appropriate for testing theory in American behavioral science. This issue will also be addressed in the last section of this chapter.

Personality Traits and Typologies

Personality is a complex and interdependent system of mental faculties, including traits, motives, emotions, attitudes, perception, motility, creativity, and so on, and behavior patterns characteristic of the person that are recognized as such by others. However, personality is not a fixed entity. It is best viewed as a system that is constantly changing in response to events occurring inside and outside the individual. Thus, there is both continuity and change in personality. The question is what changes and what tends to remain the same or continuous in this broad construction called personality. There is quite a bit of evidence to the effect that there are age-related changes in traits, motivations, and energy levels or in the "covert" personality processes that are not directly amenable to conscious control (Bengtson, 1973:33). These covert processes are more related to feelings, such as self-esteem, sense of competence, and control, than to actions, such as socialization and work. Using a combination of projective tests and in-depth interviews, Neugarten (1965) was able to explore the last two of Erikson's stages of development. Her findings have particular importance for the integrative approach of this book because they were based on data from operationalized constructs of Erikson's scheme.

Neugarten found an increased saliency of the inner life which she called "the increased interiority of personality" in old age (Neugarten, 1969). It was marked by withdrawal of ego energy from the external environment, which was seen as more dangerous and complex by the 60-year-olds than the 40-year-olds. The 40-year-olds tended to see themselves as having enough energy to take advantage of opportunities and to overcome obstacles in the outer world, whereas the 60-year-olds tended to see themselves as accommodating more to the demands of the outer world. Neugarten (1965) describes this change as a move from active to passive mastery. This concept of "passive mastery" indicates a defensive or protective adaptation as a result of the fact that the 60-year-olds felt that the environment could no longer be reformed in line with their wishes. This has been identified in the gerontological research literature as an "external locus of control" (Kivett, Watson, and Busch, 1977; Kuypers, 1972), and it has been operationalized by a measure developed by Rotter (1966) which indicates the extent to which an individual perceives rewards from the environment as resulting from his or her own behavior (an internal locus of control) versus a perception that rewards are the result of external factors beyond the control of one's own behavior (external locus). This is an important concept in the integrative approach to counseling, because enhancement of a more internal locus of control is frequently an essential intermediate objective in achieving an overall treatment goal. It is a covert aspect of personality in that it indicates how a person perceives or feels about a situation rather than how a person acts in a situation. Clearly, it strongly influences how a person will act and that is why it is so important, but it is a mediating perceptual variable rather than an overt, behavioral outcome variable.

Overall, then, the aspects of personality that appear to change most with age are those dealing with the more covert, intrapsychic elements. Conversely, the aspects of personality which show the greatest continuity tend to be those having to do with overt adaptation to the social environment. Evidence from a number of studies shows stability of personality in the adaptive qualities of interpersonal functioning, lifestyle, life satisfaction, and personality type, as determined by personality testing (Maas and Kuypers, 1974; Neugarten, Havighurst, and Tobin, 1968; Reichard, Livson, and Peterson, 1962; Williams and Wirths, 1965). There seems to be an increasing commitment to a central core of values and habitual ways of behaving and relating to the outside world. At the same time, with the turn inward and greater interiority, many of the old attachments and animosities, likes and dislikes, alliances and grudges lose their saliency. The person is therefore able to concentrate more on the central core of values, the meaning of his or her life, and the cohesion of the habitual and continuous elements of the personality.

The continuity of personality has been noted in a number of empirical studies, which has led to several typologies of personality in aging. Reichard, Livson, and Peterson (1962) studied a sample of eighty-seven men from age 55 to 84 and were able to identify five distinct personality types: "mature," "rocking chair," "armored," "angry," and "self-haters." The mature men appeared to have well-integrated personalities in the sense that they could accept and integrate their past lives, their weaknesses as well as their strengths. They enjoyed their current lives, whether retired or not, and maintained at least a few close personal relationships. The rocking-chair men tended to be somewhat passive and dependent. They were glad to take it easy in their retirement, and they showed a high degree of self-acceptance. The armored type appeared to make considerable use of defense mechanisms against negative emotions and especially dependence. They maintained very active lifestyles and were generally well-adjusted. The high level of activity appeared to be demonstrating to them and to others their continued independence. To them dependence was a state much to be feared and avoided. The angry men, in contrast to the first three types, were not well-adjusted. They were hostile toward others and the world in general. They tended to blame others, they resented their wives, and they were quite fearful of death. The self-haters, on the other hand, had turned their hatred inward. They blamed themselves for failures and transgressions and openly rejected themselves and their past lives. They were clearly demoralized, depressed, and often welcomed the prospect of death.

All these men, in their sixth, seventh, and eighth decades of life, were quite consistent in their personality functioning with their earlier years of life. There appeared to be a simplification and greater cohesion of characteristic personality elements, particularly those elements that relate to the outside world (overt), but above all there was ample evidence of continuity.

Patterns of Aging

When Neugarten, Havighurst, and Tobin (1968) analyzed the data from the Kansas City study they came up with a somewhat similar typology of personality. The personality types they identified were: the integrated, the armored defended, the passive-dependent, and the unintegrated. They were, however, interested in personality not so much in its own right as one major factor in the total pattern of aging. Havighurst defined a pattern of aging as "a coherent complex of behavior, including social interaction and use of free time, achieved by an individual through the interaction of his personality with his physical organism and with the social setting" (Havighurst, 1968:71). Neugarten and associates attempted to identify such patterns that would be discovered empirically by a factor analysis of their data. The analysis included forty-five personality variables, the extent of role activity, and the degree of life satisfaction or morale of a group of people in the 70–79-year range.

The life satisfaction or morale measure (Neugarten, Havighurst, and Tobin, 1961) contained five components: (1) the extent to which the person takes pleasure from his or her everyday round of activities; (2) the extent to which the person regards his or her life as meaningful and accepts resolutely that which life has been; (3) the extent to which the person feels that he or she has succeeded in achieving his/her life goals; (4) the degree of the person's positive self-image; and (5) the extent to which the person maintains happy and optimistic attitudes and moods. A set of twenty questions was developed to tap these components, called the Life Satisfaction Index—Form A (Appendix A), the LSI-A was used to measure the life satisfaction of many of the persons in the case illustrations to be presented in this book. It will be explored in considerably more detail in Chapters 5 and 6.

The role activity measures in the study were based on ratings of the extent and intensity of activity in eleven social roles: parent, spouse, grandparent, in-group member, worker, homemaker, citizen, friend, neighbor, club-and-association member, and church member. Consequently, in this analysis the researchers were able to look at social role activity in relation to personality type and life satisfaction, which meant that they were able to address themselves to some questions in the activity versus disengagement controversy.

They found eight distinguishable patterns, the members of the first of which, termed the reorganizers, had integrated personalities with flexibility, comfortable impulse control, and competent egos and cognitive abilities. They appeared to be involved in a wide variety of reorganized activities, but their involvement in these activities seemed to come quite naturally to them and reflected continuity in their overt personality functioning. The second, focused pattern also consisted of persons with integrated personalities and high life satisfaction. They differed from the reorganizers in that they narrowed the range of their activities to one or two selective and cherished role areas. For example, after giving up the vocational pursuits, interests, and social relations associated with work they might devote much more time and energy to their homes and families than they did when employed.

The third pattern was a truly disengaged type, very much like the one described by Cumming and Henry (1961). These were people with integrated personalities in that they were well-functioning individuals with intact and competent egos and cognitive abilities. They accepted their impulses rather than heavily defending against them, but they still maintained a comfortable degree of control over them. The persons were adaptive and open to new experiences as well as being mellow and mature. In line with the disengagement idea, they were relatively low in social role activity; yet they showed high life satisfaction. Presumably their disengagement was not forced, because they appeared to be quite content with their life circumstances in much the same way as the "rocking chair" type.

The people in the fourth, holding-on pattern seemed to come closest to the patterns of their middle age. They were evidently quite successful at this in that they had high life satisfaction scores. However, their personality type was armored-defended in that they had high defenses against anxiety and rigid controls over their impulse life. They were ambitious, striving people who would probably be quite demoralized by a major physical incapacity that would prevent them from defending against their anxieties through activity.

The fifth or constricted pattern of aging also consisted of persons who had armored-defended personalities, but they had low or at best medium activity levels. They were characterized by medium to high life satisfaction. Instead of a wide range of activities, they tended to structure their lives by restricting their social activities and by closing themselves off from experience. Although they were preoccupied by losses and physical deficits, the defensive constriction of their lives seemed to be working for them to some extent because they did not have low life satisfaction scores. Good positive memories and reminiscences often seemed to sustain their morale without the satisfactions that would come from social engagement and new experiences.

The sixth, succorance-seeking pattern of aging was represented by a group of persons whose dependency needs were such that they would seek responsiveness from others. Therefore, their activity levels were mostly in the medium but not in the low level. They also managed to maintain medium levels of life satisfaction and did reasonably well as long as they had one or two persons available to meet their emotional needs.

Closer to the demoralized end of the life satisfaction continuum, the seventh or apathetic pattern emerged from analysis of the data. As in the case of the succorance-seeking, the apathetic persons had the passive-dependent personality type, but the outstanding feature of their personalities was their passivity while the more striking feature of the succorance seekers was their dependence. The apathetic persons would passively accept the emotional and instrumental ministrations of others, usually those in the immediate family. If such provisions were not forthcoming from others, their reactions were more apathetic than the succorance-seeking. Consequently, their activity level was low, and their life satisfaction was low to medium.

By far the most demoralized group fell in the eighth or disorganized, pattern with low life satisfaction scores and uniformly low role activity. Their personality type was "unintegrated," meaning that they had major disturbances in psychological functioning which were manifested through poor control over impulses and emotions and deterioration of thought processes.

It is noteworthy that the personality types that emerged from the factor analysis done by Neugarten and associates (1968) not only were quite similar to those found by Reichard, Livson, and Peterson (1962), but also provided the same kind of evidence for continuity of the more overt aspects of personality over time. This has clear implications for the intervention model proposed in the next chapter.

Changes in Self-Concept and Lifestyle

In view of the foregoing evidence that there is apt to be more change in the covert aspects of personality than in the overt, we might expect to find some changes in how older persons perceive and feel about their "selves," since the self is an intrapsychic element of the personality. Because of the human capacity to develop abstract ideas and symbols, it is possible for the individual to think about his or her own appearance, body, and even mind and to interpret feedback from within and from others outside. This interpretation of perceived feedback is what defines the self. As Riegel (1958) has delineated, the person tries to integrate all of these perceptions, experiences, and ideas into the structural system of the self. This integration is a lifelong process, and how successfully it is done in the long run will essentially determine the issue of ego integrity versus despair. For this reason self theory is central to an integrative approach to counseling the elderly.

Perhaps more than any other theorist with an applied bent, Rogers (1965) has outlined a construct of self in line with the foregoing discussion, operationalizing the elements of the self system so as to measure changes in them. For this reason, Rogers's conception of the self system will be drawn upon most heavily in this book.

There are three major elements in the self system in this conception: (1) the self-concept; (2) the self-ideal; and (3) self-esteem. The self-concept is the cognitive element of the self system in that it is what the person thinks he or she is like. The self-ideal represents a composite of standards for behavior, performance, and achievement based on precepts and examples obtained from parents, teachers, and other role models available in the larger social and cultural milieu. Self-esteem is the affective or emotional element of the self system in that it is how the person feels about his or her self-concept in comparison to the self-ideal. It is apparent that social roles are extremely important in the development of the self-ideal, since the behavioral expectations and standards associated with social positions are what constitute a social role. How one performs one's social roles can have major impact on one's self-esteem, for to the extent that one meets or exceeds expectations with regard to role performance, one can receive positive feedback from others as well as from the self. Under such circumstances, of course, the person will feel good about himself or herself. A failure to meet expectations, conversely, is likely to result in feelings of shame and low self-esteem. Thus, self-esteem is apt to be a rather changeable element in the short as well as

the long run. The loss of social roles or the reduction of activity or performance in social roles as an inevitable part of aging can clearly pose a direct
threat to self-esteem. Furthermore, it should be noted that since self-esteem
is emotional in content, it tends to be responsive to moods and bodily states
as well as to performances and experiences in the external world. Obviously,
the bodily changes inherent in the aging process can also be related to
changes in self-esteem.

Self-concept tends to be much more stable and consistent, resisting the
losses and role changes of later life. This is because, in line with the findings
of greater interiority mentioned earlier, the self-concept becomes less dependent on external factors than on inner ones as the person enters later life.
There are, of course, individual variations. Some older people remain somewhat dependent on external factors and fail to achieve any degree of closure
on their self-concepts. The succorance seekers would tend to fit this description. Others, however, have been able to integrate prior experiences and
perceptions into their current self-system and achieve a healthy degree of
closure. These would be the integrated personality types, but closure can
also happen in other personality types. Certain defense mechanisms such as
denial can assist the older person in protecting self-esteem. The person can
refuse to perceive or accept negative feedback and may avoid or downgrade
people who would be likely to provide negative feedback.

Clearly, variations in the self system are apt to be associated with differences in lifestyle in old age. By lifestyle is meant the "observable organization of an individual's activities in terms of his use of time, investment of
energy, and his choice of interpersonal objects" (Bengtson, 1973:37). Although there is some relationship between self-concept and lifestyle, lifestyle
is associated much more with the overt aspects of personality because of its
observable nature. As such, it shows considerable continuity over time. This
was demonstrated quite clearly in a longitudinal study reported by Maas and
Kuypers (1974), in which married couples who had been interviewed in 1930
as young parents were interviewed forty years later. Ten different lifestyles
were identified in the study, four for the men and six for the women:

1. family-centered fathers: these were men whose lifestyle centered on
   their spouse-parent-grandparent roles.
2. hobbyist fathers: the lives of these men tended to be focused on
   instrumental leisure activities around the house.
3. remotely sociable fathers: these were socially active fathers without
   strong commitment to major role areas such as marriage, family, and
   work.
4. unwell-disengaged fathers: the poor health of these men resulted in
   their withdrawal from social role activity.
5. husband-centered wives: marriage was the center of activity for these
   women.

6. uncentered mothers: these women engaged in much informal visiting with family and friends, but were not involved in work or clubs.
7. visiting mothers: these were involved in both club activities and informal visiting.
8. employed (work-centered) mothers: the lives of these mothers revolved around their work.
9. disabled-disengaged mothers: these women showed withdrawal from the world in the same way as the "unwell-disengaged fathers."
10. group-centered mothers: these mothers were involved in many recreational activities outside the home.

Although these individuals were partners in marriage, there were differences between the men and the women with regard to changes in lifestyle. The lifestyles of the men tended to show more stability over time. With the women, lifestyles were more apt to be dependent upon their current life situations. "Employed mothers" showed considerable change in lifestyle in that they gained a great deal of satisfaction from increased independence and new friends in contrast to their often unsatisfactory marriages and the economic problems related to one income before they became employed. In addition, they evidently underwent some positive changes in self-concept. Given the close connection between self-concept and social role, the assumption of a new social role by these women in their work offered new referents and feedback for the development of self-concept and therefore self-esteem.

An earlier typology of lifestyle by Williams and Wirths (1965) based on the Kansas City studies found six styles represented in their analysis:

1. *World of work*. These people made up 15 percent of the group studied, and they were distinguished by their focus of attention on work to give meaning to their lives. It was the narrowest in focus of the six lifestyles and it did not allow much room for adjustment to retirement if the person did not have a rapid or readily available replacement in volunteer activity or other alternatives to work.

2. *Familism*. For a third (33 percent) of the sample, the family was the center of their lives before retirement and it became so even more afterward. The "family-centered fathers" in the Maas and Kuypers (1974) study would certainly have fit into this category.

3. *Living alone*. This group consisted of 13 percent of the sample, and it was made up of persons whose central focus in relating to the world was that of a social isolate. Although they did not all actually live alone, they were inner-directed people who liked being so. They therefore represented a form of disengagement.

4. *Couplehood*. Paired relationships, whether of spouses, siblings, or close friends, were the focus of this group. They made up 20 percent of the sample and they were in some jeopardy for later adjustment if something happened

to the partner. The "husband-centered wife" of the Maas-Kuypers typology would clearly fit in this category.

5. *Easing through.* People described as "easing through life with minimal involvement" made up 7 percent of the sample. They had shown only minimal commitment to major life roles such as work, marriage, and family. This style, like the others, tended to be somewhat consistent throughout life but if it was adopted in the later years it represented a form of disengagement.

6. *Living fully.* People who seemed to get involved on more than a superficial level in a range of activities and experiences made up 13 percent of the sample. They appear to be very similar to the "reorganizers" in the patterns of aging outlined by Neugarten, Havighurst, and Tobin (1968).

Which of these lifestyles were the most successful as far as aging is concerned? Williams and Wirths indicated that successful aging was a function of the "personal action system" of the person, of which two elements necessary for success in aging are autonomy and persistence. To the extent that an individual gives back to his or her action system as much as is taken from it, that person is autonomous. If the person takes more than he or she receives, the person is dependent. To the extent that the personal action system is stable, it shows persistence, but if it is subject to change and instability, it is precarious. Of the six groups in the typology, the living fully and familism types were the most successful in that they demonstrated the qualities of autonomy and persistence most clearly. Again, in the studies of lifestyle we see evidence of continuity in the overt aspects of personality showing up just as in the studies on patterns of aging. Clearly, this has to be taken into account in the development of any model of intervention and counseling for the aged.

The Life Review Process and the Role of Reminiscence

Another theme that comes through the literature on personality in aging is that of reminiscence and the life review process. Perhaps the earliest systematic empirical evidence of this process appeared in the work of Charlotte Buhler and Else Frenkel-Brunswick at the Psychological Institute of the University of Vienna in the 1930s (Frenkel-Brunswick, 1963). They noted that in the last of the five periods of life there was a prevalence of retrospective experiences and concerns as well as considerations of the future in terms of oncoming death. In other words, the "balance-sheet of life" is being drawn up, and this appears to be a near-universal experience. "The life review process" is a phrase most frequently associated with the name of Robert N. Butler (1963), a psychiatrist and currently director of the National Institute on Aging. On the basis of extensive work with the elderly, Butler felt that the mental process of reviewing one's life was a universal experience in older persons. He described the process as one characterized by a return to consciousness of past experiences and unresolved conflicts which can then be surveyed and reintegrated into the personality. This process can have both negative consequences, leading to panic, guilt, and depression, and positive results, leading to greater candor, serenity, and wisdom.

Butler might not be correct in his assertion that there is increased reminiscence among the aged, however. It has been found that there does not seem to be a significantly greater frequency of reminiscing in the elderly and that the quality, rather than the quantity, of the reminiscence may be the important feature (Giambra, 1977). Actually, Frenkel-Brunswick (1963) had noted much earlier that the last phase of life has "a certain parallelism, queerly enough, with the age of adolescence." Reminiscence among adolescents is evidenced by the widespread use of diaries at that stage of life. There is a parallel increase in the writing of memoirs and autobiographies among the aged. Both age groups are in transition on a similar dimension: the adolescent has to leave the life of childhood and make the transposition to adulthood. The older person has to come to terms with the past and to leave that life behind in preparation for oncoming death.

Regardless of the issue of frequency of reminiscence in old age relative to other ages, the very presence and experience of reminiscence can be an important factor in work with older persons. Havighurst and Glasser (1972) found good personal and social adjustment associated with high frequency of reminiscence with positive affect. Although they could not tell whether high-frequency, positive-affect reminiscence leads to good adjustment or vice versa, there was a significant relationship between them. How one enhances such a relationship in practice is the important question. Of possible import in this regard is the finding by C. N. Lewis (1971) that reminiscence can be ego-supportive for the person by enabling him or her to identify with past accomplishments. Thus he or she can avoid the discrepancy between self-concept and self ideal that can occur when the person retires from or loses a major social role.

The Perceptual View of Aging

In the earlier discussion of phenomenological theory the terms "perceptual" and "phenomenological" both were used to describe the same ideas. Rather than use the unwieldy fusion, "perceptual/phenomenological," I will favor the term "perceptual." There are several reasons for this preference. First, the term more directly connotes the idea that the way in which a person perceives a situation will best predict behavior in the situation. Second, the term "phenomenology" seems to connote more of a European-born philosophy than a personality theory with some empirical underpinnings. Third, the term "perceptual" more readily calls attention to the rich trove of empirical and theoretical contributions in the area of perceptual psychology: work by Jerome Bruner, Arthur Combs, Else Frenkel-Brunswick, Kurt Lewin, and others. These contributions will be used and cited in the description of the background and foundations of integrative practice provided in Chapter 3.

No matter where one turns in the field of aging, after having dropped the blinders of age stereotyping, one is struck by the great variety in types of personality and responses to significant life events among the aging. The two men described in the beginning of the book, Martin Stern and Max Kaplan, reacted with marked differences to the same kinds of life events, particularly their retirements and the deaths of their wives. As one looks more closely at these two case illustrations, it becomes more evident that the way in which the two men perceived the events and situations was markedly different and that this difference serves to explain most of the difference in their responses.

The importance of perception as a mediating variable in explaining differences in emotional and behavioral responses became abundantly clear to me in a study of the incidence and fear of crime among elderly tenants of public housing units (Sherman, Newman, and Nelson, 1976). In that study, measures of fear of crime expressed by many individuals were totally at variance with the objective incidence of crime in their respective housing situations. Very often, this finding showed up in situations in which statistics on the actual incidence of crime in and around the housing unit were the lowest in the study settings, but in which the individuals indicated a great fear of being victimized. Conversely, there were quite a few persons in settings with high crime statistics who had less fear, as indicated by the same measures, as those in the low incidence housing. Clearly, the difference was determined more by how dangerous the persons perceived the situation to be than by the objective characteristics of the situation itself.

Another study which brought this home to me was an interview survey of the meaning of cherished possessions for the elderly (Sherman and Newman, 1977). Since this was a study of the *meaning* of cherished objects, it was clearly measuring a perceptual factor. Even so, the great variety of responses, affects, and general moods evoked by the same kinds of objects seemed remarkable. In one instance, there were two women in the same section of a nursing home who identified photographs of their dead daughters as their most cherished possession. The kinds of associations the photograph evoked in one woman turned out to be very depressed ruminations about how the daughter's death ruined her own life, of how her daughter (there were other children still living) would have taken care of her so that she would not have to be in a nursing home, and so on. The photograph of the other woman's daughter evoked diametrically different thoughts and associations. First, she said that the photo reminded her that she had been a mother; the daughter had given her a great deal of satisfaction and therefore the photograph showed that her life had meaning. Not surprisingly, this woman had a very high measure on the Life Satisfaction Index, whereas the first woman had a very low one.

Perhaps the most impressive findings in gerontological research bearing on the importance of perception are those having to do with perceived age of self, or what is more commonly called self-identified or subjective age. It has been shown repeatedly that those who perceive themselves as old or elderly tend to have lower measures of morale than those who do not (Edwards and Klemmack, 1973; Linn and Hunter, 1979; Phillips, 1957). Furthermore, the person's subjective age is related more to psychological adjustment than to actual chronological age (Linn and Hunter, 1979). Specifically, there is better psychological functioning if the older person's subjective perception of age is younger rather than older.

The same phenomenon shows up in studies dealing with subjective perception of health as a variable (Maddox, 1962 and 1973; Palmore and Luikart, 1972; Tissue, 1972). Although there was generally a good correlation between subjectively perceived health and objectively (medically) determined health in these studies, there tended to be a stronger correlation between subjective health and morale than between objective health and morale. What this means again is that the subjective perception of an event or condition tends to color the mood or emotional reaction to the condition more than the objective nature of the actual condition.

It is rather remarkable that all this evidence of the explanatory power of a perceptual perspective on reactions to the events and processes of aging has not had a more formal theoretical impact on the field of social gerontology. As suggested earlier, this is probably due to the difficulty of conducting the kind of research currently deemed necessary for testing theory in the social and behavioral sciences. That type of research is largely what is called nomothetic. That is, groups of individuals (usually large survey samples in social gerontology) are tested or measured and generalizations are made from the samples to the populations they were drawn from based on averages of all the measures. It should be clear that if there are so many differences between individuals in the way they perceive any one event or condition, it is awfully hard and probably meaningless or invalid to take averages of these perceptions and attempt to generalize from them. Perceptions by their very nature are highly unique and individual; therefore, the type of research that is appropriate to their study should be one that is designed to measure that very uniqueness. This type of research is called idiographic, that is, dealing with the single individual in terms of that person's unique attributes and behaviors. The idiographic method would involve the observation, testing, and measurement of an individual in terms of his/her variability at various points in time. In a sense, then, the variable measures or observations over time can be used to generalize to the individual in terms of central tendency and also to predict likely responses in future and other circumstances. The idiographic method is indeed used in some clinical practice to evaluate the significance of changes occurring in individuals in the course of counseling or psychotherapy. Unfortunately, this type of information cannot legitimately be aggregated to generalize to entire populations (Kerlinger, 1979). Yet, it is generalization that characterizes most recognized gerontological research.

The point to be made here, however, is that an integrative practice is clinical practice with individuals or groups of individuals. Therefore, observations and instruments are used to measure client functioning for the purposes of assessment and diagnosis, as well as to evaluate the extent and type of change in functioning in the course of counseling. In general, the types of observations and instruments used in integrative counseling either come from the field of gerontology or are designed or adapted specifically for integrative practice. These will be described in Chapter 3 and their use demonstrated in case illustrations in Chapters 5 and 6.

Another possible reason for the failure of gerontologists to pursue or develop a perceptual theory of aging is that such a theory by its very nature would tend to emphasize intrinsic personality processes over the life span. Currently, theories that stress internal processes are held in some disfavor as they have been for over the past ten years (Lieberman, 1980). Mischel (1976, 1977) has noted that contextual inputs or situational contingencies must be taken into account in explaining behavior, since intrinsic personality concepts serve to explain only some of the behaviors some of the time. Mischel's influential viewpoint has had an impact on some of the most recent contributions to the applied field of gerontology (Zarit, 1980). However, although the perceptual view necessarily deals with a phenomenon that appears to reside "inside" the person, it is nevertheless not a static view of personality as are posited by those theories that emphasize one general trait or characteristic of the person (for example, introversion/extroversion) and proceed to generalize to any and all situations. By its very nature, the perceptual view takes into account contexts or situational contingencies. That is, the "external" situation and the "internal" perceptual apparatus that processes it are both part of the total perceptual field. It is this field view of personality functioning that underlies integrative practice.

This very dynamic field view of perception would appear to be so variable and so situational as to resist the notion or possibility of any consistency in or prediction of behavior. Yet, this is not so, for our perception is not only interactive with the environment, it is also constructive. Bruner (1957) has said that perception is not so much a matter of representation of either internal or external stimuli as it is a matter of "model building." That is, perception involves acts of categorization, and as we gain more and more experience in dealing with the world we try to make more consistent sense out of the myriad stimuli and masses of information that reach our receptors. We therefore develop stereotyped systems or categories for sorting out all this input, and our prior experience with objects tends to strengthen our category systems. Furthermore, predominant features of individual personality seem to exist mainly in the category system of the perceiver. Therefore, if we can accurately determine the category system of an individual, we will be quite far along in predicting the behavior of that individual. Also, since the set of categories a person develops is limited, the possibility of prediction becomes even greater. Unfortunately, this limited set also means that much of the richness and variability of input can be missed or overlooked, and stereotyping in its more pejorative sense becomes more likely. Thus, if we consider a person to be "pushy," we will tend to sort all of that person's actions in terms of that particular category.

The importance of these observations about perception for the problems of aging should be apparent. If our prior experience with objects tends to strengthen our category systems, we would expect that there would be greater rigidity in our perceptions as we age. Some research on cognitive styles does show a tendency toward greater rigidity as persons grow older (Chown, 1961; Schaie and Labouvie-Vief, 1974). However, there is inconsistency in this evidence (Zarit, 1980), and there is still much variability among the aged themselves on the rigidity dimension. At any rate, we need to know more about this dimension if we are to work effectively with the aging.

Frenkel-Brunswick has described the process of increased rigidification in terms of an intolerance of ambiguity by which an effort is made to shut out uncertainties "thus narrowing what Tolman has called the 'cognitive map' to rigidly defined tracks" (1951:395). If this is the process of rigidification, how does it differ from the process described by Neugarten and associates (1968) in which the central characteristics of the personality become more clearly delineated and the cherished values become more salient? They saw this continuity of core values and characteristics as essentially positive, whereas rigidification clearly is not. The difference between the continuity and rigidity aspects lies in their purposes and outcomes. Rigidity serves a protective or defensive purpose; it screens out unwanted or dangerous information, frequently at the expense of reality. Continuity, on the other hand, allows the individual to slough off information that is clearly unimportant and provides for actively seeking out that which is valued. It is not intended to screen out information that is feared. In other words, continuity would be characteristic of the integrated personality noted earlier, whereas rigidity would be characteristic of the armored defended. Continuity suggests a proactive rather than a reactive stance.

The Place of Values in Aging

This proactive quality implies intentionality, and there is good reason to believe that the intentional articulation of one's behavior in terms of one's goals or values is highly adaptive in the aging process. Lowenthal (1980) has developed a paradigm for the study of adaptation in aging which involves a systematic exploration for the relationship between the individual's global goals (or values) and concrete goals with behavior. The greater the congruence of expectations based upon the goals and values with actual behavior, the better the adaptation to the stresses and problems of aging. In line with the perceptual view of aging, Lowenthal observed that "among relevant self-perceptions are what might be called a stress-proneness dimension, illustrated by two individuals exposed to roughly equivalent levels of life stresses, one of whom dwells on stress in recounting his life history, whereas the other merely recounts it and goes on to other matters " (1980:6).

This is consistent with the perceptual perspective, and in fact her intentionality paradigm has been identified with phenomenology (Hendricks, 1980). At any rate, values are an important element in the perceptual view of personality. Arthur Combs, a major contributor to the literature on perceptual psychology, has noted that values are too frequently viewed as remote abstractions but that they in fact affect a wide field of behavior (Combs, Richards, and Richards, 1976). Values frequently are of a generic nature, which makes them seem abstract, but some can be as specific as disapproval of people who chew with their mouths open. Rigidity of perception in aging is apt to take the form of these highly specific preferences or values in behavior and attitude. The rigidity is a defense against underlying conflict and confusion; therefore, it is very difficult for such persons to clearly perceive and articulate their generic values. Frenkel-Brunswick has made the following observation about nonrigid perception:

> Persons with less severe underlying confusions, on the other hand, may be able to afford to face ambiguities openly, although this may mean at least a temporary facing of conflicts and anxieties as well. In this case the total pattern is that of a broader integration of reality, in which no parts are left out, and thus a more flexible adaptation to varying circumstances [Frenkel-Brunswick, 1951:395].

Max Kaplan exhibited this type of flexibility and integration in the way he adapted to the mugging experience. He has faced the ambiguity of the future openly and he has chosen (value preference) to live in the present rather than worry about the future, which he will face when the time comes. Many older people do not, however, display the kind of clarity about their own values that is posited by continuity theory. This is important for gerontological practice, because values-clarification methods have been used with some success with older persons (Weiner, Brok, and Snadowsky, 1978). A preferred approach to values clarification will be provided by case illustration in Chapter 6, but the important point at the moment is that clarification of values is likely to be only one step in extended integrative counseling. This is consistent with the point made earlier about the importance of congruence between values and behaviors (Lowenthal, 1980). From the perceptual view of integrative practice, we are interested in clarifying values so that we can assess the congruence or discrepancy between clarified values and actual behavior. We are also interested in perceived behavior, because the client's actual behavior might be at variance with his or her perception of it, and we have to look at both actual and perceived behavior in relation to explicit values in the assessment process. In one instance, the person's actual behavior might be markedly discrepant with the stated value. In another case, the client's actual behavior is not as discrepant as he perceives it to be. This will become abundantly clear in the section of the next chapter that deals with self-concept (perceived self, including behavior and attributes) and ideal self (the self one would like to be based on one's ideals or values).

Another point needs to be made about values in integrative counseling. One of the foremost figures in the study of values, Milton Rokeach, has demonstrated experimentally that values can be changed when dissonance or discordance in peoples' value systems can be exposed and presented to them in certain ways (Rokeach, 1973). The whole issue of changing values of clients in counseling poses a major value question in its own right. However, if in the process of value clarification (involving no effort to change the client's values, just to clarify them) it becomes evident to the client that certain values he holds are unrealistic, self-defeating, or self-deflating, he might be motivated to make the changes himself. This too will become abundantly clear when the value called the "functionalistic ethic" is discussed in Chapter 4.

A number of important concepts have emerged from the foregoing empirical findings and review of literature on personality development in later years. Among those that are central to or have important implications for integrative practice are the following: increased interiority, locus of control, passive and cognitive mastery, self-concept and ideal self, reminiscence and the life review process, values clarification, and congruence. All of these concepts will be addressed again in the following chapters, and all of them will have to be viewed within the basic perceptual framework that underlies integrative practice.

The reader might well wonder why so much attention was given to the perceptual view in the foregoing discussion. After all, we are all familiar with the Rashomon phenomenon in which several people who witness the same crime see it in markedly different, mutually exclusive ways. It would therefore seem self-evident that each person perceives reality differently. The answer to this is that *perceptions can be changed*, and this is central to integrative practice. This point is especially important for older persons and cannot be stressed too much, for although perceptions can be changed, reality frequently cannot. Although older persons cannot realistically control some aspects of their lives, they can control their perceptions of these aspects, and the integrative approach provides the means and techniques for helping them gain such control. It can be seen, then, that the perceptual view is central to treatment as well as assessment in integrative practice.

CHAPTER THREE

Background, Components, and Principles of the Integrative Approach

Requirements of an Integrative Approach

The foregoing review of findings concerning personality development in late adulthood was intended to outline some of the salient points that need to be considered in counseling the elderly with respect to the last task of life: attaining and sustaining a sense of integrity.

There are several reasons for selecting the term "integrative" to describe the counseling approach proposed here. First, the approach attempts to integrate certain insights and techniques from various treatment theories or schools of thought with empirical findings derived from developmental studies of the aged and knowledge gained from direct practice with elderly persons. The term "integrative" also serves to describe the process whereby the person is helped to achieve and sustain a sense of integrity as against despair about his or her life, to integrate past, present, and future in a way that is unique to the individual.

The integrative approach attempts, first of all, to be comprehensive. Although it is concerned with the ultimate problem of integrity versus despair, it takes note of the fact that there are many problems of an immediate and intermediate nature with which the elderly client needs help. Many aged persons are overwhelmed with concerns about health and financial solvency. These cannot be ignored, and they impede the attainment of integrity and increase the sense of despair. Further, there may be ongoing problems of an interpersonal nature with family, friends, and other significant persons and institutions in the client's life space.

A venerable principle in the history and literature of social work practice holds that the three elements of person, problem, and situation should all be considered in case assessment and intervention (Siporin, 1972). This certainly applies in work with the elderly client. As far as the person element is concerned, we have to be aware of the client's strengths and the capacity and motivation for change, and in the integrative approach we have to be particularly concerned with the concept of self. How does the client see himself or herself: strong or weak, young or old, competent or incompetent? In addition to this self-concept, we need to know the client's ideal self, the sort of person he or she would ideally like to be and, with many elderly, would like to have been. Finally, we have to be concerned with the discrepancy between the ideal and the real self, which should provide us with some measure of the client's self-esteem.

The element of situation calls for study and assessment of the client's social situation with regard to family and significant others and the client's physical/spatial situation with regard to housing, living circumstances and facilities, general ambience, and so on. Even the broader social or cultural context of the client cannot be ignored. The values derived from various ethnic backgrounds as well as the values and stereotypes of American society, as they impinge on the client, must be taken into account.

The Centrality of Meaning for Integrative Practice

A central theme in the integrative approach to counseling is the emphasis on the meaning of events, circumstances, and significant others to the client. It is very clear from studies of successful and unsuccessful aging that people attribute different meanings to the inevitable physical decrements and other developmental events of aging (Clark and Anderson, 1967; Williams, 1963). Those who are unsuccessful in aging see these losses as catastrophic, debilitating, and often unfair. Those who age successfully see the losses as unfortunate but not catastrophic and find ways to compensate for them. They also develop a more philosophical view of them within the perspective of their total life span.

This focus on meaning is quite consistent with the perceptual framework outlined in Chapter 2. What this means for integrative practice is that it is important to keep in the background of our thinking during assessment and intervention that the older person's subjective perception, what the person *thinks* about his or her situation (its meaning), is every bit as important for the person's morale and adjustment as the reality of the situation itself. The importance of the person's subjective perception of age (Linn and Hunter,

1979) and subjective perception of health (Palmore and Luikart, 1972) have already been mentioned, but it has also been found that "symbolic" losses (loss of sense of control, of mastery) can be just as central as "concrete" losses (loss of spouse, of health) in depression among the elderly (Salzman and Shader, 1979). In addition, something as abstract as "awareness of finitude" (perceived amount of time left to live) was found to be a much stronger predictor of activity level and disengagement that actual age or physical incapacity (Sill, 1980).

Meaning is therefore the central intervening variable in the integrative approach. The counselor has to ascertain the meaning attached to an event, action, person, or thought by the client. The self-concept is also central to the integrative approach. Meaning has to be related to the self, because it is only through a reflective self that one can make something meaningful out of an event or happening. In early childhood, when we are so dependent and impressionable, we do not yet have the wherewithal (autonomous ego functioning) to develop independent impressions. Our sense of self and meanings of self/other and inner/outer is given by others and by circumstances. We all retain to some extent these earlier meanings, impressions, and constructs, even after we develop the cognitive ego capacities to subject our often erroneous and distorted impressions and meanings to more mature scrutiny. To change this earlier meaning is extremely threatening to our very selves, because it is these attributed meanings we take to be our selves. Since we think they are our selves, we are thrown into a state of anxiety or see a need to defend our selves against the onset of anxiety when they are challenged or threatened. However, since adults have greater cognitive ego capacities (barring severe organic brain disorder) than they had as children, they can subject prior meanings to new scrutiny and reconstruction, and in this way change the meanings of their selves, others, life's events, and life itself.

One major area in which such change manifests itself in the normal course of development and aging is the letting go of illusions or dreams, often of a grandiose nature and infantile in origin, about anticipated superlative accomplishments and qualities of one's self. Birren (1964), summarizing the research findings in this area, noted that in normal aging "it was as though growing older had led to acceptance of the past and to a kind of renunciation of the unattained, perhaps somewhat irrational, goals of earlier life" (1964:234). The point of this process is that the letting go of illusions allows for the acceptance of reality, of one's self, and one's life. And this, after all, is precisely what Erikson describes as the "acceptance of one's one and only life cycle as something that had to be and ... permitted of no substitutions (1963:268). However, many of us do not let go of unrealistic goals (which are often unrecognized), and the resultant feelings of inadequacy, nonattainment, and self-denigration lead inevitably to a sense of despair.

Although this might seem to be belaboring the obvious, it is clear that many professionals in the field of human relations have not accepted or incorporated the potential capacities for change inherent in the concept of ego autonomy. Briefly stated, ego autonomy as proposed by Hartmann (1964) refers to aspects of the human ego that are autonomous or independent of instinctual forces. These are generally "executive" functions having to do with intention, perception, comprehension, and motor development. The important point for our purposes is that some of these functions can be conflict-free, that is, free of the regressive pulls of the instincts and the forces of the id. Such functions as intention, perception, and comprehension can be brought to bear by the client on the problems and dilemmas of aging, thus serving an adaptive, problem-solving purpose in the last stage of life when losses and consequent regressive pulls take place.

Pinkus (1967) argues for a developmental view of old age and is critical of practice that does not follow Hartmann's emphasis on the processes of adaptation and mastery but instead emphasizes the defense mechanisms. He claims that this has led to a view of aging that is expressed in such terms as "regression," "rigidity," and "ego disintegration." Thus, aging is viewed as a reactive set of processes rather than as inherent or developmentally controlled. But, says Pinkus, "those aspects [of personality change] such as increased introversion may be looked upon as evidence of change, redirection, and reintegration of ego energy and emotional investment rather than of decline, regression, or ego disintegration" (1967:38).

The integrative approach views these changes as normal and developmental and also in many ways as functional for adaptation to and mastery of the losses and traumas of old age and, ultimately, for the accomplishment of the last task of old age. The faculties of perception, comprehension, judgment, and intention enable the elderly client to review his or her construction of the meanings of certain prior activities and events and to reconstrue them in the light of his or her total life span and the imminence of death. Frankl (1959) noted the significance of the search for meaning for persons interned in concentration camps during the holocaust of World War II. Old age and the proximity to death should impel the same search for meaning.

The Contribution of Cognitive Approaches

Given these concerns about meaning, it is rather natural that cognitive theory and practice techniques form a central part of the integrative approach. Beck (1976), a major contributor to cognitive theory and practice, has noted that the meaning one imposes on an experience determines one's emotional response, as was true in the case of Max Kaplan's response to the mugging experience. Therefore, the negative and debilitating affects that are often associated with the problems of old age, such as depression and anxiety, can be approached through the person's cognition, or ability to think. It is after all the cognitive functions, the abilities to reason and judge, that are more likely than the sensory and physical functions to remain constant well into old age. Thus, cognitive approaches to counseling make considerable sense.

Cognitive theory, like psychoanalytic theory, is insight-oriented. As Beck (1976) notes, "insight is a cognitive process consisting of identifying thoughts, feelings, and wishes and making psychological reactions" (1976:313). A primary difference between the cognitive and psychoanalytic schools of thought lies in the affective dimension of insight.

In psychoanalytic thinking, the phenomenon of "abreaction" is highly regarded and pursued in the treatment process. Abreaction is essentially the "reliving" of an alleged traumatic event or condition in childhood or infancy. Intellectual, cognitive recognition or insight is not deemed sufficient in itself to be truly effective from a therapeutic point of view. What is necessary is to re-experience the full affective, emotional intensity of the initial and continuing anxiety associated with the event or condition and thereby defuse and neutralize it. This approach necessarily involves getting through the defense mechanisms that presumably serve to protect the individual against the overwhelming anxiety associated with the event or condition.

The cognitive approach does not require such "affective insight" and in fact largely eschews the techniques designed to obtain it. Some of the leading practitioners of cognitive approaches were themselves trained and analyzed and first practiced within the psychoanalytic school of thought. They claim, however, that even when their patients experienced abreactions they did not get any better psychologically (see Ellis, 1962; Greenwald, 1973). It has also been pointed out that there is no solid empirical evidence to support the validity or efficacy of this particular psychoanalytic principle (Beck, 1976).

There are other, more compelling reasons for not attempting to attack the defenses or otherwise to probe and interpret the unconscious of the elderly client. First, it can be dangerous to the psychological well-being of the client. As noted in the research by Busse and Pfeiffer (1969), certain defense mechanisms serve positive functions in old age. For example, temporary use of the mechanism of denial can see the person through the initial impact of a major loss of a loved one. Butler and Lewis (1977) have also noted that overwhelming feelings of guilt engendered by probing and reawakening repressed material can indeed lead to utter despair in some elderly persons.

A second compelling argument is that there simply is not enough time to do the reparative work that would be necessary to undo the effects of the emotional exposure and disarming of the individual. It is one thing to undertake such affective restructuring in a young adult, but it would seem a highly risky and irresponsible approach with a person who has but a few years remaining.

These arguments, it seems to me, apply to other affective schools of thought and regressive therapies in addition to the psychoanalytic one. The more abrasive encounter group approaches and confrontation techniques would fit into this category. Certain features of Gestalt, *est*, primal scream, and other currently popular therapies would also seem to be contraindicated.

The central thrust of the cognitive approach is that the counselor works with the conscious meanings of things, events, and persons. This is not to say that meanings not available to the person's awareness do not come into play in the course of counseling. They do, but this type of insight is achieved through the application of cognition in those areas currently available to awareness.

However, the primary value of the cognitive approach for the purposes of integrative counseling is its stand that what a person thinks or believes about an event or circumstance is more important than the event or circumstance itself. This is not a new idea; it is centuries old. Albert Ellis, the founder of Rational-Emotive Therapy, one of the major cognitive schools of thought, is fond of quoting the ancient stoic philosopher Epictetus who said, "Men are not disturbed by things, but by the views which they take of them" (Ellis, 1962:54). As Beck has noted, "the thesis that the special meaning of an event determines the emotional response forms the core of the cognitive model of emotions and emotional disorders: the meaning is encased in a cognition—a thought or an image" (1976:52).

In practice, the cognitive model of emotions involves first the client's report of introspective observations of thoughts and feelings and then clarification of the relation of thought to feeling. Finally, generalizations are derived about what kinds of meanings and thoughts lead to what emotions.

Beck presents a useful illustration comparing the cognitive model to the psychoanalytic and conditioning (behavioral) models (1976:55). This is shown in Figure 3-1.

The essential feature of this illustration is that the psychoanalytic and behavioral (conditioning) models, unlike the cognitive one, do not emphasize the importance of meanings that are accessible to conscious introspection and report. The psychoanalysts emphasize unconscious meanings and the behaviorists in effect reject meaning entirely. By dealing with accessible, conscious meanings through introspection, the cognitive model does provide the means for development of an internal locus of control and for cognitive mastery, as these were described in Chapter 2.

Another point raised in Chapter 2 that holds particular relevance for the aged has to do with the replacement of the functionalistic ethic with alternate values or self-evaluations. Here, too, the cognitive approaches have a great deal to offer. Ellis (1974, 1977), in particular, among the cognitive theorists stresses the dysfunctional effects on self-esteem and on behavior of evaluating one's self in terms of performance standards, frequently perfectionistic ones. He notes that people actively reindoctrinate themselves with self-denigrating statements, such as "I should have done better than I did" or, more generally, "I should be better than I am." A large part of Ellis's Rational-Emotive

Therapy is devoted to combating these self-depleting and self-defeating beliefs. He insists that people must recognize their own worth in terms of their very being, their essential humanity, rather than their performances.

It is a central tenet of the integrative approach that the person has value in his or her own right. Furthermore, not only the counselor but also the client must come to accept this basic principle of self-worth. The profession of social work has long expressed belief in the inherent worth of the person, regardless of performance, behavior, or history. However, this has generally been expressed as a principle for practitioners to abide by rather than as a stated goal or end-state for the client to achieve. In the integrative approach it is a cardinal principle that if possible the client should achieve this goal of basic self-acceptance. It is a prime requisite for the efficacy of the approach insofar as finding an alternative to the functionalistic ethic is concerned.

One writer and practitioner who most clearly and effectively addresses

FIGURE 3-1. *Thinking and Emotion.*

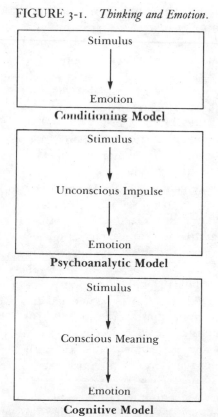

Source: Aaron T. Beck, *Cognitive Theory and the Emotional Disorders* (New York: International Universities Press, 1976). Copyright © 1976 by Aaron T. Beck, M.D. Reprinted by permission.

himself to this issue of self-evaluation and its centrality in the solution of despair is Theodore I. Rubin. In *Compassion and Self-Hate: An Alternative to Despair*, (1975) Rubin states, "Despair is directly proportional to energy and substance used in the service of self-hate" (1975:5). It should be recognized in this regard that today's aged were raised in a society replete with negative stereotypes about the aged and with a concurrent high evaluation of youth and accomplishment. Many, probably most, of today's elderly have incorporated these evaluations as part of their self systems, whether they recognize it or not. Therefore, compassionate approaches to the self such as Rubin's are essential in liberating the elderly from the functionalistic ethic.

Rubin provides many insights and self-help. His book is basically cognitive in approach, relying on the inherent common sense of the reader, and it is so clearly and humanely written that I have recommended it as "homework" to clients for discussion and working through in the counseling process.

So far, I have discussed cognitive approaches only in broad outline, stressing those aspects having to do with the functionalistic ethic, internal locus of control, and the centrality of meaning in solution of the integrity versus despair issue. There are, of course, the immediate and intermediate problems of living, having to do with interpersonal relations, fears, emotional reactions to pain and ill health, and so on. There are numerous techniques in the cognitive literature for dealing with these. Essentially, these techniques are based on the premise that faulty beliefs or convictions are responsible for a range of behavior problems and poor coping patterns, and that cognitions can control behavior and emotions. However, remediation is not just a matter of telling the client about these distortions and faulty beliefs; there is a repertoire of techniques which include such things as distancing and decentering (Beck, 1976), graded-task assignment (Beck, 1976), cognitive rehearsal (Beck, 1976), rational imagery (Lazarus, 1971), self-demonstration (Raimy, 1975), modeling or "vicariation" (Raimy, 1975) and a host of other didactic, instructional, interpretive, and cognitive review techniques (generally termed "cognitive restructuring") sometimes used in conjunction with selected behavioral techniques. We will not deal with these exhaustively here, because they are incidental to or instrumental for the basic purposes of the integrative approach. Some of these techniques will be noted as they were applied during the counseling process in the illustrative case materials to be presented later.

There are limitations to the cognitive approaches as far as work with the elderly is concerned. Other treatment theories can be helpful in providing alternative or complementary treatment approaches in areas not sufficiently handled by cognitive approaches. We turn next to the contributions other schools of thought can make to integrative counseling of the elderly. These will be viewed in the light of certain shortcomings in some of the cognitive approaches.

The Contribution of Other Approaches

Despite the earlier observations about the regressive emphasis of psychoanalytic theory, it should be noted that the developmental theory of Erikson which provides the focal concept of this book is essentially psychoanalytic. Erikson is, of course, an ego psychologist and brings a strong social and cultural perspective to bear on his view of aging, much more in line with an integrative approach than the more classical Freudian frame of reference.

One of the gaps I have found in the cognitive approaches in work with the aged is a relative lack of consideration of the differential impacts of objective events on individuals. The focus on how cognition can affect emotions, particularly in terms of faulty thinking, tends to underplay the real impact of the loss of a loved one. Cognitive theory is very clear about dealing with the endogenous factors in depression: self-hate, irrational feelings of incompetence, worthlessness, and so on. However, in true reactive depressions there is the exogenous fact of the loss of a loved one and the need for working through the grief and mourning process. In this regard, psychoanalytic theory, and in particular object relations theory (Bowlby, 1961), has much explanatory power and value for perceiving the full dimensions of such a loss, with its elements of guilt and ambivalence. Since such losses are so much at the center of the aging process, this contribution is an important one indeed.

Another important aspect of psychoanalytic theory is its emphasis on the relationship between client or patient and therapist, which is seen as the most important vehicle for therapeutic change. Of course, all of the major schools of counseling have stressed the importance of the relationship factor. However, it was Rogers (1965) in his client-centered theory who delineated the necessary conditions for a constructive therapeutic relationship. They are the need for the helping person to: (1) experience and communicate an empathic understanding of the client's internal frame of reference; (2) experience unconditional positive regard for the client; and (3) be congruent or "genuine" in the relationship. Subsequent clinical work and research has demonstrated the efficacy of these three conditions and has operationalized them in the scaled dimensions of "accurate empathy," "nonpossessive warmth," and "genuineness" (Truax and Carkhuff, 1967). These "core conditions" for a helping relationship have now become essential ingredients in many human relations training programs (Egan, 1976), and they have also been incorporated in training for work with the aged (Greenberg et al., 1976). The significance of these components in the integrative approach will be evident in the following section on the counseling process.

Another contribution of Rogerian thinking to the integrative approach is the self theory (Rogers, 1965). As a self-psychologist, Rogers has contributed conceptual and research tools for assessing self-concept, ideal self, and self-esteem. It should be mentioned, however, that Rogers's essentially nondirective approach to individual and group counseling is sometimes not applicable or constructive in work with the elderly. This, too, will become evident in the materials to be presented on the counseling process.

The earlier presentation of the conditioning or behavioral model (Figure 3-1) relative to the cognitive and the psychoanalytic models indicated that meaning is effectively absent from the behavioral model. Given the centrality of meaning in the last task of life, it is clear that behavioral approaches cannot play a major part in the integrative approach. However, there is a place for some behavioral techniques in dealing with the immediate and intermediate problems of living having to do with fears, inhibitions and maladaptive behaviors. In fact, there has been a growing attempt to integrate cognitive and behavior-modification approaches (see especially Meichenbaum, 1977). Many of the techniques of this integrated cognitive and behavioral approach are based on the recognition of the fact that a person's covert or inner speech can become an effective mediator of behavior. Thus, the mediational value of private speech (one aspect of cognition) can be used for behavior change through self-instructional training techniques (Meichenbaum, 1977:18-31). Again, some of these techniques will be evident in the case materials to follow.

If the behavioral approach is lacking in methods to deal with the issue of meaning in people's lives, the existential approach to counseling deals largely with the issue of meaning. Frankl (1959, 1965) has already been mentioned, and his method of logotherapy is an existential approach with an almost exclusive focus on meaning. Another major form of existential psychotherapy, Daseinsanalysis (Binswanger, 1963; Boss, 1963), views the person as being constantly engaged in attributing and creating meaning to self, others, and the surrounding world. These approaches have obvious implications for integrative work with the elderly. The integrative approach proposed in this book also uses the perceptual perspective, which is central to existential practice (Laing, 1960). This means that the client must be seen from his or her own unique point of view.

Although the existential approaches have a great deal of applicability to the last task of life, particularly in dealing with anxiety and the fear of death, their emphasis on choosing the future (May, 1953) through more "authentic" living and eschewing the past with its associated guilt about "inauthentic" living has its dangers. Butler and Lewis (1977:43) have noted the risk of ignoring and not working through the guilt the aged client expresses about the past. A related problem is that there may not be the time or opportunity to live the more authentic life that would allow for acceptance of the past. The significant others about whom one feels guilty are often no longer alive, the old choices about action and vocation that were not authentically made are not apt to be available in new forms, and there is simply not enough time left to overcome the despair over the past by "choosing the future." However, there are some aged clients who will have the time and the opportunity (particularly those whose spouses and children are still alive) to live more authentically, to recognize and take responsibility for the choices available to them. In these instances, the existential approach clearly has much to offer.

A number of the contributions from these various schools of thought that have been incorporated into this integrative approach were anticipated by Adler (1929, 1964). His was a cognitive approach, focusing on meaning and on conscious rather than unconscious processes. His perspective on the individual was phenomenological, and he also saw the individual in a social-psychological framework as reacting to and acting on society. This is certainly compatible with the treatment model to be presented here.

It is not my intention to review all the major personality theories and schools of thought in order to identify their potential or actual contributions to the integrative approach proposed here. My object is to identify for the reader some of the major contributions or perspectives and to provide a few pertinent references for the reader to pursue as needed. Fortunately, there has been a coming together of disparate schools of thought in the form of common practice approaches. Thus, as noted, there has been a melding of some cognitive and behavioral approaches and a more general acceptance and incorporation of the core conditions (warmth, empathy, and genuineness) in various schools of counseling and psychotherapy. It is really up to the originality, background, and creativity of the counselor as to which particular techniques he or she wishes to employ within the developmental framework outlined here. In short, it is evident that any approach capable of dealing with the immediate and intermediate problems of living while helping aging individuals in the ultimate resolution of life's last task has to be eclectic in nature. That is in fact what the integrative approach is all about.

The Social Reconstruction Syndrome

The social breakdown syndrome presented in Chapter 1 can be reversed by social system inputs. One of the most promising models for intervention in the gerontological literature is the "social reconstruction syndrome" developed by Kuypers and Bengtson (1973). Their model represents a comprehensive social psychological framework that incorporates elements of social systems, self-concept, and labeling theories as they might be applied to practical problems of adjustment in aging. Given this comprehensiveness, the model has the capacity to incorporate the person-problem-situation perspective. In addition, it potentially has both prescriptive and descriptive value: descriptive in the sense that it describes much of the process whereby older persons are able to prevent or reverse the breakdown syndrome in their lives after significant losses or traumas with formal (social and health agency) or informal (family, friends, neighbors, and self) help; prescriptive in the sense that it shows generally how and when in a total cycle certain inputs from the social system are necessary to reverse the breakdown syndrome. In order to illustrate how the model works, Figure 3-2 shows the social reconstruction syndrome.

The kinds of interventions and services necessary to reverse the breakdown cycle are apparent in their broad outlines in Figure 3-2. Input A, the first point of intervention, calls for the practitioners to help liberate the elderly person from an inappropriate self-view of low status or worth. This self-view is generally based in large part on the "functionalistic ethic" of our society, which holds that performance in economic or other socially "productive" roles defines a person's value. This is clearly an inappropriate basis for self-evaluation for retired persons whose physical decrements preclude or inhibit their functioning in such roles. What is called for is a more compassionate and humane basis for self-judgment. This can best be done by counseling, whether by a professional counselor, caseworker, occupational or recreational therapist, or nonprofessionals such as friendly visitors, confidants, or other providers in the natural helping network.

Input B shows the need for "hard" services such as income maintenance, housing, health, nutrition, and transportation to counter the negative effects of poor conditions and thereby to reduce dependence. Enhanced self-reliance results as the person is encouraged to view or label himself or herself as more

FIGURE 3-2. *The Social Reconstruction Syndrome: A Benign Cycle of Increasing Competence through Social System Inputs.*

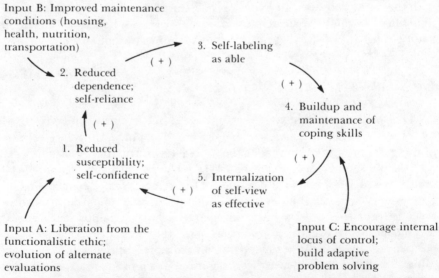

Source: V. L. Bengtson, *The Social Psychology of Aging* (Indianapolis: The Bobbs-Merrill Co., Inc., 1973). Copyright © 1973 by The Bobbs-Merrill Co. Reprinted by permission.

able and competent. The practitioners' support for growth and maintenance of coping skills (Input C) should help build adaptive problem-solving capacities that can lead to a more internal locus of control in the older person. Too frequently, elderly persons believe that their lives are controlled largely by external circumstances, events, and persons rather than by themselves. This is certainly true for persons caught up in the cycle of the breakdown syndrome. With a positive change in that perception, it is more likely that the person will incorporate a view of self as effective and competent. The consequence should be to reduce the psychological preconditions for continued breakdown or demoralization and to enhance morale in general.

The social reconstruction model is not only highly suggestive for formal intervention purposes, it also has a great deal of explanatory value for aging in general. It has been identified as an "emergent theory" of social gerontology that "provides what may be the most systematic statement of the interdependence between older people and their social world" (Hendricks and Hendricks, 1979:201). There is good reason to believe that many older people who suffer some degree of social breakdown because of age-related losses and crises are able, through informal support networks or by their own personal efforts, to reverse the breakdown cycle very much in the manner described by the social reconstruction model. This idea of people successfully coping with their problems without formal help is certainly not a new one. Gurin, Veroff, and Feld (1960) found in a nationwide mental health survey that most people tend to rely on their own inner resources to deal effectively with their own problems.

There is no question that the social reconstruction model has been most suggestive and helpful in the development of a treatment model for the integrative approach. Several concepts in the model are reflected in key components of the integrative model. These include the ideas of improved maintenance conditions, self-labeling, encouragement of an internal locus of control, and liberation from the functionalistic ethic. However, certain aspects of the original Kuypers and Bengtson model are not particularly descriptive of or prescriptive for actual practice with the aging. For example, in most cases intervention begins with tangible services of the type indicated in Input B rather than with attempts to liberate the client from the functionalistic ethic as depicted in Input A. Usually, formal intervention occurs immediately following some loss or traumatic event, frequently in the nature of crisis intervention, which also precludes providing Input A at the beginning of the intervention process. Also, a number of the suggested steps in the model need a great deal more explication in terms of what the practitioner has to do in order to implement them. It should be recognized, however, that the model was not intended to be more specific or operational. It was intended mainly to be suggestive, and it most certainly was that for the integrative treatment model which follows.

The Integrative Model

As mentioned above, most work with older persons begins with provision of maintenance services and/or a good deal of emotional support to see them through the initial crisis situation. This is reflected in the diagram of the integrative model shown in Figure 3-3.

There are four major inputs (A–D) in contrast to the three shown in the social reconstruction model. Each of the four inputs should lead to a set of objectives, as described on the arrow lines in the treatment cycle, each marking a different level of client functioning. That is, the first level achieved by the provision of maintenance condition should be the relief of immediate stress and dependency. The second level achieved by the provision of emotional support and coping strategies is one that should be marked by the re-establishment of an equilibrium, in that morale and coping strategies are sustained. The third level to be achieved by encouragement of an internal locus of control should be a higher plateau of functioning characterized by increased coping skills, problem-solving capacity, and cognitive mastery. Finally, the fourth level achieved by Input D should be marked by a major increase in the degree and quality of overall morale and life satisfaction commensurate with a general state of ego integrity.

The focus on increased morale, life satisfaction, and even ego integrity as outcomes of the whole intervention process clearly distinguishes the integrative model from the Kuypers and Bengtson model, which does not explicitly identify a morale factor. However, a basic assumption of integrative practice is that increased morale is always the final goal of intervention, even if we are more directly aiming our interventive efforts at such things as improved coping skills, more effective behavior, and so on. As Frank (1974) has noted, in the final analysis all forms of counseling and psychotherapy are intended

FIGURE 3-3. *The Integrative Treatment Model*

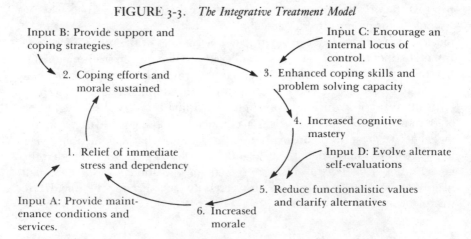

to combat and overcome demoralization. To have helped a client change into an effective but unhappy "coper" from an ineffective unhappy one leaves a distinctly negative impression. The enhanced coping ability should lead to a more satisfying, or at least less demoralized, kind of life.

The integrative model will be presented and illustrated in much more detail in the next chapter, which provides a view of the model in terms of a treatment continuum for the purposes of differential assessment. In the meantime, however, the model will be explicated here in terms of four major components. These consist of: (1) the self component; (2) locus of control component; (3) the value component; and (4) the morale component. These components are related to the counseling inputs of the model (B, C, and D in Figure 3-2). The maintenance and service input (A in Figure 3-2) has to do more with the indirect provision of services largely through the use of referrals than with direct counseling. The self component really permeates the entire treatment cycle. For example, we aim to stabilize self-esteem through emotional support early in the process whereas toward the end we are involved in changing self-concepts, self ideals, and self-esteem in the process of reducing functionalistic self-evaluations and clarifying alternative self-evaluations.

In the following explication of these components a number of instruments will be presented. Most of them come either directly from the gerontological literature or were developed specifically for integrative practice. Most of them can be used for assessment purposes and also for evaluating the extent of change in some of the major dimensions from the start (pretest), during, and at the end of counseling (posttest). Some of them can also be used to enhance the actual treatment process. At any rate, their use will be demonstrated in case illustrations, so even if the reader does not intend to use each and every one of the instruments in practice, they should serve to explicate each of the model's components in greater operational detail than a narrative description alone would.

The Self Component

Since the self component is pivotal for all the other components of the model and since it permeates the entire treatment cycle, it needs more explication here than was given to the review of findings regarding the self concept provided in Chapter 2. There are many different conceptions of the self and ways of measuring the concept in the psychological literature (Wegner and Vallacher, 1980; Wylie, 1974), so it is important to give the background, rationale, and measurement approaches to the self as it is conceived in the integrative model.

The integrative conception would have to be categorized first as a cognitive representation of the self. Consistent with the perceptual view of person-

ality underlying integrative practice, the cognitive approach assumes that if
we are to understand and hope to predict a person's behavior we must first
understand how this person cognitively represents or construes the world.
Cognition here means the act or process of knowing and is often used interchangeably with the words thinking, perception, and understanding. Basically, cognitive psychologists hold that there are structures that organize and
integrate past knowledge for use in understanding future input. The term
"schema" has been used to represent the structures that encode and represent
knowledge. A schema is a structure "internal to the perceiver, modifiable by
experience, and somehow specific to what is being perceived" (Neisser,
1976:554). Piaget (1954) also found the concept of a schema to be central to
his work on how the young child constructs reality. At first, the infant
constructs only a few simple images to which meaning is attached; these
simple structures are further elaborated and modified to become the more
complex structures (schemata) of the adult.

The theorists whose work comes closest to the cognitive conception of the
self in the integrative model are Rogers (1965) and Kelly (1955). They both
see the self as a cognitive structure or set of structures which organize,
modify, and integrate functions of the person. Markus (1980:110) has noted
that "viewing the self as a set of cognitive structures or schemas that have an
extremely important and powerful role in organizing an individual's experiences helps to demystify the concept of the self. We do not have to think of
the self as an ephemeral concept like the soul. A cognitive structure approach
helps us to be more specific about the self and allows us to investigate it."

This cognitive conception of the self is consistent with both the measurement (assessment and evaluation) and treatment processes of integrative practice. In this regard the Rogers self-paradigm outlined in Chapter 2 which
conceives of the self system as having two major elements, the actual self-
concept and the ideal self-concept, has been most helpful. For one thing,
Butler and Haigh (1954) have demonstrated in studies using measures of
these two elements that a discrepancy between the two measures can be used
as a measure of self-esteem, and it is important in the course of integrative
counseling to have a clear assessment of self-esteem. Further, research has
indicated the value of using both the actual self-concept and the ideal self-
concept because they have an empirically demonstrated link with locus of
control and environmental context (Kivett, Watson, and Busch, 1977). This
is why the actual–ideal discrepancy measure is preferred over a direct measure of self-esteem such as the widely used Rosenberg (1979) Scale. According to the discrepancy measure, if a person with a high measure of ideal self
on an evaluative self-report scale has an actual concept of self that is very
much lower, that person will have very low feelings of self-esteem. In this
sense, self-esteem is an affective variable, whereas self-concept is a more
directly descriptive, cognitive variable. This seems very much in line with
the reconstruction model and therefore suggests the kinds of measures to be

used in operationalizing the self component of the integrative model. The preferred measure is the Semantic Differential Test (Osgood, Suci, and Tannenbaum, 1957) because it is particularly suited for measuring and describing the special meaning of certain concepts (self, ideal self, other persons, ideas, things) in people's lives. As the authors of the test indicate, it can be used not only to test people's attitudes about social and political issues, but also as an assessment device in psychotherapy. It has been found particularly useful in determining the need for counseling and as an indicator of the areas to be covered and the directions to be pursued in counseling.

The essence of the Semantic Differential Test is to have the person respond to a "concept," which can be a person, idea, object, event, or any other thing that can be symbolically represented by a term (for example, "mother," "peace," "money". The person responds by making a check mark at the appropriate place on a seven-point, bipolar scale with adjectives at each end to represent the polar opposites in meaning.

Osgood and his colleagues found through repeated factor analyses of results of the test that three basic dimensions or meanings seemed to apply to the given concepts (Osgood et al., 1957). These dimensions were: evaluation, potency, and activity. The first dimension has to do with positive or negative evaluations of a concept, as in "good/bad." The potency dimension has to do with the strength or power of the concept, as in "weak/strong." The activity dimension has to do with the level of activity ascribed to the concept, as in "fast/slow." The actual scales used in the case illustration in this book, along with the scores and the dimensions noted on the side in parentheses, are given in Table 3-1.

The scale "old/young" has descriptive and assessment value in its own right and was not scored within any of the three dimensions. The evaluation, potency, and activity dimensions therefore each include four scales. Consequently, the highest score a person could get on any one of the three dimensions would be 28 (7 + 7 + 7 + 7) and the lowest would be 4 (1 + 1 + 1 + 1).

It is of great interest and value for assessment purposes to look at the dimension score separately. For example, a person who actively dislikes or hates his or her father, who has powerful (negative) valence in the person's life, might respond to the concept "My Father" by checking scale positions that would give a low score on the evaluation dimension ("extremely bad," "extremely unfair") but a high score on the potency dimension ("extremely strong," "extremely big") and the activity dimension ("extremely active," "extremely tense").

One of the strong assets of the Semantic Differential Test is its versatility; one can choose the concepts that are most important and salient for the individuals or groups one is working with (Kerlinger, 1973). In a number of case illustrations to follow, about twelve concepts, depending on the person, were used in each (before and after) administration of the test. They in-

TABLE 3.1. *Example of Semantic-Differential Test Sheet*

	(Extremely)	(Quite)	(Slightly)	(Neither or in Between)	(Slightly)	(Quite)	(Extremely)	
Large	7	6	5	4	3	2	1	Small (Potency)
Worthless	1	2	3	4	5	6	7	Valuable (Evaluative)
Fast	7	6	5	4	3	2	1	Slow (Activity)
Cold	1	2	3	4	5	6	7	Hot (Activity)
Happy	7	6	5	4	3	2	1	Sad (Evaluative)
Weak	1	2	3	4	5	6	7	Strong (Potency)
Good	7	6	5	4	3	2	1	Bad (Evaluative)
Tense	7	6	5	4	3	2	1	Relaxed (Activity)
Tough	7	6	5	4	3	2	1	Soft (Potency)
Old								Young (not scored on any of the 3 dimensions)
Active	7	6	5	4	3	2	1	Passive (Activity)
Heavy	7	6	5	4	3	2	1	Light (Potency)
Fair	7	6	5	4	3	2	1	Unfair (Evaluative)

*The numbers on the lines are inserted to indicate how the scales would be scored. They would not be on the form when it is presented to the respondent, who has to put a checkmark on the appropriate line.

cluded: My Family, My Husband (Wife), My Mother, My Father, My Sister (Brother), Me (As I am now), Ideal Me (As I would like to be), My Health, Dependency, Life, Death, and Religion. The first seven concepts listed are generally found in counseling or psychotherapeutic work because they are the significant persons (including self) in most people's lives (Osgood et al., 1957:259). The concept "Ideal Me" provides a measure of the person's aspirations, ideals, standards, in short, the ideal self. Thus, a person who gives a low evaluation score for "Me" (self-concept) and a very high evaluation score for Ideal Me (self ideal) would have a large discrepancy between the two scores and, therefore, a low self-esteem.

Another advantage of the Semantic Differential Test is that it can be plotted graphically to portray what Osgood calls a person's "semantic space," that is, the spatial arrangement and relationships of the key concepts in a person's life in terms of their semantic meanings for the person. This is very similar to Lewin's (1951) concept of "life space"; in a sense the graphic portrayal of key concepts in a person's life by semantic differential techniques can provide a helpful view of a person's psychological life space. This is done by plotting the location of each concept according to its cumulative score on each of the three dimensions (Osgood et al., 1957:95). Ideally, this should be done in three-demensional space with balls representing concepts and with connecting rods. However, the place and relationship of the concepts can be plotted on graph paper in two-dimensional form, using the critical evaluative and potency scores. The activity scores and locations can then be given in nongraphic (narrative) form. A simplified model, based on a hypothetical case and using the scoring system for this group, is shown in Figure 3-4.

The hypothetical person in this instance had very high cumulative scores on the evaluation dimension for the concepts of "Religion" and "Ideal Me." These concepts are at the very top of the evaluative continuum, with total scores of 28 (7 + 7 + 7 + 7) each. The concept "Me" on the other hand, is low on the evaluative dimension, a score of 12. The concept "Ideal Me" shows the most potency by virtue of its placement along that dimension, based on a score of 27. "Religion" is the next most potent concept (score of 24), with "Me" third (score of 10), and "My Health" last (score of 7). Even this simplified model can tell us a great deal about the person, assuming these are valid reports of the meaning of the concepts to the person. The question of validity is, of course, a critical one. It is essential for the counselor to check out his or her clinical impressions with the self-reports of the clients, to discuss the client's responses with the client, and to determine on this basis whether the self-report scores on each and all concepts can be accepted as valid.

In Figure 3-4 it is clear that the self ideal is a highly valued and potent concept in the person's life space. If we add to this the hypothetical score of 24 for "Ideal Me" on the activity dimension, we would have to say that the ideal self also is very active in the person's life space. The person's self-

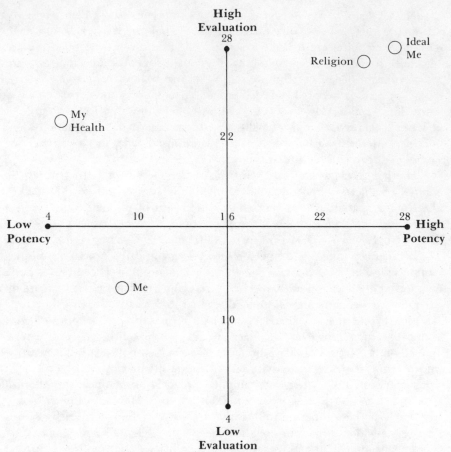

FIGURE 3-4.   *Spatial Model of Semantic Differential Test*

concept (Me) is very low in evaluative terms, although somewhat more potent; we could therefore say that there is a great discrepancy between self-
concept and high self ideal, which should mean a very poor self-esteem. This
is, of course, open to validation through the counselor's clinical impressions
based on observations of and interviews with the client. If we want an overall
measure of self-concept and ideal self, we simply sum the scores on the
twelve bipolar scales. In this case, the total score on all three factors (evaluation, potency, and activity) for "Ideal Me" is 67, whereas the total score for
"Me" is 29. If we want a measure of self-esteem, we have to subtract the score
for "Me" from the score for "Ideal Me" on *each* bipolar scale and then sum the
differences. In this case, the sum of the differences was 32. It is not correct to
simply subtract the total sum of all the scale scores for "Me" from the scale
scores for "Ideal Me," which in this case would have been 38. At any rate, a
score of 32 indicates a much lower degree of self-esteem than, say, a score of 8.

Such measures of self-concept and self-esteem have been criticized because they imply a static view of the self and consequently do not in themselves provide a satisfactory explanation of behavior (Wylie, 1974). Mischel (1976) has argued that whereas measurement of a personality dimension such as self-concept is often highly predictive of behavior in the same kind of situation in which it was first measured, there is little predictive power across a number of situations. However, this simply indicates that the individual is able to discriminate changes from one situation to another. Thus, the actual situation or context will have an effect on behavior and emotions, but it is the way in which the elements of the situation are perceived and processed by the person that will determine the nature and intensity of the resulting emotion or behavior. As Combs et al. (1976) have said, "although we may sometimes use the self-concept as a convenient device for understanding a person, it should never be forgotten that people always behave in terms of the total phenomenal field, never in terms of an isolated part" (1976:161).

What is meant by "the total phenomenal field"? It is best at this point to pull together the various concepts that have been presented so far in this discussion of the self component of the integrative model. Figure 3-5 organizes all of the concepts in the self system according to the integrative model and illustrates their relationships to one another.

To answer the earlier question about the meaning of the total phenomenal field, it can be said that it includes all of the elements. A through E, in Figure 3-5. In other words, it is the total field of phenomena available to the individual's perception at any one point in time. This includes not only phenomena in the environment outside the person but also phenomena perceived as internal to the person, such as the self-concept. The "phenomenal self" is a concept that has not been presented heretofore, but it is an essential element in the total self-system which helps to explain variations in behavior, emotions, and self-perceptions in different circumstances and times. This phenomenal or perceived self is the organization of all the ways in which a person sees himself or herself and encompasses all self-perceptions in a particular situation (Combs et al., 1976; Friedman, 1955; Hilgard, 1949; Lecky, 1961). For example, the distance (discrepancy) between the self-concept (element A) and ideal self (element B) will be indicative of self-esteem (along dimension A) within a specific situation. If we obtain measures of self-concept and ideal self as indicated in the illustrated hypothetical case in Figure 3-4, the resulting measure of self-esteem is indicative of the person's self-esteem in that specific testing situation at that time. Our hope would be to see the distance between self-concept and ideal self reduced markedly in the posttest situation at the end of counseling.

In order to illustrate the dynamic interaction of the various elements in the self system in a particular situation and at a particular time, let us take a situation in which an older person could quite conceivably find himself on our busy roads and highways. Let us assume that an elderly man and his wife

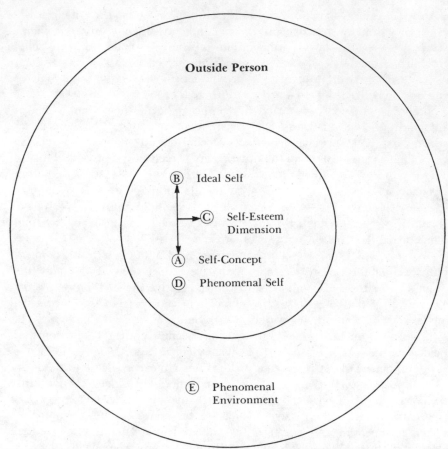

FIGURE 3-5. *The Self System in the Phenomenal Field*

are out driving and he, the driver, has stopped at a red light. He is allowed by law to make a right turn if no traffic is approaching on the left, and since he sees no such traffic, he slowly makes the turn. However, his peripheral vision is not as good as when he was younger, and he does not see a car that is approaching rapidly from the far left. When he finally does see it, he is not able to stop in time or to speed up enough to avoid the need for very rapid and severe braking on the part of the other car to prevent a major collision. His failure to react is probably a result of his slower reactivity due to the aging process, a fact of which he is aware only too much.

Let us assume further that the (younger) driver of the other car passes him at the earliest opportunity and yells out the window, "What's wrong with you, you senile old fool? Do you want to kill someone?" The elderly driver's immediate reactions to this are mixed, with some elements of anger for being called a "senile old fool" and some sheepishness and guilt about having come close to causing an accident. It is the phenomenal self (D) which processes all of this. It perceives what is going on in the environment (the near collision, the hurtful name-calling by the other driver) and it also perceives the dynamic internal structure of the self at that moment: the self-concept (A), the ideal self (B), and the discrepancy between them (C).

Let us assume that the elderly driver has an ideal view of himself as somewhat younger than his years, or at least not old, and as alert rather than senile. Assume also that the new, negative input from the environment has been received and processed by the phenomenal self and has been registered and perceived as a lower self-concept, that is, the man's own descriptive view of himself at that time. In short, the phenomenal self perceives a much greater discrepancy between the ideal self (rather young and alert) and the self-concept as a result of the new input ("old," "senile," and near-perpetrator of an accident). As mentioned earlier, self-esteem is the affective element of the self system and tends to be more volatile and changeable than the self-concept or the ideal self. Therefore, the elderly driver experiences an almost immediate emotional letdown. He feels somewhat deflated and saddened.

Now let us assume that his wife, sensing his frame of mind, says, "Don't pay any attention to him, dear; he was driving far too fast for you to see him in time. You are a good driver and you know it." He does in fact know it and begins to process this information about his driving ability. In other words, his phenomenal self processes the support and information from his wife (who is part of his phenomenal environment) together with information from the past. He realizes that he has not had a serious accident in over forty years of driving and that in fact he is a careful driver. He also recognizes that the other driver must have been driving too fast, and although his own reflexes are not what they used to be he did look carefully before he turned. As a result of this processing of information from both outside and inside the self, the perceived discrepancy between the self-concept and the ideal self has been significantly diminished and the elderly man's mood has lifted considerably in a short period of time.

The reason for this illustration and discussion is to underline the importance of the concept of the phenomenal self. Although self-report measures of self-concept and ideal self give us some estimates of clients' self-esteem and self-perception, it is really the phenomenal self that is most important to us in clinical practice. Since it is the phenomenal self that does the processing or perceiving of the discrepancy between the self-concept and the ideal self, we should be warned not to take the difference between static measures and graphic representations of self and ideal as necessarily valid indicators of self-esteem. We need to check them against our clinical impressions and, in order to get at what is going on in the phenomenal self, we need to engage in more phenomenological methods in practice. I refer to the kinds of methods that go into accurate empathy: the attending behaviors, the sensing and reflecting back of your impressions of what the client is feeling or perceiving in order to verify that your impressions are essentially the same as the client's.

The Locus of Control Component

It has been noted that perceived control over events may have an important effect on the way in which older persons respond to stressful situations and on their self-esteem (Zarit, 1980). The locus of control concept is central to the integrative model (see Input C, Figure 3-3). The internal/external locus of control framework developed by Rotter (1966) has been particularly useful because it assesses the extent to which a person feels in control over events and is able to obtain rewards from the environment based on one's behaviors. To put it another way, it assesses the individual's perception of self as a powerful or powerless person. Much of the work that has been done to study the effects of locus of control and aging has included Rotter's measures of locus. These studies indicate that individuals generally perceive themselves to be more powerful with age, up to about fifty years old (Penke, 1969; Bradley and Webb, 1976). Evidence on age-related differences after age 50 is conflicting. Certainly the loss of important roles and decline in physical well-being would contribute to a decreased belief in personal control over one's fate. It is as yet unclear whether this is a generalized decrease in the belief in personal control or whether it is confined to certain areas. At any rate, locus of control is closely linked to personal style and self-concept. Kuypers (1972) explored ego functioning and personality correlates of the control dimension in persons over 65. He found that individuals with an internal locus of control were characterized by greater activity and adaptiveness to stress. Those who held an external locus of control were characterized as closed, defensive, and nonadaptive in their interaction with the environment.

In order to give the reader some idea of how one can determine whether a person has an internal or an external locus of control, let us take a look at several key statements from the Rotter (1966) Scale:

1. a. In the long run people get the respect they deserve in this world.
   b. Unfortunately, an individual's worth often passes unrecognized no matter how hard he tries.
2. a. Becoming a success is a matter of hard work, luck has little or nothing to do with it.
   b. Getting a good job depends mainly on being in the right place at the right time.
3. a. Many times I feel that I have little influence over the things that happen to me.
   b. It is impossible for me to believe that chance or luck plays an important role in my life.

4. a. What happens to me is my own doing.
   b. Sometimes I feel that I don't have enough control over the direction my life is taking.

The respondents to these questions are asked to circle the letter (a or b) that comes closest to their opinions. Internal locus responses would be: 1.a., 2.a., 3.b., and 4.a., whereas the external locus responses would be: 1.b., 2 b., 3.a., and 4.b. The feelings of control or lack of control of events should be quite apparent in these responses. A number of social gerontologists have used a shortened version of the scale (Valecha, 1972) rather then the full 29-item scale (Rotter, 1966) because it is less demanding in terms of time, energy, and attention for elderly respondents.

It is interesting that Kuypers (1972) found that the variables distinguishing internals from externals were ego/cognitive variables as opposed to interpersonal or affective (emotional) variables. This indicates that internals and externals differ in their basic cognitive perception of the world and not only do their perceptions differ, but the strategies which they use to mediate between the self and the environment also differ. It appears that internals have learned more strategies for coping. Such individuals, one would expect, would be less vulnerable both physically and psychologically to the stresses of aging and would feel more positive about their lives in general. Palmore and Luikart (1972) in fact found that in persons over 60 internal control orientation ranked second as the factor accounting for variance in life satisfaction. Self-rated health ranked first. Thus, those who have an internal locus of control are likely to be perceived as more adjusted and to perceive themselves as healthier and more satisfied than those who have an external locus of control.

In addition to the empirical evidence of the importance of locus of control as far as gerontological studies are concerned, it has been found that Rotter's locus of control measure is a good predictor of how well clients will do in counseling or psychotherapy (Rabkin, 1977). Rabkin notes that

> because "internals" are more prone than "externals" to try to shape events, they are more likely to participate actively in a treatment plan suggested by a psychotherapist. A patient with an internal locus of control will accept a proposed task as something he can do himself to improve his condition; the therapist is seen as a facilitator who "helps him to help himself." In contrast, the patient with an external locus of control is likely to expect a "wonder session," in which the therapist's actions are entirely responsible for whatever change occurs. For such a patient therapeutic prescriptions must entail simple, passive acts which allow the outside force, the therapist, to cure him [1977:25].

This makes it abundantly clear why it is necessary to encourage an internal locus of control in order to achieve the ultimate goal and objectives of the integrative model.

As valuable as it is, something is needed in addition to asking questions like those in the Rotter Scale in order to assess adequately the older person's sense of control or mastery over the circumstances of his or her life. The ideas of passive mastery and cognitive mastery come into play here. It has already been noted that the move from active to passive mastery found by Neugarten (1965) represented a defensive or protective adaptation to the fact that older persons felt their environments were less controllable and that they were developing a more external locus of control. Active mastery would of course be associated with an internal locus of control. What is needed in addition to a more internal locus of control for the older client is not passive mastery but rather "cognitive mastery." This is reflected in Kuypers's (1972) findings on ego/cognitive variables and their association with an internal locus of control and greater life satisfaction.

To make this issue of cognitive versus passive mastery more concrete, the case illustration of Max Kaplan indicated cognitive mastery on his part over the mugging event. If he had gone the route of passive mastery, he would have kept himself shut up in his apartment much more and would have ventured out much less. Another example of passive mastery can be seen in the illustration of the elderly driver which was just given. His reduced peripheral vision and slower reflexes which led to feelings of less internal control, are compensated for by driving more slowly and more carefully. It would be an even more clear-cut case of passive mastery if he began driving much less frequently as a result of the fright he experienced in the incident.

Max Kaplan did not show much evidence of the defensive type of reaction to the mugging incident that would be characteristic of passive mastery. It is not that his locus of control shifted from an internal to an external one. In a sense, he had transcended that issue by his affective and intellectual recognition that he could not have total control over the events of his life. Apropos of this, a completely internal score on the Rotter Scale (all internal items circled and no external ones) is considered atypical, unrealistic, and rather grandiose (Rotter, 1966). What Max Kaplan demonstrated was cognitive mastery in that he recognized and accepted the fact that he did not and could not have total control. He showed cognitive mastery also in his ability to live more in the present than in the future or the past. It is the theme of acceptance of the actual limitations of one's power as well as a transcending of the issues of power, dominance, submission, and so on, that Peck (1968) delineated in his concept of ego transcendence versus ego preoccupation.

This kind of acceptance partakes of the wisdom inherent in the famous prayer by Saint Francis: "God grant me the serenity to accept the things I cannot change, courage to change the things I can, and the wisdom to know the difference." Bateson (1972) has said that the ability to put the formula of the prayer into practice can prevent "the conclusion of despair," namely, that there are no more alternatives available. Thus, cognitive mastery could conceivably enable the person to avoid the conclusion of despair in favor of ego integrity.

How can a practitioner assess the relative presence or absence of cognitive mastery in the client's coping efforts? First, one can obtain information directly from the client about his or her reaction to incidents involving dramatic recognition of loss of one's powers, control, or capacities, as in the mugging incident with Max Kaplan and the driving incident with the elderly man. Just how the client reacts to the incident and the recognition in terms of thoughts, feelings, and behavior should tell the practitioner a great deal. If information about such incidents is lacking or if one needs supportive data to verify clinical impressions, I have found it helpful to ask clients whether they agree with, disagree, or cannot decide about the following statements:

1. I find that I am not much bothered by the fact that there are things in my life over which I have no control.
2. It is hard to feel good when there are certain things in life I can no longer influence or change.
3. I feel very bad when there are things I want to have or want to change and I am not able to do so.

If the client either agrees or disagrees, it is helpful to ask whether he or she strongly agrees or disagrees or "just" agrees or disagrees. If the person agrees with statement 1 and disagrees with statements 2 or 3, the responses are indicative of some degree of cognitive mastery. However, if the client strongly disagrees with statement 1 and strongly agrees with 2 and 3, the responses indicate little or no cognitive mastery and are also probably indicative of an external locus of control with some attendant demoralization. However, these two latter impressions could be checked out directly by asking some locus of control questions and one of the morale measures that will be presented shortly. If one wants a quantitative measure of the client's cognitive mastery, one can use the Cognitive Mastery Assessment Questionnaire and scoring instructions given in Appendix B.

The Value Component

When the role of values in the aging process was discussed near the end of Chapter 2, it was noted that values could affect a wide field of behavior (Combs et al., 1976; Lowenthal, 1980; Rokeach, 1973). It is particularly important to emphasize that values that impinge most closely on or are intrinsic parts of the self system have the most saliency and are most likely to affect behavior (Combs et al., 1976; Rokeach, 1973; Rosenberg, 1979). Certain values are inextricably tied up with self-concepts and are evident in such evaluative adjectives as honest, moral, good, conscientious, hard-working, and compassionate. Rosenberg (1979) refers to these as "self-values" and he has found empirically that their significance is particularly striking with regard to negative self-assessments. It does not take much imagination to see that the values inherent in the functionalistic ethic when incorporated as self-values, as they are for most of us, can serve to create negative self-assessments. That is why Kuypers and Bengtson (1973) made "liberation from the functionalistic ethic" a centerpiece of their reconstruction model and why "evolv[ing] alternate self-evaluations" is a major input in the integrative model.

Fortunately, many of the self-values associated with the functionalistic ethic are instrumental rather than terminal values. Instrumental values are beliefs concerning desirable modes of conduct, whereas terminal values are beliefs concerning desirable end-states of existence (Rokeach, 1973). The importance of this distinction for our purposes is that some studies have shown a decreasing preference for instrumental values and an increasing preference for terminal values as people move into late adulthood (Neugarten et al., 1968; Ryff and Baltes, 1976). Furthermore, Rokeach (1973) has found experimentally that it is easier to change instrumental values and that one way of bringing about value change in general is by showing the person the inconsistencies or lack of congruence between his or her instrumental values and their related end-state or terminal values.

To make instrumental and terminal values more explicit, let us look at the actual list of terms Rokeach (1973) has developed in his research to describe the two types of values. It is a widely used classification scheme in current social science research. His list of instrumental values is the following:

> ambitious (hard-working, aspiring)
> broadminded (open-minded)
> capable (competent, effective)
> cheerful (lighthearted, joyful)
> clean (neat, tidy)
> courageous (standing up for your beliefs)
> forgiving (willing to pardon others)
> helpful (working for the welfare of others)
> honest (sincere, truthful)
> imaginative (daring, creative)
> independent (self-reliant, self-sufficient)
> intellectual (intelligent, reflective)
> logical (consistent, rational)
> loving (affectionate, tender)
> obedient (dutiful, respectful)
> polite (courteous, well-mannered)
> responsible (dependable, reliable)
> self-controlled (restrained, self-disciplined)

It should be noted that these eighteen terms are adjectives describing characteristic behavior. This is consistent with the concept of instrumental values as preferred "modes of conduct" that should be instrumental in achieving certain end-state or terminal values.

The list of terminal values is as follows:

a comfortable life (a prosperous life)
an exciting life (a stimulating, active life)
a sense of accomplishment (lasting contribution)
a world at peace (free of war and conflict)
a world of beauty (beauty of nature and the arts)
equality (brotherhood, equal opportunity for all)
family security (taking care of loved ones)
freedom (independence, free choice)
happiness (contentedness)
inner harmony (freedom from inner conflict)
mature love (sexual and spiritual intimacy)
national security (protection from attack)
pleasure (an enjoyable, leisurely life)
salvation (saved, eternal life)
self-respect (self-esteem)
social recognition (respect, admiration)
true friendship (close companionship)
wisdom (a mature understanding of life).

The reader has probably noticed that terminal values are stated in terms using nouns, which is consistent with the idea of a terminal value expressing a life goal or end state. Another feature of these two lists of values that should be noted is that some instrumental values are much more congruent than others with certain terminal values. For example, the instrumental value "self-controlled (restrained, self-disciplined)" is not really congruent with the terminal value "an exciting life (a stimulating, active life)," whereas the instrumental value "imaginative (daring, creative)" is much more so. The significance of this for treatment as well as assessment in integrative practice is that we can help older clients not only to clarify their values but to reorder them in terms of an overall value organization that is much more consistent with where they are in their lives from a developmental, physical, and situational point of view. In this process, they can find inconsistencies between their instrumental and terminal values and among their terminal values in terms of their priorities or rankings with respect to their current life circumstances. For example, a person of, say, 60 years of age suffers a serious heart attack which causes some permanent structural damage. Let us say that the highest ranked terminal value for this person is "an exciting life (a stimulating, active life)." It is clear that this value can no longer be the salient one in his or her life and that a different one, say, "happiness (contentedness)" or "inner harmony (freedom from inner conflict)" would be much more achievable and consistent with that person's life and actual (physical) existence. Furthermore, if that person has been helped to clarify this and chooses to work toward either of the two alternatives as a primary life goal, there may be need to clarify inconsistencies between instrumental and terminal values as a result of this shift in preferred terminal values. Let us assume that this person's highest ranked instrumental value had been "ambitious (hard-working, aspiring)" and that the "exciting life" was equated with dramatic successes and accomplishments in the corporate world. It is clear that "ambitious and hardworking" can no longer be the preferred mode of conduct for this person. It is not only incongruent with the newly chosen terminal value, but it could also be a threat to the person's very existence by risking a fatal heart attack.

The process of values clarification in integrative practice means that the client clarifies and then decides upon his or her *own* values. The counselor does not give or recommend the values to the client. The client must freely and committedly decide upon his or her own value priorities and their organization; else, the whole values-clarification process will be ineffective.

How does a counselor help the client to clarify personal values? This is really the assessment part of the process; the actual decision making about and implementation of value priorities is the treatment part. I have found the above lists of instrumental and terminal values to be helpful in assessment. The client can be asked to rank the eighteen values in each list from 1 (the most preferred) down to 18 (least preferred). The clients should be allowed to do this ranking in their own selected place and time so that the rankings become as much as possible their own self-constructed hierarchies of values. This in itself is likely to be very helpful to the clients, and they certainly seem to find it interesting and stimulating. They begin to think of issues that had been dormant or subliminal for them. At any rate, the counselor goes over the list with the client to be sure that the current organization of values has indeed been clarified. This, then, is the assessment piece. Next, any inconsistencies need to be pointed out and decisions about reordering made. An example of this whole process will be given in a case illustration in Chapter 6. In the meantime, it should be mentioned that if the client is not able to work with written lists because of visual or other problems with reading or writing, the same kind of process can go on orally between the counselor who refers to the lists and the client who responds orally. In such a situation, the counselor has to be careful not to intrude on the client's autonomous processing and ranking by inadvertent cues or suggestions. Also, it might not be necessary to go over the complete lists, especially if this impedes the client–counselor relationship, and the lists can simply serve as guides in the discussion and clarification of values.

Another way of getting at the salience of certain values in a client's life space is to include them in the Semantic Differential Test. For example, instrumental values, stated in noun form such as "honesty," "cleanliness," "imagination," and so on, can be put at the top of the semantic differential sheet with the bipolar adjective scales (see Table 3-1). Any of the terminal values can also be put at the top of the sheets. In this way one obtains a measure of the salience of the values in terms of the evaluation, potency, and activity dimensions of the Semantic Differential Test. Their relative salience could then be shown graphically in a spatial model of the Semantic Differential Test (see Figure 3-4).

The evaluation of self in terms of the functionalistic ethic is an area that needs some exploration and assessment in integrative practice. Older clients do vary on this dimension, as should be evident from the findings mentioned in Chapter 2 on patterns of aging in which those in the "holding-on" pattern demonstrated a stronger functionalistic orientation in their preferred modes of conduct than did persons in the other identified patterns. At any rate, the extent to which the functionalistic orientation prevails in the client's life can be assessed in a number of ways. First of all, much can be learned in the early history-taking, information-gathering state of counseling. Then there might be need for a more explicit process of values clarification, possibly using the above lists as either guides or actual instruments in the process. It is also possible to get more directly and specifically at the functionalistic dimension by asking the clients whether they agree with, disagree, or cannot decide about the following statements:

1. A person isn't worth much when he or she is no longer able to carry on as a productive member of the community.
2. Unless I feel that I have accomplished or done something that other people value, I feel quite worthless.
3. When you are no longer a contributing member of society by functioning in such roles as worker, parent, etcetera, you can't really feel that you have value as a person.
4. A person's worth does not depend on how good a citizen, parent, or worker he or she is, but simply that he or she is a human being.

The last statement attempts to reflect the more humane, compassionate view of self that Kuypers and Bengtson (1973) say should replace the functionalistic self-view. The two values are specifically contrasted in question 4, so that the client makes an explicit value choice in responding to it. The counselor should also try to assess the *degree* of agreement or disagreement on these four questions by asking the clients whether they strongly agree or just agree, strongly disagree or just disagree. These questions might not be understood in the same way by each and every client, so it is important that the counselor is sure that the client understands the meaning of each question. This can be done by asking clients if they are clear about the questions and then clarifying the questions, preferably by paraphrasing, in a way that will not be indicative or suggestive of a preferred response on the part of the counselor. To be consistent with the perceptual approach, it is more important to understand the client's own unique perception of phenomena (in this instance structured questions and response options) than to adhere to an inflexible, verbatim reading of questions and responses as would be done with structured questions in the usual type of survey research. The purposes of such questions are for assessment and treatment of a specific person, not to generalize to other older persons as a whole. With these provisos in mind, a quantitative measure of the degree of belief in the functionalistic ethic can be obtained by using the Functionalistic Ethic Assessment Questionnaire and scoring instructions given in Appendix C.

The Morale Component

We noted earlier that integrative practice is in agreement with Frank's (1974) view that all counseling and psychotherapy are ultimately intended to reverse the process or state of demoralization. This was not an explicit part of the social reconstruction syndrome but it is the critical outcome or dependent variable in the integrative model of practice. Even if a client asks only for "hard" services such as housing or financial assistance, our intent is that the provision of these services will lead to greater client satisfaction with at least current life circumstances, if not with life in general. In most cases we explicitly intend that clients should feel better about themselves as well as about their life circumstances, and in many cases our goal is a greater general life satisfaction that is not restricted to specific current circumstances. Ultimately, of course, we would hope that our clients could achieve a state of ego integrity that would of necessity include a good deal of life satisfaction and relatively high morale.

Consistent with its grounding in gerontological literature and research, the integrative approach should draw upon concepts and measures of morale from the field of gerontology. While recognizing methodological questions about existing measures of morale, Lawton (1977) noted in his review of morale measures in gerontological research that the Life Satisfaction Index (Neugarten et al., 1961) can be recommended if one's interest is in a general criterion of morale for normally responsive subjects.

The LSI (Form A) has the added advantage of a great deal of past and present usage and published findings with which to compare one's own findings in practice. It was also the basis for many of the influential findings on personality and patterns of aging presented in Chapter 2. Considerable reference will be made to the LSIA (see Appendix A) with regard to specific clients when case illustrations are provided later in the text.

It can be seen from Appendix A that the statements in this form are quite clear in their intent. In addition, it is obvious that most of the statements tap dimensions of general morale and contentment while a few others go directly to the issue of integrity versus despair. The LSIA contains twenty statements. A response indicating a positive attitude toward aging is scored as 1. A negative or doubtful response receives a zero.

Statement 1, "As I grow older, things seem better than I thought they would be," obviously taps one's attitude toward aging. An "agree" response is scored as positive. A "disagree" response would obviously indicate a negative attitude toward aging, and no point credit is given. If the person is not sure how to respond and checks the "?" space, it is scored as a "disagree" response. That is, unless there is an emphatic positive response to each statement, it is not scored as a positive indicator of life satisfaction.

Statement 2, "I have gotten more of the breaks in life than most of the people I know," is an indicator of life satisfaction. Many individuals who have not aged successfully, who are in some degree of despair, think that they had bad breaks, were unlucky, or were victimized by life circumstances.

Statement 3, "This is the dreariest time of my life," is a morale statement that requires a "disagree" response in order to score as a positive indicator of life satisfaction.

Statement 4, "I am just as happy as when I was younger," is scored positively if there is an "agree" response. It should be noted in regard to this statement that a person may be even happier in old age than in his or her youth, and this could be indicative of a positive attitude toward aging. It is extremely important to check back with clients in the counseling process to be sure about the meaning of these responses. This might not be feasible in a large-scale survey, but when forms are being used for assessment purposes in individual or group counseling it is essential to verify the meaning of the responses.

Statement 5, "My life could be happier than it is now," requires a "disagree" response to qualify as a positive indicator, whereas Statement 6, "These are the best years of my life," requires an "agree" response. Statement 7, "Most of the things I do are boring or monotonous," taps a measure of current attitude or morale rather than a retroactive comparative one, and it requires a "disagree" response for a positive score. On the other hand, Statement 8, "I expect some interesting and pleasant things to happen to me in the future," taps a future-oriented, hopeful dimension.

Statement 9, "The things I do are as interesting to me as they ever were," is almost the direct opposite of Statement 7; it is scored positively if "agree" is checked. The reader has probably noted that some of the statements are essentially the same as others, but stated positively rather than negatively or vice versa, as in Questions 7 and 9. This is intended as a check on consistency of response. In a counseling situation the client should be asked about any apparent inconsistency on such items. It could simply be a random checking error, or it could mean a genuine inconsistency or ambivalence in attitude which it is important to pick up in the counseling process. For example, a client might agree with Statement 7, "Most of the things I do are boring or monotonous," and also agree with Statement 9, "The things I do are as interesting to me as they ever were." These seem to be contradictory and should be checked, because there is the unlikely but logical possibility that the client has always found the things he or she does boring or monotonous, so things are "as interesting" as ever.

Statement 10, "I feel old and somewhat tired," is a sensitive indicator of morale. Studies have quite consistently shown that people who characterize themselves as "old" are generally apt to be low in other indicators of morale. The positive answer to Statement 10 would therefore be "disagree."

Statement 11, "I feel my age, but it does not bother me," is tapping basically the same "feeling old" dimension as Statement 10. Although the statement is somewhat qualified by the phrase "but it doesn't bother me," the positive response in this instance would be "disagree." A person may feel his age and finds that it does bother him so "disagree" is checked for essentially negative reasons. Therefore, in a counseling situation it is important to check the meaning of this response to the client.

Statement 12, "As I look back on my life, I am fairly well satisfied," of course, calls for an "agree" response in order to be scored positively. The positive response to Question 13, "I would not change my past life even if I could," is also "agree." It should be noted that this statement is directly consistent with one of Erikson's descriptive statements about ego integrity as "the acceptance of one's one and only life cycle as something that had to be and that, by necessity, permitted no substitutions" (1963:268).

Statement 14, "Compared to other people my age, I've made a lot of foolish decisions in my life," is indicative of regret and lack of acceptance of certain aspects of one's life, so the positive response would be "disagree." Statement 15, "Compared to other people my age, I make a good appearance," has to do with body image, which has been identified as important for self-esteem. Consequently, the positive response to this statement would be "agree."

"I have made plans for things I'll be doing a month or a year from now," Statement 16, expresses a degree of future orientation in much the same way as did Statement 8, which can be seen as hopeful and therefore positive, if the response is "agree." On the other hand, Statement 17, "When I think over my life, I didn't get most of the important things I wanted," requires a "disagree" response. It clearly indicates a sense of regret rather than acceptance.

Statement 18, "Compared to other people, I get down in the dumps too often," is a straightforward indicator of feelings of depression and to be positive the response would have to be "disagree." On the other hand, Statement 19, "I've gotten pretty much what I expected out of life," requires an "agree" response to be scored positively since it is the obverse of Statement 17. Finally, Statement 20, "In spite of what people say, the lot of the average man is getting worse, not better," expresses a societal dimension of life satisfaction. In general, it is more likely for a despairing person than for an integrated person to see things in society as going to pot or perdition, so the positive response to this question would be "disagree."

Another morale or "happiness" measure that can be used in place of or in addition to the LSIA is one that was used in a nationwide mental health survey (Gurin, Veroff, and Feld, 1960). The measure is easy to understand and to administer and is therefore quite appropriate for many older clients. The question or measure is:

> Taking all things together, how would you say things are these days—would you say you're *very* happy, *pretty* happy, or *not too* happy these days?
>
> Check one below:
>
> These days I am very happy   _____
> These days I am pretty happy   _____
> These days I am not too happy   _____

The meaning of the responses to this question should be self-evident, even though the question is quite general and subjective in nature. It should be noted that although people who are not generally happy might check that they are happy, giving what they think is the socially approved response, it is likely that those who indicate that they are "not too happy" are indeed not generally happy.

Lawton (1977) has noted that "positive self-concept" or self-esteem is another measure of morale, but one that has not received much systematic attention in gerontological research. Gaitz and Scott (1972) developed a self-esteem question and measure very similar to the above "happiness' measure: "How do you feel about yourself as a person—pretty good, just okay, could be better, or not so good?" Another, more comprehensive self-esteem measure is the Rosenberg (1979) Self-Esteem Scale. The discrepancy score between the self-concept and ideal self measure on the Semantic Differential Test is preferable for assessment purposes in integrative practice because it is consistent with the self system model outlined earlier in this chapter (see Figure 3-5).

The Use of Instruments in Integrative Practice

Many practitioners might feel that it is not necessary to use morale instruments in order to determine the extent to which clients are demoralized about their situations, selves, or lives. This is probably true generally, although measures such as the self-esteem discrepancy score have particular meaning in the integrative practice model. Actually, the whole issue of the use of instruments in integrative practice needs to be considered at this point. There are those who would say that such devices are not necessary in any form of counseling or psychotherapy. Szasz (1965:36-37), for example, has said that such tests tend to provide a mystique of expertise, a scientific aura that is in fact pseudoscientific and unnecessary. There is certainly some truth to this, and the testing can imply that the counselor has some kind of arcane and secret knowledge about the client that the client is not privy to. This could, of course, increase the distance between the helper and the helped, which is contrary to the development of a sound therapeutic relationship. Consequently, all the tests mentioned here were self-report instruments in which the intent of the questions can be readily understood by clients with little or no interpretation by the counselor. Furthermore, the clients' responses to the instruments are used in the counseling process as a basis for exploration, discussion, and further mutual work and understanding. They are thus a means of clarifying and validating clinical impressions gained through verbal and observational techniques. By using these instruments directly with the clients and checking responses for validity, there is a demystification of the whole process.

Therefore, the use of instruments is not an either/or question. It is a matter of selected and differential use. In very short-term counseling in cases involving crisis situations or those involving predominant use of hard services and minimal counseling, there is no need for the use of instruments for assessment purposes. The problems and needs in such cases are evident and immediate. However, when we get beyond the Input A stage of the integrative model (see Figure 3-3), we have counseling objectives involving the stabilization and sustaining of morale and self-esteem, concepts for which there are appropriate assessment instruments. Even before we get to the stage of Input C, "encouraging an internal locus of control," a measure of the locus of control factor would give us an early indication of prognosis and sense of the extent to which the client will see himself or herself as the one most responsible for bringing about necessary changes and seeing the counselor as facilitator in the process (Rabkin, 1977).

One has to consider carefully the advisability of using instruments in any case. Development of a sound relationship with the client has first priority, and instruments should be used only if they do not detract from that relationship. For whatever reason, a client might be fearful or suspicious of the instruments or the use to which they might be put, and this has to be respected. In the very large majority of cases, though, clients will be more than willing to respond to the instruments after an explanation of their purpose and after seeing the questions themselves. Most of these instruments are clearly designed to explore questions about which the clients themselves are intensely interested—their morale, their veiws of themselves and others, and the attitudes that have particular meaning at this stage of their lives. Consequently, most clients see the instruments as distinct assets in the counseling situation.

One must always make it clear to clients in the very beginning that responding to the instruments is purely voluntary and that they can choose not to respond at any point in the assessment process without jeopardizing the services they seek. The clients should also be told that they will have an opportunity to see the results of the tests and to discuss their responses. They should know that this sharing of results is part and parcel of the counseling process. We should be open in saying that we know that the predetermined response categories in some of the instruments often do not adequately represent their own particular attitudes about the questions being asked. That is why we want to go over their responses with them, so that their own unique attitudes can be clarified. In addition, we should indicate that the form in which some of the results can be presented (diagrams, rankings) can also be an aid in the counseling process.

It is certainly true that a number of the concepts that are central to integrative practice (self-concept, ideal self, self-esteem) can be seen as abstract until seen in graphic form by the client. In fact, diagrammatic assessment instruments are being used increasingly to enhance client understanding as well as to aid practitioners in the assessment process (Hartman, 1978).

In addition to their assessment uses, these instruments can be used to evaluate the extent of change (pretest to posttest) on key variables in the integrative model in the course of counseling. Finally, the instruments presented here, since they come largely from the gerontological literature, enable one to relate the findings from practice cases to the larger body of knowledge and research on aging. This should help to inform practice and keep it relevant to and current with the burgeoning field of gerontology.

Principles of Integrative Practice

The salient points from Chapters 2 and 3 can be summarized in a set of principles that can serve as a general guide to integrative practice.

The first of these principles upholds the intrinsic worth of the client. This means that the client is valued regardless of his or her attributes, achievements, or performances. This is more than a guide for the practitioner, it is a value which we hope the client will incorporate so as to have a more compassionate view of self and others in the latter stages of life. It is the antidote to a functionalistic evaluation of persons.

The second principle is client self-determination. This means that our work with clients is determined largely by the client's expressed wishes in the sense that they should be permitted to make decisions for themselves, to become what they wish, and to determine their own lifestyles. Thus, if the client's immediate expressed wishes are for hard services (transportation, housing, medical care), these must be met first. If we see the need for intensive counseling in addition to the hard services, we can communicate this to the client, but if the client does not want intensive counseling, we should respect that decision. Thus, the principle of self-determination could mean the client's right to fail, if he or she so chooses, but it also means that we recognize the fact that the client and not the counselor is the primary problem solver in the counseling process.

The third principle states a belief in the uniqueness of each individual.

This is consistent with the perceptual perspective that underlies integrative practice, in which each person has a uniquely different view of self and the surrounding world. In practice, this means that we use assessment methods that maximize individuality and minimize categorization or generalized labeling of the client.

The fourth principle of integrative practice has to do with the focus on meaning. The practitioners must always determine as much as possible the meaning of events, circumstances, and other persons in the client's life space. This sensitizes the practitioner to the manner in which the client perceives or construes his or her own reality. Accurate empathy becomes a requisite for the realization of this principle.

The fifth principle of integrative practice has to do with the centrality of the self-concept in assessing, working with, and evaluating one's work with the aging client. The client, as well as the practitioner, needs to know the importance of maintaining and enhancing self-esteem in order to carry out the change process and to attain the morale and integrity that are the ultimate objectives of counseling. Thus, discussion of concepts of the self, the ideal self, and self-esteem is apt to be part of the ongoing dialogue between practitioner and client.

Finally, there is a sixth principle which I have not directly addressed up to this point. For lack of a better term, I am calling it the "androgogy principle." It comes from the field of adult education, in which there is a primary tenet that older adult students should function as teachers and learners at the same time, using their experiences to facilitate the learning process (Ingalls, 1973). Although this educational meaning of the principle has direct transferability to integrative work with groups—in which the experiences of the members are used in this didactic sense—its more general meaning has applicability for integrative practice with individuals as well.

There is explicit recognition that the traditional role of the older person as teacher and adviser has been largely lost in our modern technological society, with its proliferation of new fields, specialties, and "experts" for what used to be considered normal problems of everyday living. From a developmental perspective, the integrative approach holds that there is natural need and inclination in the older person to fill the role of teacher and adviser. As Nouwen and Gaffney (1976:153) put it, "only when we are able to receive the elderly as our teachers will it be possible to offer the help they are looking for. As long as we continue to divide the world into the strong and the weak, the helpers and the helped, the givers and the receivers, the independent and the dependent, real care will not be possible, because then we keep broadening the dividing lines that caused the suffering of the elderly in the first place."

Thus, the counselor must acknowledge directly to each older client recognition of the experience and accumulated life knowledge she or he has. Whenever possible, the practitioner should attempt to draw upon this background of the client. This can be done most obviously in group situations, in which the client's prior experience can be drawn upon to help and support others in the group, but it can also be applied in encouraging an individual client to engage in helping, teaching, or advising functions (as a volunteer in a foster grandparent program, friendly visitor for other older persons, and so on). This serves a number of functions. It enhances self-esteem, restores and strengthens atrophied social competencies, and increases the likelihood of greater client self-determination and independence.

There are of course many elderly who are dependent and who would prefer to have someone else take responsibility and make decisions for them. Rather than acting as teachers or advisers they appear to be acting as children or pupils. The androgogy principle can be applied realistically to activate potentials in many clients who have assumed dependent roles, as well as to enable the more independent client to function as an "elder" in the traditional, positive sense of that term, as a respected guide or teacher.

The central theme that runs through these principles of integrative practice is that they seek to take advantage of the natural developments of the later stages of life, to recognize them as natural and normal, and, where they are lacking or stunted, to enhance them. It will be recalled that research has generally found evidence of change in the covert aspects of personality and evidence of continuity in the more overt aspects of personality. The implications of this for integrative practice are that we should generally try to support and sustain rather than change such overt areas of functioning as interpersonal relations, lifestyle, and person/environment transactions. For example, we seek to support and enhance family relations where these have been an essential ingredient in the life of a client. We attempt to sustain a certain level of social interaction through group methods for those clients who, through death of friends, relocation, or loss of old work associations, have increased affiliative and emotional support needs.

Conversely, we tend to work for positive change in covert areas of personality functioning, particularly those areas indicated by the integrative model: enhancement of self-esteem, development of a more internal locus of control, and internalization of more positive self-evaluations. This is not to say that one would never work toward change in the overt aspects of personality functioning. We should be alert, for example, to the potential need for a group experience for a client who is depressed in reaction to the loss of a loved one.

These generalizations about overt and covert aspects of personality and the generalized guides for practice provided by the principles of integrative practice cannot, of course, speak to the specifics of practice. That is what will be done in the next three chapters. The specifics will be given in the light of a treatment continuum based on the integrative model presented earlier in this chapter. This continuum will be explicated in the next chapter.

CHAPTER FOUR

The Methods and Techniques of Integrative Practice

THE TERMS methods and techniques are frequently used interchangeably in the counseling and psychotherapy literature, but they are differentiated within the perspective of integrative practice. For our purposes, a method is a general procedure or process for attaining an objective. Techniques and skills are much more specific and are subsumed under or part of a larger process which is the method. Differential objectives, and therefore methods, are determined by a number of factors among which the type of problem and time factors are most prominent. There are, for example, cases in which the primary problem is lack of certain basic resources. In such cases, the primary method or process is the provision of the needed resources and services, either directly or indirectly by referral to agencies that can provide the needed service. In addition, the counseling methods that complement the provision of such services tend to be supportive in nature. In another case, the primary problem may be a family one and the family itself may become the vehicle for change, either through the use of family treatment methods or the use of the family for support and maintenance. Sometimes, informal methods of help other than the family are most appropriate for the presenting problem, for example self-help groups or informal helping networks of friends and neighbors.

Time factors are also very important in determining methods. Thus, the methods used in short-term counseling, whether in individual, small group, or family modalities, will differ in type, emphasis, and intensity from long-term treatment. Supportive methods and techniques might predominate in the short run, whereas methods oriented toward client insight would predominate in the long run. This will become clearer in the treatment continuum which follows.

Treatment Continuum of the Integrative Model

The continuum of integrative practice reflects the time dimension that is inherent in the integrative treatment model shown in Figure 3-3, and it explicates the input objectives in somewhat more detail. However, the continuum does not just reflect the model, it has a basic underlying assumption of its own that has not yet been made explicit. The assumption is that there are "deficit" needs and "growth" needs in older persons just as there are in younger ones (Maslow, 1970). Deficit needs are basic requirements for physiological well-being and safety. The basic needs for adequate rest, nourishment, and shelter have to be met before people can achieve a sense of security and safety, which in turn allows them to strive for belongingness and love to meet their needs to be part of a group and to have an affective relationship with others. Through affiliation with others it is possible to meet a fourth need in Maslow's hierarchy, the need for esteem. This is accomplished by individuals receiving feedback from others in order to realize that they are competent and of value. This formulation is actually quite consistent with the self-concept theory presented in Chapter 2. The feedback can be provided by a counselor as well as by significant others in the lives of the individuals. Groups, whether therapeutic, support, peer, or a combination of these, are obviously powerful mechanisms for such feedback.

Maslow's fifth need is self-actualization, which means fulfilling one's nature and potential. There is a good deal of professional disagreement with Maslow and other humanistic psychologists who posit a fundamental and universal human motive for self-actualization in the sense of fulfilling all of one's potentials in all aspects. Without engaging in that debate, I will simply state that for the purposes of the integrative model the fifth need or goal is achievement of ego integrity as it has been defined and discussed in this book.

It can be seen that there is a kind of progression in terms of the inputs needed to move an individual client from the basic deficit needs to the growth needs. This is why "improved maintenance conditions" is the first input on the treatment continuum of the integrative model. Deficit need conditions and motives call for a reduction of tension and stress and for the restoration of equilibrium. Growth motives, on the other hand, call for gains to achieve a new level of functioning or equilibrium. This is reflected in Table 4-1. Objectives 1 through 6 indicate the need for reduction of stress and stabilization of functioning, while Objectives 7 through 12 indicate gains and increments in functioning.

TABLE 4-1. *Treatment Continuum of the Inegrative Model (Inputs)*

A. Provide Maintenance Conditions and Services

   Objectives:

   1. reduce stress due to situational crisis or problem
   2. remove impediments in person-situation configuration
   3. reduce dependence on emergency supports

B. Provide Support and Coping Strategies

   Objectives:

   4. stabilize self-esteem
   5. sustain morale
   6. sustain coping efforts

C. Encourage Internal Locus of Control

   Objectives:

   7. enhance coping skills
   8. increase problem-solving capacity
   9. increase cognitive mastery

D. Evolve Alternate Self-Evaluations

   Objectives:

   10. reduce functionalistic self-evaluations
   11. clarify alternative self-evaluations
   12. increase life satisfaction/ego integrity

The initial inputs in A above are most responsive to the immediate critical needs in the situation. It should be helpful at this point to return to the person-problem-situation concept mentioned earlier. The problems in the beginning of the breakdown cycle are likely to be critical rather than chronic, and there is generally an immediate focal need that is evident in the person-situation nexus. Usually, the most immediate need is for a change in the *situation*. Thus, in the case of an elderly person whose heat has been shut off for nonpayment of the utility bill, it is first necessary to see to it that the heat is restored. The cause of the nonpayment, which is part of the *person* element, is not treated first.

Indeed, a great many elderly persons are in poverty or near-poverty, and all they need is the provision of financial or other concrete assistance without any counseling. It is obviously an intrusion and unethical to foist counseling on such persons. However, in protective work with the elderly it has frequently been found that they suffer from mental confusion due to acute (and reversible) organic brain syndrome caused by malnutrition precisely because of their poverty. Whenever the person is confused by a condition such as that or simply overwhelmed by the force of circumstances related to poverty, poor housing, ill health, and so on, there may be a need for supportive and informational counseling in addition to the initial need for material resources. Since this is a book on counseling, it is addressed to these situations rather than to the majority of older persons who are not confused and whose problems are directly and simply related to economic need.

We tend to consider the function of counseling as bringing about changes in how the client thinks, feels, and behaves. Even if the individual's situation presents cause for concern, the objective in counseling is apt to be to change his behavior so as to enable him or her to change the situation. We have emphasized that the integrative model focuses first on the client's deficit needs as they are contained in the situation. However, in meeting the need for nutrition and safety we are also reducing the stress brought on by the situation. Therefore, we state the first objective in Table 4-1 as a person-objective: "reduce stress (in the person) due to situational crisis or problem." It should be noted that for the most part all the objectives are stated in terms of the person. Thus, item 3, "reduce dependence on emergency supports" is an aspect of the person even though "emergency supports" are aspects of the situation. It should be noted that both the inputs and attendant objectives shift more toward the person than the situation as the continuum progresses, with Input D and its objectives the most personal and least situational.

Input B has as its objectives a set of maintenance states representing equilibrium in the person's functioning with regard to mood and attitude (self-esteem and morale) and behavioral functioning (coping efforts).

Input C, on the other hand, has as its objectives positive change (enhancement, increases) that represents a move from coping to some mastery or control. By the time we move to Input D it is clear that deficit needs have receded into the background and growth needs related to self-concept and integrity are in the foreground as counseling objectives.

Differential Objectives and Methods in Integrative Practice

It is important to recognize that we cannot always be certain at the time that we enter into intervention with an older person whether the situation will be short-term or whether it will lead to an extended period of practice and counseling. We can give brief service, including concrete maintenance services and counseling, and then discontinue them when the situation has stabilized and the immediate crisis-oriented objectives have been met. Whether we continue beyond the short term depends primarily on the client's expressed desire and the need for extended counseling. Another factor is the setting in which the service is provided. Some settings provide an opportunity for the delivery of the necessary Input A type of services in the short run as well as for continuation of counseling on an extended basis, with the availability of concrete maintenance services on an as-needed basis. Some local offices for the aging, departments of public welfare, and departments of social services are of this type.

The following case illustrates how such an option for short-term or extended work might come about; this case is also intended to provide a more specific understanding of how the inputs and objectives identified in Table 4-1 are actually brought into operation.

Constance Jennings was a 77-year-old single woman who was living alone in a large single room in an old boarding house in a city in western New York State. The rooming house was a large old home in a residential section of the city which had once been very affluent and stylish. However, the neighborhood and the buildings were deteriorating, and most of the fine old homes had long before been broken up into small apartments and single rooms for rental. The area could not yet be considered a slum, but it was populated mostly by older retired persons on fixed incomes and some younger transients.

Miss J.'s landlady called the Adult Services Unit of the local Department of Social Services to report that Miss J. was in need of protective services because she had not paid her rent in four months and seemed quite confused and forgetful. The landlady was aware of the availibility of protective services because of prior experience with other elderly tenants. She said that she could not afford to permit Miss J. to keep her room any longer without payment of rent. She had allowed Miss J. to stay this long because of her previous good record of prompt payment of rent for almost ten years.

A protective worker was sent out the following day, and she first spoke at length to the landlady before talking to Miss J. The worker found out that when the nonpayment of rent first started Miss J. just seemed to be forgetful about paying it. However, as the landlady continued reminding her of it, Miss J. began claiming that she had indeed paid the rent and she appeared to become suspicious of the landlady's motives. She would not let the landlady into her room, and she would sit at the top of the stairs and watch the landlady "like a hawk" all day long.

The landlady was also fearful that Miss J.'s mental state had deteriorated to such an extent that she might represent a safety or fire hazard by leaving on the hot plate or toaster in her room. The landlady also thought that Miss J was not taking care of herself adequately. She did not seem to go out more than once a week, and then only for very light grocery shopping, judging by the small packages she would bring back. The landlady therefore doubted that she was eating properly.

After their discussion, the landlady started to take the worker up to Miss J.'s room, but they found Miss J. at her post at the top of the stairs. The worker identified herself and indicated that she would like to talk to Miss J. to see if she could help straighten out the rent situation. Miss J. appeared very doubtful and peered suspiciously over the worker's shoulder at the landlady.

It was only after the landlady went back into her own apartment that the worker was able to convince Miss J. to let her talk to her in her room.

The room was not badly kept up, but the worker noted that the only food Miss J. seemed to have on hand was some bread, some jam, and tea. When she asked Miss J. if she cooked everything in her room or went out for some meals, Miss J. replied that she could not afford to eat out. It was quickly apparent to the worker that although Miss J. was somewhat suspicious and confused, she was above all fearful and lonely. Through patient and calm expression of her warmth and concern for Miss J., together with reassurances that she was not there to place Miss J. elsewhere at the landlady's behest, the worker got the client to confide that she had become fearful about being placed elsewhere several months earlier when another woman in the apartment house was taken to the county nursing home because she was no longer able to care for herself. Miss J. felt that the landlady was instrumental in that woman's placement and wanted to do the same thing to her. She thought the rent issue was the landlady's way of getting rid of her.

When the worker indicated that she has seen the landlady's rent book, and that it looked indeed as though Miss J. was four months behind, Miss J. admitted that she might be, but said she doubted that the landlady would let her stay even if she paid the rent. The worker pointed out that not paying the rent would be one sure way of having the landlady evict her.

Miss J.'s despair and loneliness overcame her suspicions at this point, and she related the following facts about her current situation to the worker. Her only source of income was a small amount of Social Security, which was far below the maximum allowed payment because her employment as a clerk-typist in a small business concern had not been covered by Social Security until very late into her work career. Both her parents had died in her early adulthood and the small amount of money and insurance they had left her had been used up long ago. Her only sibling, a younger sister, had died of rheumatic fever at age six. Consequently since she had never married, Miss J. had no close relatives to whom she could turn in her retirement years. She did have some modest savings at retirement which she had slowly eaten into over the years.

She confided to the worker that she still had over $1,000 put away in various parts of her room, in the corners of drawers, in boxes in the clothes closet. She had retained this sum despite her low social security payments by eating virtually nothing but toast with a little jam and tea for the past few months. She had stopped going out to eat in restaurants even though all she had in her room to cook with was a two-burner hot plate and a toaster. And, of course, she had not paid her rent for several months.

Other concerns besides her financial situation were physical complaints about dizziness and some pains in her legs and arms from time to time. These complaints, as well as her suspicions that the landlady wanted the money she had hidden away in her room, were also responsible for her staying in the house and restricting her outings to occasional grocery shopping. When Miss J. and the worker together searched her room, it turned out that Miss J. had over $2,000 hidden in various places, enough to pay her back rent and still have over $1,000 left. She would also still be eligible for Supplemental Security Insurance (SSI) since the leftover money was within SSI limits. Miss J. said she did not want SSI because it was "welfare," and she and her family had never been on welfare, no matter how hard the times were.

For the time being, rather than try to convince Miss J. of her entitlement to SSI, the worker got her to agree to pay the back rent from her savings if she could be assured that the landlady would not try to have her evicted. In turn, the worker got the landlady to agree to allow Miss J. to remain, if she paid her rent and if it could be determined that she was physically and mentally able to care for herself with outpatient health and/or mental health services.

The worker was able in subsequent visits to establish a relationship of trust with Miss J. and took her for a physical checkup at a nearby medical center, where they were able to give Miss J. an unobtrusive mental status evaluation as well. It was found that she was suffering from malnutrition due to her inadequate diet and that she had some circulatory difficulties, which could be treated through medication. It was also determined that she probably had acute brain syndrome as a result of the malnutrition and circulatory problems. However, the syndrome was reversible through vitamin therapy, an adequate diet, and medication for the circulatory problems. At first, the worker took Miss J. to the medical center for her medication and checkups, but as she got better Miss J. chose to walk there herself.

Given the payment of the overdue rent and the reassurance that Miss J. was mentally competent, the landlady was quite agreeable to her remaining in the rooming house.

In all, the worker had twenty-two contacts with Miss J., including visits to the clinic and other offices with regard to SSI and related financial matters, which extended over a three-and-one-half-month period. It took quite a few meetings with Miss J. before the worker convinced her to apply for SSI. The worker had to assure her that SSI was not welfare, that Miss J. was entitled to it by virtue of her many years of work, and that it was not her fault that her employment did not have Social Security coverage in the earlier years of her working life. The worker repeatedly reminded her of her good work record and her history of self-support and independence as sources of legitimate pride and worthiness for SSI. With the worker's support and reassurance and the success of her medical treatment, her fearfulness and suspicion left and she felt more hopeful. However, even though she accepted the SSI, she continued to be concerned that the worker was from the "old welfare department," which had been renamed the Department of Social Services some years before. Miss J. said that even if her neighbors did not know the worker was from the "welfare department," she herself knew it, and she asked to have her case closed in DSS, although she was clearly very grateful for the help the worker had provided at this critical time in her life. The worker respected her reasons and accordingly closed the case. Although Miss J.'s association of DSS with the old welfare department was not entirely realistic, the worker was aware that Miss J. was concerned about remaining in a state of dependency, even if it was only symbolic.

Looking back at this case from its beginning, one realizes that it was not clear at first whether Constance Jennings would be a candidate for short-term or any kind of counseling. There was a strong possibility that she might require placement in a psychiatric setting or might need some other non-voluntary protective services in the community, such as conservatorship or trusteeship. If it had been found that she was not mentally competent to manage her money but that she could function otherwise in the community, as a New York State resident she could have had a conservator appointed (probably DSS, since she had no relatives or lawyer) to manage her funds. Regardless of the type of nonvoluntary alternative, integrative counseling would not have been possible because she would not have had the freedom of choice or cognitive capacity (because of mental incompetence) to benefit from such treatment.

As it turned out, her mental status imporved enough for her to benefit from short-term counseling along with the concrete services of the worker. Let us trace the developments and inputs in her case in terms of the integrative continuum in Table 4-1. First, the worker was able to reduce the stress caused by the crisis of possible eviction or involuntary placement (Objective 1). Secondly, the worker removed the "impediments in the person-situation" (Objective 2) by getting Miss J. to pay and the landlady to accept the back rent, while assessment of Miss J.'s mental and physical status were undertaken. The regular allowance reduced "dependence on emergency support" (Objective 3).

As far as Input B is concerned, the worker clearly provided reassurance to Miss J. about her worthiness, stressing her past record of employment and of independence and self-support in order to stabilize her self-esteem (Objective 4). The worker also helped to sustain Miss J.'s morale (Objective 5) by visiting her and supporting her emotionally to counteract her sense of isolation and her feelings of loss of control over finances, her landlady, and her circumstances generally.

The worker also helped Miss J. to regain and sustain her coping efforts (Objective 6) by getting her examined and registered at the local medical center and then encouraging and supporting her regular visits to the center. In this regard, the worker was actually in the beginning stages of Input C-encouraging an internal locus of control. However, it would have taken more extended counseling to achieve the objectives related to the internal locus of control.

Given Miss J.'s accomplishments in the short run, it would appear that she was an "internal" to begin with. This raises the interesting question, as far as the integrative treatment continuum is concerned, as to which clients need more than the practical services and emotional support Miss J. received in order to receive the objectives of higher morale and greater life satisfaction. We are still collecting and analyzing data on this question and do not yet have a definitive answer. However, some empirical findings in England (Goldberg, Mortimer, and Williams, 1970) suggest that many elderly probably need more than practical, concrete services in order to achieve significantly higher levels of morale. Goldberg and her colleagues assessed the social and medical condition of 300 older persons who were referred to the welfare department of a borough of London. Half of the clients were randomly assigned to trained social workers and the other half to regular Department of Social Welfare officers. Both groups were very similar in regard to their physical, emotional, financial, and environmental conditions at the start of service. After ten months of service the clients were evaluated again. It was found that both groups had significantly fewer practical needs; in fact, the input of practical services by the trained social workers and the welfare officers were about the same. The big difference in input was that the trained social workers spent much more time on casework counseling with the clients and with their relatives. It was found on reassessment that the clients served by the trained workers had fewer worries, were less depressed, were more active, and had higher life satisfaction than those served by the welfare officers.

What this suggests, then, is that in a good integrative practice, even in short-term cases requiring mostly concrete, material help, there is need for supportive counseling as well as the provision of hard services to meet deficit needs. The kind of supportive counseling offered to Constance Jennings as part of Input A consisted of reassurance, warm concern, and recognition. The need for the core conditions of warmth, empathy, and genuineness (Truax and Carkhuff, 1967) holds true throughout counseling, of course, but the strong emphasis on rather heavy emotional support and reassurance has to shift as we move in the continuum toward encouragement of the client to use his or her own initiatives and abilities. Input C requires a type of counseling that provides for development of certain kinds of problem-solving abilities that finally move the client toward mastery and control rather than simply "coping." If counseling remained at the heavy emotional support and reassurance stage of Input A, there would be an increased chance of incurring greater dependency in the client. One study of protective services to the elderly suggests that we might be encouraging dependency by such an approach (Blenkner, Bloom, and Nielsen, 1971).

In sum, there are differential methods as well as objectives as we move through Inputs A, B, and into C in applying the integrative approach in short-term practice and counseling. At first, in Input A, we offer much emotional support, reassurance, and direct or indirect (referral) provision of practical services to meet the objectives of reduced stress, removal of person-situation impediments, and reduced dependence on irregular or emergency forms of help. Then, as we move through Input B, there is more emphasis on encouragement of self-efforts than on simple, unconditional reassurance in order to achieve the objectives related to stabilization and equilibrium in the person-situation configuration: sustained morale, stabilized self-esteem, and sustained coping efforts. Much of this reassurance in counseling in this stage involves coping statements on the part of the counselor, such as: "You *can* do it." "You have done it in the past." "Good! You've gotten yourself back on track by your own efforts," etc. There is also an explicit effort by the counselor to have the clients incorporate these coping statements and to consciously use them on themselves. An essential part of the integrative approach at this time is to tell the clients that in crisis situations such as the one they are facing, there is always a tendency toward loss of self-esteem and that it is necessary to recognize that this is a subjective emotional state that is transient if they do not let it get them down. There is a need to consciously counteract this state by reminding themselves that they *do* have competence and skills and that they have demonstrated these in the past. This should help to buttress their self-esteem and their morale.

As we move into the Input C stage, there is still the need for this encouraging kind of support and even for some reassurance as the clients struggle to retain their balance and equilibrium. However, now the emphasis is more on achieving change rather than stabilizing the situation and this means that the counselor must more actively and explicitly encourage and enhance the development of skills, problem solving capacities, and greater behavioral and cognitive mastery and control on the part of the client to provide more of an internal locus of control. How much such control should be emphasized depends on the individual and the circumstances, but as far as short-term counseling is concerned it should be enough to avoid dependency and enable the client to do some independent problem solving. Whether or not the client ever achieves ego-integrity we will probably never know, because he or she will no longer be in counseling. It is only in extended integrative counseling that ego integrity is apt to be an explicit objective and an observed outcome. In short-term practice we are looking for increments in problem-solving abilities, in certain skills, and in self-initiated control and mastery to the extent possible. This means that in addition to providing the kind of encouragement and support mentioned earlier, the counselor has to enable the client to obtain or develop the necessary skills and sense of mastery or control. This might have to be done through referral in cases in which it is realistic to expect clients to develop new or different vocational aptitudes and skills; or it might have to be for rehabilitation services when there is need for development of physical skills and functioning.

It should be useful at this point to consider the whole question of what constitutes short-term counseling versus extended or long-term counseling as far as the actual time frame is concerned. Butcher and Koss (1978) reported on the basis of a survey of almost a million patients in psychotherapy that "most therapists structure brief treatment as about 6 to 10 sessions of 50 minutes in length once a week. Most therapists inform the patient of the time limitations in advance and expect that the focused and limited goals will be achieved in that period" (1978:739). They found the upper limit of short-term therapy to be 25 sessions or about six months.

Several points should be made about these findings with regard to treatment of the aged. First, given the different settings of the sessions with the elderly (client's own home, hospital, nursing and rehabilitative settings), the 50-minute office session cannot be held as the norm. Particularly in group counseling, sessions are apt to be longer, though many are not. Six sessions would have to be the lower limit for short-term integrative counseling. Another point to be made is that although focused and time-limited goals will frequently be established in the integrative approach with the aging, it is very possible that counseling continues over a longer period, particularly in cases of chronic physical and practical problems that will require ancillary services over the long run in addition to counseling.

Generally, the time limits of short-term integrative practice are from six weeks to six months. Most cases involve six to fifteen sessions within a period of from six weeks to three or four months. The short-term version of integrative practice is therefore similar in time and frequency dimensions to other brief therapies. It tends to differ in regard to the range of settings in which it is used, the use of referral and practical services, and the particular emphases of some of the supportive techniques used. The last two points will be explored in more detail in the next section.

Referral and Support

I have already emphasized that the elderly are often in need of concrete services and that their deficit needs for these services must be given priority if any progress is going to be made. Therefore, even if the counselor's primary or sole function is to counsel people, it is essential that he or she is knowledgeable about programs and services for older persons available in the community in order to make the necessary referrals before, during, and after counseling.

Pfeiffer (1975) has standardized an approach to assessing the need for community services by older persons. His "Functional Assessment" scheme lists the following kinds of formal and informal services: transportation, social/recreational services, employment (job finding and counseling), occupational or job training, remedial training (in basic personal skills), mental health, psychotropic drugs, personal care (help in bathing, dressing, feeding), nursing care, physical therapy, continuous supervision (live-in person to supervise), checking services (someone to "check in" periodically), relocation and placement services (new housing, including institutional placement), homemaker-household services, meal preparation (in and out of home), legal or protective services (managing legal or personal business affairs), and information and referral services. This is a rather generic list and some communities might not have all of them, particularly smaller communities. Therefore, it is highly advisable for the counselor to develop a "service inventory" for his or her community such as the one outlined below.

Service Inventory

Direct Services
1. Information and referral
2. Counseling
3. Transportation
4. Home services (Family & Child Service Co.)
5. Legal services (Legal Aid Society)

Indirect Services
1. Educational services
   a. Vocational education assistance
   b. Continuing education
   c. Public library
2. Financial Services
   a. Discounts
   b. Financial counseling
   c. Food stamps
   d. Insurance counseling
   e. Manpower services training
   f. Employment service of the state department of labor
   g. Property tax relief
   h. Social Security
3. Health Services
   a. Adult health screening
   b. Alcohol abuse care
   c. Ambulance services
   d. Community health center
   e. Emergency food services
   f. Home health and homemaker services
   g. Health insurance counseling
   h. Hospitals
   i. Long-term care facilities
   j. Medicaid
   k. Medicare
   l. Mental health care
   m. County nutrition program
   n. Veteran's benefits
   o. Voluntary health services
4. Housing Services
   a. Emergency fuel payment loan program of Community Action Program
   b. Home maintenance program
   c. Homes for the aged

    d. Housing brokerage service
    e. Municipal housing
    f. Veterans' benefits
    g. Winterization program
5. Legal Services
    a. Attorney court services
    b. Advocacy
6. Recreational Services
    a. Church activities
    b. County nutrition program—social rather than nutritional
    c. Senior citizen and retirement organizations
7. Social Services
    a. Supportive counseling
    b. Friendly visiting and escort service of volunteers
    c. Telephone reassurance
8. Transportation Services
    a. CDTA—special rate
    b. Ambulance service

This inventory was prepared by a Title XX–funded protective service unit staffed by graduate social work students under the supervision of a faculty member of the School of Social Welfare at the State University of New York at Albany. The field instruction unit was located in the Schenectady County Department of Social Services, which was mandated under New York State law to provide protective services to residents of Schenectady County. In line with the purposes of its Title XX funding, the field instruction unit was organized to make service more accessible to older clients through outreach programs, as well as to mobilize community resources to allow the clients to remain in the community. If the client had a family, an attempt was made to strengthen family ties. Because this unit provided such a variety of services, including counseling, referral, and the use of family and other informal support networks, the disguised case illustrations in the remainder of this chapter are based on work done in that unit.

As far as the service inventory is concerned, it reflects the actual services available in Schenectady County for older persons at the time of the field project. The direct services were those which could be provided directly by the Schenectady County DSS. The indirect services were those provided elsewhere to which the students often had to refer clients. A copy of the inventory was filed in each case folder for periodic checks as to the need for and use of the listed services.

Too often, a counselor will simply provide information to the client about available services on the premise that the client will follow through. Although we do not want to foster dependency in our older clients by doing everything for them in obtaining outside services, it should also be recognized that "a period of dependency is often a necessary part of the recovery process after a traumatic event" (Lemon and Goldstein, 1978:591), even in short-term counseling situations. It might therefore be necessary to contact the agency providing the service, take the client there to apply for the service, and then follow up to see that the service was provided.

Lowy (1979) has talked about the social worker's responsibility in the referral process, but what he has said applies equally well to anyone working in a formal helping relationship with older persons:

> Responsibility does not end with the referral. Social workers must assume responsibility for the results of their judgments and actions when making a referral. A worker must recognize that asking for help from others is not simple for older people, and the time of referral is a vulnerable period; clients are open to suggestions and ready to work, but they can become easily discouraged if movement is not felt by them. The more threatening the problem, the less prone is the person to go somewhere else again and rehash it. Referral involves not only sending the person to another agency, but also follow-up, making sure the client got there and is receiving the necessary service [1979:229–230].

Frequently it is difficult to make referrals for older persons, because they have been independent all their lives and feel that accepting service would make them or mark them as dependent. The following case illustration is an example of such a situation, but it also shows which services can be provided once the client can be convinced that he or she is entitled to such services without the stigma of dependency.

Mrs. McCall was a 65-year-old widow who had worked all her life supporting and helping others. Her husband had been disabled in an accident early in their marriage, and she had to raise their son singlehandedly while caring for her husband. Still, she managed to earn extra money beyond her husband's disability payments by working as a practical nurse. When her husband died and her son left home, she worked as a live-in nurse with various disabled people. However, Mrs. McCall developed a serious heart condition along with other serious vascular ailments, and she could no longer adequately care for herself and her apartment, much less support herself.

Her neighbors noticed that she had become housebound and largely bedridden, but she would not apply for any help. It was a neighbor who finally contacted the Department of Social Services, and a student social worker from the special protective services unit was assigned to Mrs. McCall. Mrs. McCall politely told the worker that she did not need any help from Social Services, that when she felt better she would go to work again. The worker appealed to Mrs. McCall's professional judgment as a practical nurse to get her to see the need for a complete checkup and medical advice as to when and what she could do. After considerable persuasion on the part of the worker, Mrs. McCall agreed to go with her to a local comprehensive health center for a thorough work-up. The worker also learned that Mrs. McCall had "not gotten around" to applying for social security, even though she was eligible for it. She was not against Social Security, since she recognized that she was entitled to it for her years of covered employment. It did not have the stigma of "welfare" for her. However, she still had hopes of going back to work, in which case she thought she would not be entitled to it.

After several visits to the health center for the complete battery of physical tests, Mrs. McCall was told by the doctors that she should not work again. The kind of work she did as a practical nurse, lifting and moving people about, would surely lead to a heart attack or a stroke, in which case she would have to be hospitalized. The threat of this even greater dependency finally persuaded her to accept some of the services the worker mentioned. The worker used an oral contractual arrangement with Mrs. McCall in which the two of them agreed as to which tasks each of them would carry out in the process of obtaining the needed services. This approach seemed to suit Mrs. McCall's need for autonomy.

While Mrs. McCall's Social Security application was being processed, the worker was able to get her approved for food stamps, for she had very little in savings. In addition, an application for Medicaid was processed so that she could be provided with homemaker services, which the physician at the health center insisted she must have several days a week. After a while, she came to appreciate that she could keep up her apartment much better with her own light housekeeping efforts as long as the heavier work was done by the homemaker.

Thus, in less than two months the worker in this case was able to provide the following services by referral: food stamps, Social Security, health, Medicaid and homemaker, as well as counseling and transportation, which were provided directly. Throughout all this, the worker had to focus on Mrs. McCall's depleted feelings of self-esteem because of her perceived dependency. The worker drew heavily on the client's past record of hard work and support of others so that she could accept those accomplishments as permanent parts of her self-concept. The worker's argument was essentially that Mrs. McCall had shown great compassion for others all her life and that she should reserve some of that compassion for herself now that she needed it. Mrs. McCall did accept and come to terms with the ongoing services she had been provided by the referrals. However, she and the worker agreed mutually that the counseling services would end after two months. If she needed help later, she would know where to turn. This was all quite consistent with Mrs. McCall's character and her desire to remain as independent as possible, even though she was very appreciative of the help she had received.

Referral and supportive counseling are not really separable in practice with the aging. That is why this section is entitled "Referral *and* Support." Mrs. McCall clearly needed supportive counseling just to recognize her entitlement to services and to bring herself to accept them.

Mr. Roland represented a different type of referral problem. It was not so much that he resisted referral services as that he was too traumatized or too disorganized to use services effectively without supportive counseling. He was an 80-year-old widower who was referred to the Department of Social

Services by a friend who was concerned about his depressed state and the fact that he was not taking care of himself or his apartment. Although he was in good physical condition for his age and fully ambulatory, he had never recovered from the death of his wife a year and a half before. He had a daughter in the Midwest who wanted him to live with her. He was briefly hospitalized for a reactive depression. The plan was for him to go to her home after he had been stabilized following discharge to the community and after some outpatient psychiatric care. However, Mr. Roland did not keep his psychiatric clinic appointments and he did not take his prescribed doses of antidepressant medication. Things dragged on for more than a year because he had not been given psychiatric clearance to move.

When the student worker was assigned to his case by the Department of Social Services, he was barely eating anything and was staying in bed most of the time. The worker made an appointment for him at the mental health clinic for the following day and took him there in person. He was again given medication and an appointment for two weeks hence. The worker made a notation of the appointment and the medication for Mr. Roland so that he could keep track of them. The worker also arranged for a homemaker to come in five days a week, not only to clean up and maintain the apartment, which was in a bad state of disarray, but also to see that Mr. Roland did not stay in bed all the time and that he took his medication.

Mr. Roland's emotional problem was related to the fact that he was still mourning for his dead wife. Although the antidepressant medication helped with his symptoms, he needed supportive counseling to work through his grief reaction. Since he was not receiving psychotherapy at the mental health center, his worker saw him twice weekly for a month and a half. During this time, Mr. Roland reminisced a great deal about his dead wife and their life together. In addition to the counseling, the worker took him for his clinic visits, kept an eye on his medication, and contacted his daughter to plan for his eventual move to the Midwest with her.

In a month and a half, Mr. Roland recovered emotionally as a result of medication and the counseling to the point where he was stable enough to work out the remaining plans for his move without the worker's assistance. It took a period of twelve weeks from the worker's first visit to the time Mr. Roland's daughter picked him up and took him home with her.

The Family as a Problem Source and Resource

Mr. Roland's case illustrates not only the need for support in using referral services but also the need from time to time for intervention by professionals of the formal helping network in order to facilitate help from the informal helping network, in this case the family.

There are many popular misconceptions about the aged and their family situations in our society. One of these misconceptions is that most aged persons are living alone with little or no contact with their children or other living relatives. In fact, more than eight of every ten men aged 65 and over and six out of ten older women lived in families in the beginning of the 1970s. The majority of these families consisted of the aged couple. Only 7 percent of the men and 15 percent of the women lived with relatives other than the spouse (Lowy, 1979:34–35). However, whereas 79.3 percent of the men 65 and over were married in 1975, only 39.1 percent of the women were; to put this differently, only 13.6 percent of the men but over half (52.5 percent) of the women were widowed (U.S. Department of Health, Education, and Welfare, 1976). Because of this fact, we frequently encounter aged widows who are living alone as recipients of gerontological services and counseling. Often there are children living nearby, since over three-quarters of persons over 65 in the United States live within thirty minutes of at least one child. However, there are often problems in the relationships between the older person and the children who live in close proximity.

In a survey of problems between aging parents and their adult children, Simos (1973) identified some common misconceptions on the part of the children which created difficulties. One was the children's belief that their parents would be happier if they were more socially involved, even if this was not at all an expressed interest of the parent. Another problem was that the children were uncomfortable just sitting with their parents; they tended to feel that there should be more active social interaction between them, without realizing that they were offering emotional support by their mere presence and interest. Also, when a parent dies, the adult child feels compelled to "take over" and sometimes precipitously moves the surviving parent into his or her home. The adult child may inadvertently foster repression of the normal grief reaction by offering the survivor a variety of diversions. The children also failed to recognize the genuine grief reactions of their elderly parents over losses like the death of a pet, the right to drive a car, a house, furnishings, or other cherished possessions.

The parents in their turn also presented some recurrent obstacles to good ·family relationships. Chief among them was the tendency to retain the old parental control behaviors, such as offering unwanted advice and guidance and making demands when in fact they were often in dependent positions vis-à-vis their children. Another frequent problem was the tendency for the parent to generate guilt in the adult children, usually for alleged oversights or failures to meet filial responsibilities.

The case of Mrs. Quinn illustrates a number of these points. She was a 75-year-old widow who was living alone in an apartment. Her son lived in a nearby suburb with his wife and two children but was visiting his mother less and less frequently. She had lived in his home for almost a year two years earlier, when she was recuperating from a broken hip. As soon as she felt strong enough, she moved into an apartment of her own. However, her hip had not mended well, and she was in considerable pain most of the time. This prevented her from keeping up her apartment in the manner she wished.

A student social worker from the special unit in the Department of Social Services contacted her in an outreach effort. A neighbor who knew of its services had notified the unit that Mrs. Quinn seemed to be getting more and more depressed and withdrawn since she had moved in just over a year ago. When the worker called on her, Mrs. Quinn welcomed the chance to talk to someone about her dissatisfaction with her present circumstances. She told the worker that she had a lovely home before she fell and broke her hip, and although she had been a widow for almost ten years she had continued to be very sociable and entertained a lot of people. She considered herself an excellent cook and hostess. Her biggest pleasure and source of pride had been entertaining others in her home.

After she broke her hip and had to go and live with her son, things went badly for her. She could not entertain others, she tried to encourage her daughter-in-law to do so. However, her daughter-in-law was not interested in entertaining and could not understand why it was so important to Mrs. Quinn. A strained relationship developed between them, and Mrs. Quinn thought this also included her son, who seemed to be relieved when she said she wanted to move out.

Moving out did not help, though, because her bad hip did not permit her to fix up her apartment, cook, and entertain as she liked. Because she could not entertain as in the past, she did not feel that she could really socialize with other people. She would not be able to reciprocate if they showed her any hospitality.

Rather than question Mrs. Quinn's assumption that people would not want to socialize with her unless she entertained them, the worker asked whether she would accept homemaker help in maintaining her apartment in the way she wanted. Mrs. Quinn agreed to this gladly, and within a matter of two weeks she was having her neighbors and some of her old friends for tea and lunches. She always managed to have tea and cookies or cake when Mrs. Kay, her worker, would visit.

As is often the case, the provision of a hard service such as the homemaker in this instance led to a productive counseling relationship. The worker visited Mrs. Quinn at least once a week, and their discussions turned to the thing that was now most troubling to Mrs. Quinn, her relationship with her son and his family. Her son called her only about every other week and visited only once a month, usually by himself or with one or the other of his teenaged sons. The visits were always rather short and uncomfortable. Mrs. Quinn said she was very hurt by her son's lack of attention, and she had told him so quite a few times, but it did not seem to do any good. She asked whether Mrs. Kay would be willing to talk to her son about this, because it was causing her a great deal of distress.

Mrs. Kay agreed to do this and worked out an appointment with Mr. Quinn and his wife. At first, both of them seemed a bit defensive and edgy. Mr. Quinn claimed that they were under a good deal of strain lately, largely of a financial nature. With one son in college and another one getting ready to go, as well as a house to pay for, his salary as a bank teller was inadequate, so his wife had to go out to work as a sales clerk in a local thrift store. She was usually tired at the end of the day and did not look forward to entertaining anyone, particularly his mother, who was a "fanatic" about the way the table was set and what was served.

Mrs. Kay shared with them the changes that had come about in Mrs. Quinn as a result of the housekeeper. The daughter-in-law remarked that she had not realized how central to Mrs. Quinn's self-confidence this entertaining business was. She had always thought it was a little frivolous on Mrs. Quinn's part, but she understood it better now that Mrs. Kay explained it. Mr. Quinn said he was really pleased his mother was feeling better and that he would like to see more of her, but he had to admit she made him feel so guilty by her continual references to his lack of attention that he found himself visiting her less and less.

Mrs. Kay said she thought that her relationship with Mrs. Quinn was good enough to work with her on her guilt-provoking and critical comments. However, it would be necessary for Mr. Quinn and his wife to contact and exchange visits more often. In fact, now that Mrs. Quinn had the house-keeper and was entertaining more, perhaps she could have them over to her place on a more regular basis. Mr. Quinn and his wife thought this idea was worth a try, and Mr. Quinn said he would call his mother the next day to see what could be set up.

The worker then met with Mrs. Quinn and interpreted some of the pressures her son and his wife were under, as well as the discomfort her son felt over her comments about his lack of attention. That these comments might be driving him away rather than having the intended effect of en-couraging him to visit more often came as something of a shock to Mrs. Quinn. At any rate, she invited her son and daughter-in-law over for dinner on the following Saturday, and Saturday dinners at her apartment soon became a regular feature of their relationship. Since the two teenage boys were out on dates most Saturdays this provided a relaxing time for Mr. Quinn and his wife, since his mother was in good spirits while entertaining them.

There were fewer visits by Mrs. Quinn to them, because it was acknowl-edged by all of them that her daughter-in-law had neither the inclination nor the energy to entertain. On the occasions when she did visit, things did not go entirely smoothly. Although Mrs. Quinn tried to be less critical, she tended to be somewhat patronizing toward her daughter-in-law's efforts. Fortunately, her daughter-in-law was more tolerant of this behavior as a result of Mrs. Kay's interpretation of its meaning to Mrs. Quinn.

Mrs. Kay provided a total of eight weeks of service in this case. With the provision of the homemaking services and the supportive counseling, she was able to achieve all of the objectives of Input B (Table 4-1); that is, she stabilized Mrs. Quinn's self-esteem and sustained her morale and coping efforts.

This case illustrates a number of points about older persons and their adult children in our society. The adult children are apt to find themselves pulled in several directions as a result of life transition problems experienced in the three-generation family. The children are usually going through a mid-life crisis of their own, while their adolescent children are going through the identity and other crises of their age group. In addition to being concerned about their offspring and themselves, they are concerned about their aging parents. At best this has to be a somewhat stressful situation. If, in addition, the aged parent (or parents) is demanding and guilt-provoking, alienation will develop. Mrs. Kay had a good relationship with Mrs. Quinn and was able to interpret this to her. There is a recurrent need for this type of interpretation in work with older persons and their adult children.

On the positive side, there is a good deal of evidence of filial responsibility on the part of adult children for their aging parents, and there is considerable interaction between older parents and their children (Adams, 1970; Troll, 1971). What is called for is "filial maturity," a term coined by Blenkner (1965), on the part of the adult children. This is a quality which can be drawn upon as a resource for the older parent. Filial maturity for the middle-aged child involves being dependable as well as depended upon by the parent, and it means that the child has to work through his or her ambivalent and immature parental ties in order to be free to help the parent as an individual with his/her own rights, needs, and limitations. It is frequently the task of the counselor to assist the middle-aged children in achieving this type of maturity. Mrs. Kay accomplished this to some degree in the case of Mrs. Quinn.

Self-Help and Other Informal Resources

The family has been a frequent informal source of help for older persons in periods of trauma and crisis, despite the high mobility of families in our industrial society (Litwak, 1960). However, it should not be forgotten that the elderly themselves are the most frequent source of their own help. They still overwhelmingly choose to live with a spouse or alone in preference to living with their children, unless the only other choice is a nursing home (Butler and Lewis, 1977). I have already indicated that many if not most older persons undertake their own social reconstruction, sometimes almost entirely by themselves and sometimes with other informal sources of help such as family, friends, neighbors, and peers. Although family is the first source of informal support, about 20 percent of the elderly do not have children living close enough for frequent visits and another one-quarter to one-third do not have living children (Shanas, 1968).

A number of gerontological investigations have noted the presence of informal support systems exclusive of families in the lives of older persons. One of these investigators, Helena Lopata, defined a support system as a "set of relations involving the giving and receiving of objects, services, social and emotional support defined by the giver and the receiver as necessary or at least helpful in maintaining a style of life" (Lopata, 1975:1).

One type of support system is the self-help group, a type of mutual aid group that emphasizes personal participation and action-orientation much in the style of a consumer action group (Gartner and Riesmann, 1977; Hess, 1976). An example might be a group of elderly tenants organizing to obtain reasonable rents, and repairs. It is this social action orientation that distinguishes the self-help group from the mutual support group, which tends to stress mutual emotional support for persons experiencing the same types of problems, as in the Widow-to-Widow program, in which widows who have gone successfully through the mourning process provide support to new widows in their grief and mourning (Caplan and Killilea, 1976).

The self-help reflects the fact that old people are likely to develop spontaneous helping patterns which are very similar to those of extended families. Sometimes it may be necessary for the gerontological practitioner to initiate the helping interaction or to provide for continuity in the informal helping process (Smith, 1975).

These points about the informal support system are illustrated in the case of Thomas Donello, an 68-year-old man who had never married and was living alone in a small apartment in an apartment building with a large number of elderly tenants. He came to the attention of the student unit of the Department of Social Services because his landlord was planning to evict him. The worker who was assigned to his case found Mr. D. outside his apartment talking to several of his neighbors at the time of the first home visit. Mr. D. was quite obese and obviously had difficulty moving about. When they went into Mr. D.'s apartment to talk in private, the worker was taken aback by its condition. Magazines, newspapers, and books were stacked high along the walls and even in high piles in the middle of the living room floor. The same was true of his bedroom. In the kitchen bags of garbage were leaning against each other and taking up most of the floor space. The odor from the garbage was quite unpleasant. It was as though Mr. Donello was being slowly pushed out of his apartment by all of the paraphernalia piling up in it.

The worker told Mr. Donello that DSS had received a call from a fellow tenant who was concerned about the landlord's plans to evict Mr. Donello. The landlord claimed that the conditions of his apartment made it a fire hazard. Mr. Donello acknowledged that this was true, but said that he found it very difficult to do anything about the situation. He noted that his physical condition was not good; he had diabetes, which he was not regulating adequately, as well as poor mobility because of obesity. He added somewhat sheepishly that he found it almost impossible to get rid of things. He said he "couldn't bear to waste anything," and that was why things had piled up so much. He seemed genuinely overwhelmed by it all and was quite agreeable to having the worker assist him in doing something about the apartment situation and his physical condition.

The worker first got the landlord to agree somewhat reluctantly to put off the eviction if Mr. D.'s apartment could be cleaned up in the next week or two. Next, a request was made for a visiting nurse to see Mr. Donello regularly to help him regulate his diet and insulin. Then, a young man employed under the CETA program was brought in to help with housekeeping and errands. The worker made arrangements for Mr. Donello to donate his surplus books and magazines to a local nursing home. When the CETA worker began carrying the books and magazines out, he was joined by a number of the neighbors, who helped with the lifting and carrying.

Mr. D. promised that he would throw a big spaghetti dinner for his neighbors when his apartment was all cleared out. He had been a cook most of his life, he told the worker, first in the navy and then in a number of restaurants until his retirement two years earlier. He said that his neighbors knew they would be getting a good meal when the job was done. It was evident that Mr. Donello was well-liked by the neighbors, and one of them told the worker that they were very angry at the landlord for planning to evict Mr. Donello as well as for his failure to keep the building in a good state of repair.

The garbage was quickly cleared out along with the books and magazines, while the newspapers and other magazines were taken to a recycling plant. However, there was still a strong odor in Mr. Donello's kitchen as a result of the accumulation of garbage. The neighbors jokingly told him that even his spaghetti would not be good enough to make them want to eat in his kitchen. Soon, however, the neighbors came to the serious conclusion that the landlord should make some needed repairs as well as paint Mr. Donello's kitchen. The neighbor who had called DSS about Mr. Donello, a man who appeared to be in his middle sixties, was the most vocal and planful in this discussion. He noted that the walls of Mr. Donello's living room and bedroom were also in need of painting because of the discoloration marks where all the books and magazines used to be.

When the worker visited Mr. Donello the following week he found that repair and painting of the client's apartment had indeed begun as a result of pressure on the landlord by the other tenants. Mr. Donello was already planning for the big spaghetti dinner when the painting would be finished. The worker visited him several more times thereafter and then closed the case because his field instruction was coming to an end and the client was not in need of continued counseling.

This case gives some indication of the potential for self-help groups among the elderly. In this instance, the action by the tenants was spontaneous and the worker did not get involved in a direct, systematic way in the informal support system, but it can be seen that such an arrangement might be indicated in other similar circumstances.

The common features of all the cases presented so far in this chapter, regardless of whether they involved just the practitioner and the client, the client's family, or other support systems, are that they were short-term within our definition, involved referral and provision of practical services, and accomplished the objectives of at least maintenance and stabilization (Inputs A and B) in the treatment continuum of the integrative model.

Specific Techniques of Integrative Practice

The counseling methods mentioned in the foregoing cases were essentially supportive and geared toward stabilizing the psychosocial functioning of the client rather than toward bringing about significant improvements in behavioral, emotional, or cognitive functioning. In the third phase (Input C) of the integrative model the counselor has to enable the client to feel and be more in control of his or her current life situation. Although this can and should be accomplished within the defined time limits of short-term counseling, it requires more than supportive methods. It calls for techniques that will increase the client's coping skills, problem-solving capacities, and cognitive mastery.

In developing skills and the sense of mastery directly within the context of integrative counseling rather than through referral, some of the cognitive techniques are quite helpful, and some of the newer cognitive-behavioral techniques are also viable. Mahoney and Arnkoff (1978) have identified three major types of cognitive therapies: rational psychotherapies, coping skills therapies, and problem-solving therapies. The rational type, represented by Ellis (1962) and Beck (1976 and 1979) has application in both short-term and extended integrative counseling, but the techniques of rational therapy are used differentially for short-term and extended counseling. The coping skills and problem-solving therapies, on the other hand, are intended essentially for short-term counseling and are particularly appropriate for the Input C stage of the integrative continuum. I should emphasize, however, that these techniques might also be used in the short run in extended counseling cases. Thus, when the clients' deficit needs are met through Inputs A, B, and C of the integrative model, they might want and be able to meet their growth needs through Input D of the model in extended counseling.

The cognitive and cognitive-behavioral techniques presented here by no means represent the total repertoire of such techniques, but they are the ones I have found most useful and appropriate for developing social and daily living skills along with a sense of mastery and control in the elderly (Sherman, 1979). The following descriptions of the techniques will be complemented by illustrations of their application in cases provided later in this chapter and in Chapters 5 and 6.

One technique is the identification by the client of automatic thoughts (Beck, 1976 and 1979) that create negative emotions such as anxiety, sadness, and anger and of negative behavior such as avoidance and lashing out verbally or physically. The client is given a form (see Appendix D) for the monitoring of "homework" assignments in which she/he is asked to keep a daily record of dysfunctional thoughts in the following manner:

1. Describe actual events or thoughts and daydreams of the day leading to unpleasant emotions.
2. Describe the type of emotion (sad, angry) and rate the degree of emotion involved on a scale of 1 to 100.
3. Write down the automatic thought(s) and rate the degree of belief in the thought on a scale of 1 to 100.
4. Then write a rational response to the irrational automatic thought(s) and rate the degree of belief in the rational response (1–100).
5. Re-rate the belief in the automatic thought (1–100) and specify and rate the subsequent emotions (1–100).

In identifying and disputing the negative cognitions leading to the negative emotions, the client should be able to gradually decrease the intensity and incidence of those emotions. This is actually a form of rational self-disputation that is very similar to Ellis's A-B-C method of disputation (Ellis, 1974), which is illustrated in a group context in Chapter 5.

Another technique is cognitive rehearsal (Beck, 1976) in which the client imagines him/herself going through the steps of some selected activity and reports the anticipated obstacles and conflicts. This, of course, allows for some advance preparation of coping and problem-solving strategies. This can also be used in the form of an "as if" technique (Beck and Emery, 1979) in a retrospective rather than an anticipatory sense. When the client is able to recount the past but is unable to identify a clear-cut cognition, she/he is asked to re-experience or imagine the event as if it were happening right now. This enables the client to pinpoint the automatic thought that represents an obstacle in the situation.

The technique of changing attributions (Mahoney, 1974) is based on the idea that people's behaviors and emotions are influenced by perceived causality. For example, a client's belief that certain physical symptoms such as hyperventilation or rapid heart beat are caused by physical dysfunction (heart or lung problems) might be changed to a recognition that they are symptoms of anxiety. This is particularly useful in self-control programs in which clients are helped to view themselves as responsible for their improvement. This enhances feelings of mastery and helps to maintain gains.

Bibliotherapy is a very common type of cognitive approach in which readings specific to the clients' problems and information about the emotional and behavioral effects of dysfunctional cognitions are assigned as homework. Clients are asked to read the materials and be prepared to discuss them in individual or group counseling with respect to their own problems. This calls for awareness on the part of the counselor of the client's degree of literacy, as well as his or her potential resistance to this highly didactic technique. It can be quite effective when pertinent readings are used in conjunction with certain other cognitive techniques.

Some of the cognitive techniques are particularly well suited to work on the problem of anxiety in older persons, whereas others are especially good for depressed moods or actual clinical depression. One of the better ones for dealing with anxiety is rational imagery (Lazarus, 1971), but it can also be used to deal with other dysfunctional feelings. In this technique the client is asked to fantasize as vividly as possible the details of an unpleasant event and to feel as anxious, depressed, or ashamed as such an event would make the person feel in fact. Then, the client is asked to try very hard, to push him or herself to feel only somewhat tense, regretful, disappointed, or annoyed at the event, rather than feel the more upsetting, disproportionate and disabling kinds of emotion that were first experienced. Lazarus also used a "step-up" technique in this approach in which the client is asked to outline all of the negative things that could happen and then imagine the worst thing that could occur. Anything different from this represents a "step up," because nothing could be as bad as what was imagined.

Vicariation (Raimy, 1975) is a technique that can be used to counteract the anxiety and concern that prevent people from performing a behavior they see as too frightening or too difficult. This is done by having the person observe the counselor, another client (in a group situation), or some other person perform or model the problematic behavior. The client thereby obtains evidence to dispute the belief that the behavior cannot be performed without incurring a disaster. When the client's misconceptions have been altered, she/he is encouraged to perform the behavior.

Systematic rational restructuring (Goldfried, Decenteco, and Weinberg, 1974) calls for rational re-evaluation by the client of the irrational ideas she/he is thinking when feeling a negative emotion. In this respect, it is somewhat like the technique of identification of automatic dysfunctional thoughts. However, in this approach the client and counselor together construct a hierarchy of difficult situations, with successful coping at one level a prerequisite for progression to the next more difficult situation. This use of a hierarchy is similar to the behavioral technique of systematic desensitization, but rational re-evaluation is used in place of relaxation. That is, the client actively determines what irrational ideas she/he is thinking when anxious or depressed and then re-evaluates the situation in more rational terms, noting any changes in subjective units of disturbance (SUDS). The case of Miriam Jones to follow in this chapter illustrates this technique.

Another technique particularly helpful in dealing with depression and feelings of uselessness and incompetence is mastery and pleasure therapy (Beck, 1976) in which the client keeps a daily record of activities and marks down an "M" for every activity that provided a sense of mastery and "P" for every activity that provided some pleasure. This is particularly effective for depressed people who characteristically believe that there is nothing they enjoy any more and nothing they can do with any competence or mastery. However, it can also be used with older persons who have to begin again to master some of the simple skills of daily living after suffering a stroke, acute arthritis, or other disease.

A technique for coping with the tasks of daily living as well as the weight of depression is graded task assignment (Beck, 1976). This is sometimes called "success therapy" in that the client begins with a simple assignment or task the counselor knows she/he can do and then accomplishes increasingly difficult tasks. Care has to be taken that the tasks are not too difficult and not likely to produce feelings of failure and incompetence.

Problem-solving therapy has been referred to as a form of cognitive therapy (Mahoney and Arnkoff, 1978), but it includes a diverse collection of procedures that are related to various behavioral approaches such as assertiveness training, modeling, and positive reinforcement through praise for effective responses to problematic situations. It is essentially a behavioral process which trains clients in how to solve problems, generate alternative effective ways for dealing with problematic situations, and make decisions about the most effective response to specific problems from the various alternative responses (D'Zurilla and Goldfried, 1971). There has not yet been much empirical evidence of the effectiveness of this approach, although Toseland (1980) reported some success using group problem solving with the elderly.

Overall, I have found that techniques of cognitive restructuring have the greatest ultimate applicability to the issue of integrity versus despair. "Cognitive restructuring" is a generic term for a number of essentially cognitive (as distinct from combined cognitive-behavioral) techniques and procedures. Some of those already presented, such as cognitive rehearsal, rational imagery, and identifying and disputing dysfunctional thoughts, are cognitive restructuring techniques that have particular applicability in short-term practice situations.

Two other cognitive restructuring techniques are essential to integrative counseling. They are distancing and decentering (Beck, 1976). Distancing is the process whereby the client learns to view his or her thoughts objectively, which means of course an increase in the ability to sort out rational versus irrational and functional versus dysfunctional thoughts and beliefs. Decentering is the process whereby the client is enabled to separate himself or herself from the impact and occurrence of external events. This is particularly useful for situations in which clients personalize external events. In such instances, the counselor points this tendency out to the client and encourages the client to evaluate the event more realistically.

Distancing and decentering techniques are particularly suited for extended counseling where the identified goal is the overcoming of despair in favor of greater life satisfaction and ego integrity. Variations in these techniques will be illustrated in the extended counseling case materials in Chapter 6.

Case Illustrations of Applied Techniques

The following case of a 74-year-old woman who was treated in the outpatient psychiatric clinic of a city hospital illustrates the use of the techniques of changing attributions, rational imagery, and systematic rational restructuring. The client, Miriam Jones, was recovering from an operation three weeks before on a carotid artery on the left side of her neck. A small package of plaque had accumulated in the artery and although it was not yet large enough to cause an occlusion or a stroke it was ulcerous and small globules of blood and plaque had broken off and gone into the brain causing a brief blackout and certain other symptoms of a stroke. The surgery had been exceptionally successful, and the surgeon who performed the operation was very pleased with the results and told Mrs. Jones that her artery was "clean as a whistle" and that there should be no concern about a recurrence since she did not show evidence of any significant atherosclerosis.

In her physical checkups following the operation Mrs. Jones was given a clean bill of health and except for the admonition to take it easy for a while she was told she could resume her full and normal round of activities without any restrictions in just a few weeks. Despite these reassurances she said she had a "terrible fear" which would not leave her and which forced her to ask friends and relatives and finally a paid companion to stay with her every night since her return home from the hospital two weeks before. She was given a prescription for Valium, but this did not seem to help her general anxiety. She complained of a queasy stomach and an inability to keep food down, a tightening in the throat where the operation had occurred, and transient pains on the left side of her head. She was acutely attuned to any physiological changes such as "hot flashes," heart palpitations, sweaty palms, trembling hands, and so on. Because of the persistence of these complaints despite the Valium, she was referred to the outpatient psychiatric clinic.

The counselor to which she was assigned quickly assessed Mrs. Jones as a bright, articulate woman who had a history of capacity for independent decision making and problem solving. She had been a supervisor of sales personnel in a section of a large department store until her retirement ten years ago. After her husband had a massive stroke five years ago, she cared for him very competently at home with only occasional professional home care help. Her two adult children both lived in distant states, and there were no other close relatives in the area. Her husband needed help in and out of his wheelchair, his bed, the bath, and so on. Yet, she was able to handle him up to the time of his death two years ago.

When the counselor asked her to tell him what was troubling her she said that she had a terrible fear most of the time and did not know how to describe it. When he asked her to try to tell him her clearest recent experiencing of it, she said that she had a very strong fear about coming to the clinic alone on this day, so she asked a neighbor to drive her. The neighbor was waiting outside for her, and Mrs. Jones said she felt very bad about imposing on her neighbor this way, but her fear of coming to the clinic alone was just too great. In the course of the first session, Mrs. Jones indicated that she felt trapped by her fears.

The counselor attempted to see whether the client's capacity for imagery could be used for treatment as well as assessment purposes. He asked Mrs. Jones to imagine coming to the clinic alone and to tell him how anxious she would be on a scale going from zero (absolute calm) to 100 (absolute panic). She said it depended on whether she took a bus, a cab, or drove herself. Taking a cab would be the best, but even that she gave a rating of 60 on the Subjective Units of Disturbance Scale (SUDS). She said she was most fearful of driving herself (95 on the SUDS) because she was afraid of driving as well as being alone, so that was the worst imaginable combination.

Since taking a cab provoked the least anxiety, the counselor asked her what she feared would happen in the cab to account for the rating of 60 she gave on the SUDS. She said that she feared she might have a blackout similar to the one she had before her operation. When asked to fantasize this as vividly as possible, she reported feeling a sensation on the left side of her head, of blacking out, and then coming to and not being able to think clearly or to know her whereabouts. If this happened with a friend or neighbor driving her, she would feel a bit more secure than with a cab driver, who would be a stranger and not know anything about what had happened to her. If it happened in a bus, there would be many more strangers and more confusion, which would be more frightening and embarrassing.

The counselor questioned Mrs. Jones about her ability to speak and to make her needs known immediately after her earlier attack. She reported that she felt a tingling on the whole right side of her body. She found that she could not move her leg, her arm, and her fingers with ease or without concentration. She then tried to talk, because she was most fearful of being unable to speak. She found she was able to, but the right side of her mouth felt numb, as though she had been given an injection of Novocain. However, she remembered being relieved that her spoken words were intelligible, although she felt they were a bit slurred. The counselor remarked at this point that given the surgeon's report about the success of the surgery and her fine prognosis that it was highly unlikely that another such attack would occur. However, he asked her to close her eyes and fantasize again as vividly as possible all the details of such an attack in a cab. When she had done that, he asked her to try very hard to feel only "somewhat tense" about the possibility of such an attack. After she had concentrated on this with her eyes closed for about two minutes the counselor asked her to rate her anxiety on the SUDS again, and she said it had gone down to about 15.

This technique of rational imagery seemed to have worked well in the first session, so that this together with the good rapport that had been established with Mrs. Jones enabled the counselor to ask her if she would be willing to make her next trip to the clinic three days hence in a taxicab. Mrs. Jones asked if she should use the same device of trying hard to be just somewhat tense. The counselor said yes and indicated that they would work together in their next sessions to come up with some other devices to help her cope with her fear. Mrs. Jones agreed to take the cab next time and said that she would try the device of imagining herself only somewhat tense when she experienced some of the other fears.

Mrs. Jones came to the second session by cab and was pleased that she had felt only a slight anxiety in the process. She reported a SUDS rating of 5 as she imagined her next trip in the cab. The counselor remarked that this showed good capacity on her part to put these rational techniques into practice. He then asked her how things had gone otherwise for the past three days. Mrs. Jones said that her fears of being alone at home still continued because of the physical symptoms she was experiencing, which seemed to her to be related to her operation. She tended to focus on the fact that the surgeon told her to take it easy in terms of activities and exercises after the operation. It was as though she had blocked out the remaining information that the operation was a complete success and that she would be able to go back to her *full* preoperation round of activities in a few weeks.

The counselor had been able to discuss Mrs. Jones's physical condition with the surgeon and her attending physician at the hospital before the second session, and he was told that Mrs. Jones's prognosis was excellent. Her reported symptoms were clearly related to anxiety rather than an actual physical condition. With this in mind the counselor explored with Mrs. Jones the kinds of fears that were associated with the physical symptoms she was experiencing. She spoke at length about these; they related primarily to her husband's massive stroke five years before and what happened to him. He, too, had an operation on the same carotid artery, and he had a massive stroke immediately following the surgery. That was why she was terrified of the operation. She was dismayed by the fact that she did not feel totally relieved by the success of the operation, but instead was very fearful. She said that all she could think of was how helpless and dependent her husband was after his stroke, so she could not help imagining herself having a stroke like that alone. At least her husband had her to care for him, but she was really all alone. It became clear that the thing Mrs. Jones feared most was having a stroke at home alone and remaining there perhaps for days because she could not move or speak.

With the medical information in hand the counselor was able to use the technique of changing attributions in this second session. He went over each of her symptoms, such as transient headaches on the left side of her head, "funny sensations" in her right arm and leg, and came back to the clear medical fact that the surgery was completely successful and could therefore not be associated with her symptoms. Further, all the tests showed that she had no significant atherosclerosis, so there was no foreseeable danger of a stroke. Then the counselor suggested that her symptoms might be a result of the anxiety about what she had just gone through and its terrible associations with what happened to her husband. He added that this would be quite understandable, but it could also be quite debilitating in its own right. Mrs. Jones said that she certainly could believe that, because it seemed that her thoughts rather than her physical symptoms frightened her the most.

The counselor mentioned some of the common physiological manifestations of anxiety, and Mrs. Jones was quite sure that these were what she was experiencing. However, her intense preoccupation with physical symptoms did not go away immediately. She wanted to discuss these symptoms in each succeeding session in the first month of counseling, just as if the original discussion about anxiety as the cause of her symptoms had never taken place. The counselor repeatedly reminded Mrs. Jones to attribute her physiological symptoms to her anxiety instead of to her physical condition. He would also ask her to make a conscious effort to work on changing her attributions outside of the counseling sessions as well. The need to redirect her attributions began to taper off after the third session until it was not at all necessary by the eighth session.

In the fourth session, the client and counselor worked up a hierarchy of anxiety-provoking situations so as to undertake systematic rational restructuring in which Mrs. Jones would rationally re-evaluate the irrational ideas she was thinking when she experienced the anxiety associated with each difficult situation. The hierarchy contained ten items that began with taking the bus to the clinic. Mrs. Jones lived by a bus line that went directly to the hospital, so she could save quite a bit of money by not taking a cab to the clinic. By the fourth session, the bus situation had a SUDS rating of only 10 for her. The hierarchy contained other items such as walking to the Senior Center (near her home) by herself (30 SUD), driving her car in the neighborhood (50), driving her car to the clinic (70) on a busy main street, and driving her car into her garage (80). Mrs. Jones's garage had a very narrow door with just a few inches to spare on each side of her car, and she still complained about feeling somewhat shaky in her hands and in her coordination. Finally, the item at the top of the hierarchy was staying home alone at night with her fears.

The counselor would have Mrs. Jones imagine each difficult situation and report her SUDS rating. Then she would identify the irrational thoughts associated with the anxiety and re-evaluate them in a more factual, realistic light. Then she would be asked to imagine the situation again and to report her SUDS rating. If it had gone down to a zero or 5, the counselor would ask her to carry out the actual difficult action in the week between their sessions. For example, Mrs. Jones drove her car to the clinic for the fifth session and reported a SUDS rating of 10 in the process.

When she imagined doing it again in the session the rating dropped to zero, and she and the counselor decided to go on to the next item on the hierarchy. In all, it took eleven sessions to complete the hierarchy. In all, Miriam Jones received counseling for sixteen weeks. All of the manifest symptoms of anxiety were gone and she was essentially back to her preoperative lifestyle.

The second case illustrates the following techniques: mastery and pleasure therapy, graded task assignment, homework, bibliotherapy, identification of automatic thoughts, and cognitive rehearsal. In addition to this range of cognitive techniques, the case also illustrates a task-centered approach to practice which is particularly promising for short-term counseling with the aging (Cormican, 1977). The task-centered model was developed in social agency settings in which referral and provision of maintenance services are as important as counseling (Reid and Shyne, 1969; Reid and Epstein, 1972; Reid and Epstein, 1977; Reid, 1978; and Epstein 1980).

Reid and Epstein (1977) have indicated that task-centered work normally consists of six to twelve sessions (with related environmental work) once or twice a week in two to four months. The general approach is to develop a case plan that consists of (1) assessment and (2) a problem-reduction program of action which focuses on client's target problems (Epstein, 1980). Assessment is concentrated in the first two sessions with emphasis on exploration and specification of the problems. The identified problems are purposely limited in number, usually one or two but no more than three.

The next step involves setting target problem priorities, setting goals, and specifying the particular client and practitioner tasks to be carried out. A task states a general direction for action, and these general tasks are broken down into more concrete task specifications. For example, the major target problem in a case might be a lack of appropriate assertiveness on the client's part in social situations. Therefore, the general task for the client would be to increase social assertiveness and specified client subtasks would involve such things as role-playing self-assertion with the counselor in a session, or reading literature on assertiveness skills outside the session as "homework," or actually trying out those skills. Practitioner tasks would be related to training the client in assertiveness such as modeling certain assertiveness skills.

This second step also includes contracting with the client about the duration, scheduling, and conditions of the course of treatment. This does not have to be a written contract, although it can be if the client so desires. However, the conditions and specification of client and practitioner tasks, as well as any third party involvements (family members, referring agencies) have to be mutually and explicitly agreed upon and spelled out. The whole emphasis in the early stages of the task-centered approach is to identify and then quickly work on the problems that the *client* sees as most pressing. This means that the contract should preferably be worked out by the end of the second interview.

The third major step or stage is the implementation and problem-solving part of treatment. In this stage, the practitioner fosters a favorable relationship and climate for problem solving and task performance. Although problems, goals, and tasks are explicitly set, there is room for flexibility and change, if circumstances change significantly. The practitioner obtains the necessary resources and maintenance services and/or instructs the client in the skills required to accomplish the stipulated tasks. The client's task performance is reviewed in each session and adjustments are made as necessary.

In the fourth and last stage, there is a progress review on alleviation of the target problems. If sufficient progress has occurred, arrangements are made to terminate completely or to follow up at a later date with some monitoring of client task functioning.

Let us now take a look at the specific case illustration of the range of cognitive techniques outlined earlier and how they were applied within a task-centered framework. The case is that of a 66-year-old woman who went to a family service agency at the suggestion of the director of a senior service center she had been attending on and off over the past three years. The director had informed the agency that the client, Mary Rozek, had run into a series of problems over the past year which had made her quite "depressed and discouraged." It began eleven months before when Mrs. Rozek fell and broke her hip, which required extensive surgery and extended recuperation. Then, six months ago her closest and dearest friend died. Mrs. R. had tried to get herself more active in the senior center over the past few months to lift and maintain her spirits, but just one month ago her 10-year-old dog died. She had been very attached to the dog, and this seemed to be the proverbial straw in her case. She began feeling more blue than ever and claimed she was not even able to keep up her social contacts and activities at the center. She told the director that she would like to get help for her problem, but she balked at the idea of a psychiatric clinic because of her concern about the possible stigma involved. The director then told her that the family agency provided individual counseling, and Mrs. Rozek agreed to go there if the center director would set up the appointment and tell the agency something about the onset of her problem.

Even before the first session with Mrs. Rozek, the agency practitioner assigned to her case knew that she had a depression of sorts. He also knew that it would be important to determine whether it was of severe or moderate dimensions, for in less than a year she had suffered some losses that would be considered significant psychosocial stressors according to the *Diagnostic and Statistical Manual of Mental Disorders* (American Psychiatric Association, 1980). The broken hip and surgery could be classified as at least a "moderate" if not a "severe" stressor and the death of her close friend would be classified as a "moderate" rather than just a "mild" or "minimal" stressor. Finally, the death of her dog, although it is not classified by the Diagnostic and Statistical Manual, probably had a marked impact on her, which was magnified by the cumulative effect of the three events. It was therefore decided to have Mrs. Rozek fill out the Beck Depression Inventory (Beck et al., 1979) so as to determine the severity of her depression. If she was found to have a severe clinical depression and/or suicidal tendencies, it would be necessary to convince Mrs. Rozek to go to a psychiatric setting for evaluation and treatment.

Before the Beck Inventory was administered, Mrs. Rozek was encouraged to discuss her current feelings and reactions to recent events. She said that she did feel depressed as a result of the death of her friend and her dog, but in addition to that she felt as though she had lost whatever self-confidence she had previously. She claimed to feel uncertain of herself in making some of the simplest decisions and seemed to have lost the capacity to handle uncomplicated matters like bank balances, medical bills, and so on. She felt particularly unsure of herself in social situations and this, added to her general lack of energy, pleasure, and interest, led her to avoid going to the senior center. She added that she was not sure whether her sadness or her feelings of insecurity and lack of self-confidence were the worst.

She explained that she had not felt so lacking in self-confidence since her marriage and then went on to explain that her husband had been the dominant one in the household. She confided half-jokingly that he was Polish and acted just like a Polish man in the house, and her parents were also from Poland so she was "trained to be the good housewife." She went on to say that she was responsible, under his general direction, for raising the children and keeping the house. When the children grew up and left home, her first taste of any independence was a part-time job as a cashier in a local retail store. She liked the outside associations and the fact that she was earning some money of her own. Shortly after her husband died eight years ago, she began working full time and did so to the time of her retirement and entitlement to Social Security at age 62.

She said that she missed her husband and his companionship when he died. It was not easy emotionally, but she was surprised that she did not feel more lost and helpless without him, given the nature of their relationship. After the first few months following his death, she began feeling some sense of pleasure and accomplishment in working and supporting herself. That continued up to the time of her retirement, and she continued feeling quite good about herself after retirement when she became active in the senior center. However, since the hip injury and operation everything had been downhill.

At this point in the initial session, the Beck Depression Inventory was administered to her, and it took only about eight minutes. In addition to a rapid assessment of the severity of the depression, the inventory also provided a lead into the client's perceived problems such as view of self as a failure or incompetent, not being able to do anything without help, despair about the future, and so on. Mrs. Rozek's first inventory showed that she was not severely depressed but that she was moderately so with an inventory score of 23. The counselor was quickly able to obtain a profile of those areas that were problematic and those that were not. First, there were no reported thoughts of suicide and there were no major physiological complaints about health, constipation, insomnia, and appetite. Her major complaints were in the three general areas of sadness, failure or incompetence, and inertia or passivity. In terms of sadness she checked off the following items: "I am sad all the time and I can't snap out of it" and "I cry all the time now."

Her general feelings of incompetence and failure were expressed in the following items: "As I look back over my life, all I can see is a lot of failures" and "I have greater difficulty in making decisions than before." The intertia/ passivity problem was reflected in the following items: "I have to push myself very hard to do anything" and "I get tired from doing almost anything."

Beck et al. (1979) note the need to identify and address "target symptoms" in the initial phases of the treatment process. This is done by determining which symptoms are most distressing to the patient and which are most amenable to therapeutic intervention. This is very much analogous to the task-centered approach in which the "target problem" is identified as the one most emergent and important for the client and most amenable to effective task-oriented solutions (Reid and Epstein, 1977). And in the case of Mrs. Rozek, she agreed that the three areas identified on the Depression Inventory were the ones which caused her the most distress. She said that she did have difficulty managing simple tasks, making decisions, and so on. She did not seem to have the energy or the confidence to undertake them, and she wished somebody else would do them for her the way her husband did in the past. The counselor asked specifically what kinds of things. She said that he made most of the decisions about what they would do and where they would go, and he would take care of the simple business tasks of the household such as paying the bills, balancing the checkbook, how much insurance to carry, and so on.

She said that she recognizes the best thing for her to do would be to pick herself up and go to the senior center and force herself to participate in activities. However, she did not have the energy and the social confidence she used to have so she was afraid of feeling even worse because she would not be socially adept or "fun to be around." She said this was especially true because she could not stop herself from "crying all the time." The counselor asked her what she meant by "all the time" and then proceeded to have Mrs. Rozek do a retrospective, day-by-day frequency count of the number of times she cried in the week immediately preceding this initial session. Reid (1978) has advised that it is very helpful in task-centered practice to get such retrospective baseline information, if possible, because it adds precision to specifying the target problem. Although such retrospective data are not as precise as on-the-spot behavioral frequency counts, it has the advantage of not delaying treatment for the sake of obtaining current baseline measures.

Mrs. Rozek was quite able to reconstruct the incidents of crying during the prior week because she was all alone at home and had very little else to remember. It averaged out to about six crying episodes per day with a range of 3 to 10, with the highest incidence of 10 on the day before this session. On the basis of this information, the first target problem was identified as Mrs. Rozek's excessive crying and the goal was to reduce the incidence of crying so that she could go to the senior center without fear of crying while there. The client tasks related to this were two in number. First, Mrs. Rozek would keep a log of the time, frequency, and circumstances of her crying each day until her next session on the following week. Second, she would use a self-control procedure suggested by the counselor which involved an active self-instruction not to cry and setting a time limit on the amount of crying (Beck et al., 1979). At the same time she was asked to try to keep track of what thoughts were going through her mind each time she felt like crying. It should be noted that these tasks constituted the technique of "homework," since the client had to carry them on outside of the counseling sessions. Also, the self-control procedure got the client involved in working on her own problems beginning with the very first session, an approach highly recommended both in task-centered practice (Reid, 1978) and cognitive therapy (Beck, 1976; Beck et al., 1979).

The second target problem Mrs. Rozek decided to work on was her lack of self-confidence with regard to simple task performance. The goal here was to increase her feelings of competence and mastery. The client's first task with regard to this problem was to balance her checkbook, which she had not felt up to doing for the past two months. The counselor commented to Mrs. Rozek that she had obviously been competent with figures since she had been a cashier for a number of years. Mrs. Rozek admitted that she had been able to perform well and she agreed to carry out the task before the next session. This particular task assignment represents the technique of "graded task assignment," in which the practitioner sees to it that "the task is so structured that the chances of its being accomplished, in whole or in part, are high" (Reid and Epstein, 1972:106). As mentioned earlier, this is also a preferred technique in cognitive therapy (Beck, 1976).

The final homework assignment Mrs. Rozek was given actually represented the technique of "bibliotherapy," which simply means giving the client some written material bearing on the client's problem. In this case, Mrs. Rozek was given a booklet entitled *Coping with Depression* (Beck and Greenberg, 1974) which Beck recommends for assigned bibliotherapy for depressed patients between the first and second sessions (Beck et al., 1979). The counselor explained that the booklet would help Mrs. Rozek deal with her depression, which was not a severe one, but which accounted for her two target problems. He noted that the booklet would explain that negative thinking about her abilities, her self-worth, her future, and so on is a definite part of the depressive disorder and that the procedures they would be working out together would be designed to counteract that negative thinking.

It might seem that Mrs. Rozek was given a rather large amount of homework in the very first session. However, it has been noted that this is usually beneficial for older clients in task-centered work because "it will ease the feeling experienced by many elderly of having too much time to put to satisfying use" (Cormican, 1977:492). Also, it should be noted that in this case the counselor did not get Mrs. Rozek involved in "mastery and pleasure therapy," which involves homework and is ordinarily assigned in the first session of cognitive therapy (Beck et al., 1979). The counselor held off on this until the next session because the assignment of tasks to monitor the crying and balance the checkbook were given in the first session.

On the basis of information gathered in this first session the counselor made the following assessment. First, not only was Mrs. R. not severely depressed, but she also seemed to have worked through most of the grief over the loss of her friend. She seemed still to be mourning somewhat for her dog, and she did not appear to have any great hypochondriacal concerns as a result of her hip injury and surgery. The cumulative effect of the three events led to a sort of regression to a cognitive set characterized by relatively low self-confidence and self-esteem and a tendency toward dependency and passivity such as she demonstrated in her marriage.

It should be noted here that this regression closely fits the social breakdown model (see Figure 1-1). There was first of all a precondition or susceptibility to this type of breakdown when the three events hit, as evidenced by some of Mrs. Rozek's psychosocial functioning during her marriage. Second, there was inevitably some social labeling of her as "sick," if not deficient or incompetent, as a result of her hip surgery, rehabilitation, and prolonged recuperation. She was not socially active during this recuperation period and as a result of her induction into the sick and dependent role (having to be cared for by nurses and various aides) and the lengthy time period, there was obviously an atrophy of previous skills. She therefore arrived at the fourth point in the breakdown cycle which involved her self-identification as sick or inadequate, which in turn fed back into her predisposition toward greater dependency and feelings of insecurity and incompetence. However, the positive feature of all this was that Mrs. Rozek had already demonstrated a capacity for greater independence, problem solving and decision making after the death of her husband. This was something she and the counselor could draw upon in the counseling process.

In the second session, Mrs. Rozek reported in the log she was keeping that her crying episodes had been reduced to an average of three per day with a range from one to four for the week. Furthermore, she noted that the duration of each crying spell had shortened considerably. The counselor asked her to continue monitoring her crying and using the self-control procedure. Also, the technique of "mastery and pleasure therapy" (Beck, 1976) was now introduced. In this procedure, Mrs. Rozek was instructed to keep a daily record of the activities she engaged in and to note those that gave her a sense of mastery or pleasure. If it gave her a sense of mastery, she should mark down a "M" after her notation of the activity. Then she should try to indicate her sense of the degree of mastery represented by the activity by using a scale going from 0 (no sense of mastery at all) to 5 (very high degree of mastery). For example, if she used the self-control procedure to control her crying, she would rate her sense of mastery in engaging in that activity. Obviously, there would be some variability in her sense of mastery in that activity depending on how successful she thought it was in each episode of crying.

She was supposed to do the same thing for activities that would ordinarily give pleasure and put a "P" after the noted activity and a rating (0 for no pleasure at all and 5 for a great deal of pleasure). This procedure had been explained in the booklet she read, *Coping with Depression*. In the booklet she was made aware of the tendency of depressed people not to recognize or remember things as pleasurable that were viewed as pleasurable before the depression. In fact, much of the technique is based on the idea that depressed persons tend to generalize negatively in retrospect. They will say that nothing pleasurable happened during the day when in fact they did experience some things as pleasurable when they occurred but had forgotten about the pleasure by the end of the day. Keeping a record gives visual proof of any pleasure, however small in amount.

Since Mrs. Rozek had been able to balance her checkbook during the week, she was to undertake another task in the graded task assignment. This was somewhat more difficult than balancing the bank book, but the counselor judged that Mrs. Rozek would be able to do it. The task was to straighten out her medical bills which involved filling out the necessary medical insurance coverage forms. This had gotten somewhat complicated as a result of her surgery and the subsequent rehabilitation and practitioner expenses. However, it was not judged to be beyond Mrs. Rozek's capabilities at this time.

Mrs. Rozek seemed to have little difficulty in comprehending and implementing the procedures covered in the first two sessions, so an explicit (though unwritten) contract was developed at the end of the second interview. It was agreed that the course of treatment would involve a total of twelve weekly one-hour sessions in the counselor's office. The goals to be achieved in that period of time included a reduction of crying episodes to the point where they would not prevent Mrs. Rozek's engagement in activities at the senior center. Thus, engagement in center activities was also a contracted goal, and it was agreed that Mrs. Rozek would attend the center at least six times before the end of treatment.

She agreed to carry out mutually agreed-upon tasks involving homework, self-monitoring, filling out instruments such as the Depression Inventory, and so on. The counselor agreed to facilitate the client's accomplishment of the contracted goals by providing her with the techniques, procedures, and information she would need.

In the third session, the client was introduced to the technique of "identifying automatic thoughts." Mrs. Rozek was already monitoring her thoughts in conjunction with her crying episodes. Now she was asked to record any other negative emotions on a form called the "Daily Record of Dysfunctional Thoughts" (see form in Appendix D). In this session, she was asked to fill out only the first three columns of the form which include notations on (1) the *situation* in which the emotion occurred; (2) the *emotion* itself; and (3) the automatic thought associated with the negative emotion. The counselor explained to Mrs. Rozek that most people engage in a subvocal type of "self-talk" when they are experiencing certain emotions, and it has been found that this self-talk is usually a negative or dysfunctional type of thinking that actually leads to the negative emotion. If the person can record those thoughts, which are usually irrational, they can be brought to light to be disputed and corrected. The client was to monitor and note those thoughts during the week, and in the next session they would work on disputing and correcting them.

By the fourth session, she reported having had only three crying episodes during the previous week with none of them on consecutive days. She also reported on her weekly record form that she had a sense of mastery with a rating of 3 when she completed the straightening out of her medical bills and forms. In fact, she also experienced some pleasure in the process and she gave it a pleasure rating of 2. In addition, she was going out for walks now and experiencing moderate pleasure (ratings of 1 and 2) while taking them.

The client and counselor then went over the Daily Record of Dysfunctional Thoughts and she began to dispute the dysfunctional thoughts and find more rational responses to the situations in which the thoughts occurred. The first emotion identified on the record was "sad, crying" and it occurred in the early morning while she was having breakfast alone at home. The automatic thoughts she reported were: "I feel miserable," "I shouldn't be all alone like this," and "I should have someone to take care of me." The counselor then asked her to identify the degree of belief she had in those thoughts *at the time she had them* on a percentage scale of 1 to 100. She estimated the degree of belief as about 95. Then she was asked to consider some alternative, rational responses to the automatic thoughts. She gave this some thought and then indicated the following responses: "I should remember that I tend to feel miserable in the morning and that my mood will get better late on," "I don't have to have someone take care of me; I lived alone after my husband's death and I survived," and "I can do it again."

The counselor then asked her to estimate her degree of belief in the rational responses, and she indicated 60. Then she was asked to re-estimate her belief in the original automatic thoughts. She estimated 30, which was a considerable reduction from the original 95. This was noted under "Outcome," the last column on the Daily Record form.

The client and counselor then took the next entry on the form, and the emotion described was "disgust with myself," experienced while she was sitting at home watching T.V. by herself.

Her automatic thoughts were: "Why can't I get up and do some of that paperwork (the medical bills and forms)," "I can't seem to handle things on my own," and "I'm just incompetent, a failure." When the counselor asked her to consider rational responses to these automatic thoughts, she said, "I've handled these kinds of things before," "This feeling of failure is just part of the negative thinking in depression, and I have to remember that," and "I really can do these things because I did them in the past." She had given a rating of 75 to the emotion of self-disgust, a rating of 90 to her belief in the automatic thoughts at the time, 60 to her rational responses, and an outcome rating of 40 for her original dysfunctional thoughts. After this exercise, Mrs. Rozek was asked to fill out the complete Daily Record form and do all the rating calculations from this session on.

Mrs. Rozek reported in the fifth session that she had not cried at all during the past week, and she seemed quite pleased with this accomplishment. The counselor said he was pleased too and wondered whether she felt like trying a visit to the senior center now that the crying was under control. Mrs. Rozek seemed quite hesitant about this, so the counselor asked her to rate her readiness to undertake the task of going to the center on a "readiness scale" of 1 to 10, with 10 representing complete readiness (Hepworth, 1979). Mrs. Rozek said she felt her readiness was "only a 2 or 3." When asked why she gave this response, she said that she didn't feel comfortable approaching the people involved in the group activities after so long, even though she was not worried about crying anymore.

The counselor then had her use the technique of cognitive rehearsal in which Mrs. Rozek was asked to go through the steps in getting involved in group activities at the center and identify the obstacles and conflicts she was concerned about. She said that the group she would like to get active in again was the sewing group, but it was also a "great talking group." She could just imagine going into the room with all the women looking at her expectantly and asking her why she hadn't been attending and what she had been doing. She said it scared her, and she didn't see how she could handle all their questions all at once. It would be better if she could do it somewhat gradually, only talking to one or two at a time. She and the counselor explored the possibility of doing it piecemeal. They came up with the idea that she could first go to the noon meal at the center and talk to one or two of the women at a time during the meal and let them know she was coming back to the group on the following week. She should let them know the truth, that the death of her dog after the death of her good friend had made her feel very blue and unable to participate in any social activities up to now. She figured that everyone in the sewing group would know about her situation by "word of mouth" by the time she arrived the following week, and they would be more careful and considerate about asking her questions. When asked how ready she felt about approaching it in this way, she indicated a rating of 7 on the readiness scale, a rating the counselor felt was sufficient for her to undertake that task the following week.

Mrs. Rozek was able to carry through on this and got involved again in the sewing group. In the seventh session, she was given another Beck Depression Inventory, and she had a scale score of 12, down 11 points from the initial 23. She was able to discontinue the monitoring of her crying right after her first visit to the center. Then as she began attending the center regularly she became involved in other group activities, and her mastery and pleasure ratings were higher and more frequent on the weekly activity schedule. Also, she attended the center many more times than the minimum of six indicated in the contract. Her Daily Record of Dysfunctional Thoughts showed fewer depressogenic, irrational thoughts while her degree of belief in them when they did occur was much lower than at first. When she was given the Depression Inventory in her last session, she had a score of 4, which was well down into the normal range.

It can be seen from the Rozek case that there is a close correspondence between the task-centered model of practice and the time-limited type of cognitive therapy for depression as outlined by Beck and his colleagues (1979). The task-centered model has a number of features that make it particularly helpful as a framework for short-term integrative counseling with the aging. First, it is particularly well-suited for the provision of "hard," tangible services which are so frequently needed in brief intervention with the elderly. Second, it can be used entirely for counseling purposes and it allows for the application of various techniques, cognitive, behavioral, and others. Obviously, it can also be used to structure cases involving a combination of counseling and tangible services.

The task-centered approach has three other features which research has shown to be attributes of effectiveness in intervention. The characteristics most likely to lead to successful outcomes in intervention are structure, specificity, and congruence (Bergin and Lambert, 1978; Gambrill, 1977; Goldstein, 1973; Mayer and Timms, 1970; Phillips and Wiener, 1966). Structure is the arrangement of a set of interventions according to the dominant goals. Specificity means clearly defined goals and actions to be taken by the client, the counselor, and other involved parties. Congruence refers to the degree of correspondence between the client and the practitioner on the defined problems and actions to be taken in reducing the problems. It is easy to see that by their very nature these three features would be associated with effective intervention and would thus enhance the task-centered approach.

The case of Mrs. Rozek illustrates the application of the task-centered framework to a pure counseling situation involving cognitive techniques and no tangible services. However, it is easy to imagine a situation in which the task-centered approach would be used entirely for the provision of tangible services. For example, in the situation of an elderly client who is ready to return home from a rehabilitation setting after a stroke and is ambulatory and able to take care of most personal needs, there might be need for some visiting nursing services and assistance with heavy household work. In such a case there should be good client–practitioner congruence on the target problem, namely, lack of necessary maintenance services for return home. There should also be congruence on the goal—maintenance of the client in own home—as well as agreement about client and worker tasks. In order to maximize the client's own initiative in the intervention situation, the client tasks could include making the telephone contacts and arrangements with the Visiting Nurses Association and the agency which would provide homemaker services. The practitioner tasks could include providing the client with information about available resources and services and to see to it that any appropriate case information required by the provider agencies is given to them.

It can be seen that all three features of congruence, structure, and specificity were present in the above example of the task-centered approach. These features should be present in short-term integrative counseling even when the task-centered approach is not used. For example, the case of Mrs. McCall illustrated earlier in this chapter had all three features even though it was not handled specifically within the task-centered framework.

So far, all of the approaches, techniques, and illustrations presented have involved counseling of individual clients. Yet, most of the same principles and techniques can be applied to group situations. Integrative group counseling is also apt to be short-term by our earlier definition, although there are a few exceptions and variations in this. It is timely, therefore, to consider the methods used in integrative counseling of groups. After these methods are presented, a case of an integrative counseling group from its formation to its termination will be illustrated in Chapter 5.

Group Methods

There is one feature that might be said to distinguish the integrative approach to group counseling from other group approaches: the members of the group are viewed and act as auxiliary counselors for one another. Although this use of group participants is also true of cognitive group therapy (Holon and Shaw, 1979) and behavior modification groups (Goldstein, Heller, and Sechrest, 1969), it is not just a technical matter of method or approach; it is a matter of principle as well in the integrative approach. The androgogy principle delineated in Chapter 3 alerts us to the capacity and need of older persons to be teachers and role models, not only for younger persons but for one another. The group is an excellent modality for this role performance, as will be seen shortly.

Before getting into the "how to" questions of group formation and approaches to leading integrative counseling groups, there should be some consideration of working with older persons in groups generally. In the past two decades a variety of group approaches to work with older persons have been developed ranging in goals and objectives from achievement of the most basic skills in daily living to "life enrichment" and "self-fulfillment" (Weiner, Brok, and Snadowsky, 1978). Thus, in institutional settings, sensory training groups have been established with the objective of bringing the patient back in touch with his/her environment through experiences that use all five senses. Patients who are somewhat less regressed can participate in reality orientation groups in which a structured behavioral approach is used to improve their general orientation to and awareness of time, place, and person. At an even less regressed level, patients can engage in remotivation therapy, which is a group program using structured group discussion with the objective of motivating a renewed interest in their environments, having them think about and discuss topics about the real world, helping them in relating to other people and enhancing their ability to communicate with others.

These group approaches are generally used in long-term care facilities, where the degree of regression and/or organic brain dysfunction in the clients rules out the kind of cognitive activity required in the integrative approach. Much more in line with the purposes and approaches of integrative practice are support groups or supportive group therapy. They are psychotherapeutic in that they are geared toward alleviating mild or moderate depression and anxiety as well as loneliness and social isolation, but there is no effort to bring about significant personality change or to deal with defenses, and the assumption is made that the group members have developed lifestyles and ways of interacting that protect them from injuries to their self-esteem (Goldfarb, 1974). Emotional support, reassurance, and guidance are offered by the group therapist or counselor.

For the most part, support groups have been conducted in institutional settings, but they have been developed in the community as well. For example, a number of support groups were developed from a patient population screened through a pilot geriatric arthritis program (Petty, Moeller, and Campbell, 1976). It is noteworthy that the members of these groups were reluctant to inquire about community mental health programs inasmuch as they did not see themselves as having problems serious enough to require counseling. Their expressed concerns were generally in the areas of health, sensory changes, mobility, and family relationships. It was necessary to develop outreach strategies in order to involve these clients in the supportive groups. That is, a staff member had to make home visits and develop a prior relationship with these individuals. Outreach efforts were also needed to maintain group participation. The general reluctance of these clients to seek counseling and the need for outreach are very common problems in developing therapeutic groups with the elderly in community settings. This is why most such groups are in institutional settings, where it is much easier to recruit and maintain groups.

The supportive group overlaps in some respects with the integrative counseling group. There is a need for the kind of emotional support and encouragement characteristic of the supportive group when conducting integrative groups, particularly in the early stages of group development.

Another group approach aims at the enhancement of social functioning and interaction through skills training, particularly assertiveness training, whereby the members learn to communicate their wishes and feelings clearly and effectively (Toseland and Rose, 1978). Development of skills to deal with everyday problems of living involving sales clerks, other service people, landlords, neighbors, and so on, clearly has practical value for older persons. Group approaches emphasizing social skill development and adaptive problem solving also have clear implications for the locus of control factor in the integrative model. Interestingly, despite their practical value and apparent appeal, these group approaches, require strenuous outreach efforts to recruit group members and maintain group attendance. Enrichment groups have as their objective the creative use of leisure time through a guided discussion format that includes relevant psychosocial issues (Weiner, Brok, and Snadowsky, 1978). These groups are not really rehabilitative or psychotherapeutic in intent or format but represent a form of leisure time activity for relatively well-functioning individuals.

The integrative approach to group counseling shares a number of objectives with several of the approaches just mentioned. It seeks to provide emotional support and nurturance as well as opportunities for socialization, just as supportive groups do. It aims at developing and strengthening social skills so as to enhance feelings of competence and an internal locus of control. However, it should move beyond these objectives to Objective 6 in the integrative treatment model (see Figure 3-3)—increased morale. There should also be some clarification of meaning in the lives of the clients and movement toward the development of their capacities for working on the issue of integrity versus despair. In fact, group practitioners have noted that the issue of integrity versus despair almost invariably becomes an area of concern in group work with older persons (Lowy, 1962; Brearley, 1975).

Thus, the focus on meaning, cognitive restructuring, and other integrative techniques for dealing with the problem of despair have to be brought to bear in the group process.

The objectives of integrative practice apply to the life situations and problems of a great many noninstitutionalized older persons. National Institute of Mental Health data indicate that new cases of psychopathology in persons 65 and over are two-and-one-half times higher than for persons in the 35–54-age range (Butler, 1974). Yet, there has been an underuse of needed mental health services, as noted earlier (Lowy, 1979). One of the most promising settings to locate persons in need of mental health services is not being used for those purposes, and that is the senior service center. People who come to senior service centers and are in need of such services can be identified by program staff who have had considerable opportunity to observe them. Further, there is less stigma attached to receiving service in a senior center than is attached to a psychiatric setting.

The group format is the normal one in senior centers and thus reduces the potential for stigma even further. The need for support among the identified clients, with their varying degrees of loneliness, depression, and anxiety, also indicates that a group approach would be the best way to start. The availability of members who have had personal experience with similar problems and issues and can serve as role models and informants, in line with the androgogy principle, also speaks to the use of the group.

It could be argued that persons who voluntarily come to a senior center are generally less demoralized than those who remain isolated and uninvolved in their communities. Although this is probably true, anyone who has worked in a center knows that there is a great deal of variation in the amount of individual involvement. In fact, the center provides a setting in which one can identify individuals who have problems with human relationships, regardless of their degree of involvement with others. Nowadays, the larger senior centers in urban areas have diversified activities and facilities that do attract those who are socially isolated as well as those who wish to be socially involved. The hot meals offered at centers under the Title VII Nutrition Program of the Older Americans Act attract some who are otherwise isolated, and the availability of reading materials and other "anonymous" facilities are also an attraction to them. Actually, senior centers are more and more becoming the setting for various social and human services, as well as the source of referral for others.

In addition to the setting selected, there are other considerations in attempting to establish groups of older persons to deal with intrapersonal and interpersonal problems. One is that there are often overwhelming concerns with financial solvency and medical care which can prevent the groups from getting beyond these concerns. Many practitioners who have attempted to form counseling or psychotherapeutic groups with the elderly have had the common experience of becoming so involved in providing information, making referrals, and intervening in problems of finances and health that the groups never became more than a source of information and referral services. There is a primary need for these hard services and they have to be taken care of outside the group in the early stages if the group is going to get on with the problems for which it is intended. The task-centered approach is well-suited for handling referrals as task assignments in individual counseling with group members outside of group sessions. This is not to say that issues concerning these services and the needs that require them should not be the subject of discussion in group sessions. In fact, other group members are often helpful informants about available services.

Another special consideration about working with older persons is that they might prefer a slower pace and speed of verbal interaction than would a group of young adults. One also has to be concerned about hearing loss. Maintaining eye contact with the client is important because it enhances lip reading and is an important ingredient in skillful helping relations generally. As I mentioned earlier, these helping skills and the core conditions of warmth, empathy, and genuineness should inform practice with the elderly as it should with every other age group (Egan, 1975a). For those who are not familiar with them, there are programmed exercises that can enhance the counselor's use of them (Egan, 1975b). It is not my intent to provide an exhaustive review of the special concerns and approaches in interpersonal work with the elderly, for there are helpful programmed texts in this more specialized area (Greenberg, Fatula, Hameister, and Hickey, 1976). I would add only one thing in this regard: a small, intimate-sized group (five to eight members) is better designed to handle some of the problems of hearing and cognitive speed than are larger groups. There is less pressure to quickly interject one's thoughts, feelings, or responses, and there is closer physical proximity to enhance hearing.

Formation of groups for integrative counseling with older persons generally follows the guidelines that have been found to lead to effective groups (Bertscher and Maple, 1977). Outcome research has shown that the most effective groups tend to be those whose members are homogeneous on descriptive attributes and heterogeneous with regard to behavioral attributes (Fairweather, 1964; Shaw, 1976; Yalom, 1975). Common examples of descriptive attributes would be age, sex, and marital status. Examples of behavioral attributes that would be important in group formation would be talkativeness, helpfulness, combativeness, inquisitiveness, aggressiveness or passiveness, use of humor, and so on. Obviously, integrative groups of older persons meet the criterion of homogeneity on the descriptive attribute of age by definition. Of course, there may be some variability in the older age range, especially in different settings. In senior service centers, most group members tend to be in the young-old category, whereas groups in nursing homes are mostly in the old-old category, but the criterion of homogeneity is generally met in each setting.

One descriptive attribute which can present problems for group formation in settings for the aging is sex. There is almost invariably a smaller number of men, frequently too few to form an adequate pool to draw from in group formation. This is not an uncommon problem in senior service centers, and in fact the case illustration in Chapter 5 reflects its rather common occurrence. Lack of men in a group does not in itself represent a problem, since a group made up entirely of women would also meet the criterion of homogeneity on descriptive characteristics. It can represent a problem if much of the work in the group focuses on the relationships between men and women in the setting. Indeed, in senior centers there is a good deal of dating, mating, pairing off, and general discussion about the relationships between members of the opposite sex. These are not frivolous matters as far as the older persons themselves are concerned, although it might be a source of some humor for younger persons with stereotyped attitudes toward the aged. Therefore, it is quite conceivable that one would want to form a group with a view to some relative balance between the sexes, in which case the shortage of men is problematic. Again, however, this observation has to be tempered by the fact that there is a shortage of men in the lives of many, perhaps most, of the women in these settings. That fact in itself will become a focal concern in a group made up entirely or mostly of older women. The central question then becomes how one lives or prepares oneself to live without a man in the later years of life.

This point about the shortage of men can be stated from another perspective as far as senior service centers are concerned. Even though women generally outnumber the men, there are quite a few married couples attending centers, and this is becoming increasingly so as more and more "younger young-old" (55 to 65) participate in and influence senior center programs. This means that the counselor has to be aware that potential group members who are married might participate in a group only if the spouse does. The inclusion of these couples can clearly influence the focus and dynamics of work in the group. In fact, they can add a beneficial heterogeneity to groups with mixed (married, widowed, never married) marital status. This goes along somewhat with the group formation criterion of heterogeneity in behavior, which holds also for performance or experience. For example, a widowed member who had a good marriage can be a role model and informant for a married member or couple in the group. Expanding on this idea beyond the marital situation, some members or potential members of groups have weathered the events and losses of aging better than others, even though there might be a good deal of homogeneity in the actual range of events and losses an older group has encountered. This should be kept in mind in forming groups.

There are some additional points about group formation that are not unique to the integrative approach but which bear mentioning. First, one should determine how much a potential member wants to be included in the group, because this is a significant behavioral attribute (Bertscher and Maple, 1977). This means that, if at all possible, the counselor should interview all potential members before adding them to the group. Also, the immediate environment should be selected to provide a group atmosphere that enhances group effectiveness, and group size should likewise be determined so that it will enhance group effectiveness. These last two points about environment and size are stated generally, so they do have to be specified with regard to their application to integrative groups.

"A consensus of the clinical literature suggest that the ideal size of an interactional therapy group is approximately seven, with an acceptable range of five to ten members" (Yalom, 1975:284). An integrative group is indeed an interactional therapy group, and these figures do apply. Given this size and the highly personal nature of the problems to be worked on in the group, the immediate environment should provide privacy and protection against outside observation and disturbance. Also, it would be preferable to have a smaller more intimate room rather than a large one so as to enhance closer interaction.

As far as duration of meetings is concerned, Yalom (1975:278) made the following observation: "There also is some consensus among therapists that after about two hours a point of diminishing returns is reached; the group becomes weary, repetitious, and inefficient. Furthermore, many therapists appear to function best in segments of eighty to ninety minutes." My practice has been to leave it up to the group members to decide whether they want one-and-a-half hours without a break or two hours with a break of about ten minutes in the middle. With older persons, problems of arthritis and other physical conditions might make a session without a break too uncomfortable. If none of the members indicate such physical concerns, my preference is to have a 90-minute session without a break.

Ordinarily, one meeting a week is frequent enough for the purposes of integrative groups. With younger age groups, two meetings a week might be necessary because the pace and elements of their lives almost take on the character of recurrent crises which need more frequent attention for resolution. The tempo of the lives of older persons in integrative groups is apt to be slower. Nevertheless, if the makeup of the group is such that there are crisis-ridden members or situations two sessions per week would be indicated.

Given the highly structured nature of cognitive therapy and the task-centered approach, one might assume that one begins immediately with the specification of problems, goals, and tasks in integrative group practice. That is not the case. The androgogy principle suggests that older persons should not only be self-determining as far as problem identification is concerned but should also have something to say about the way the group will be conducted. Also, there is good reason to believe that the highly structured approach in behavioral-cognitive groups (S. D. Rose, 1977 and 1980) may be experienced as aversive by older persons. In a study conducted in senior service settings, my colleagues and I (Toseland, Sherman, and Bliven, in press) found that highly structured groups oriented toward behavioral skills training and problem solving were not only not effective, but were met with a good deal of resistance. In one group, it took the form of overtly expressed anger and frustration, in another the members simply dropped out and never returned after a few sessions. The explicit complaints were that the group participants felt like children who were back in school as they were being taught social and problem-solving skills. They especially disliked the role modeling assignments, and they complained that they had lived a long time, had a lot of life experience, and had some knowledge and skills of their own. It would be hard to find a better argument in favor of the androgogical principle in practice. The one structured group that did not die from member attrition demanded that they have an open discussion format for their group, which they got.

The contrast groups in the study were open-ended and process-oriented rather than goal-oriented from the beginning. The more process-oriented group practice thus appears to have a great deal more appeal for older persons in senior service settings. With the advantage of hindsight it can be seen why this is so. The process group literature came out of neighborhood house and community center settings and would thus appear to have a good deal of applicability to senior service settings (Middleman, 1978; Northen, 1969; Trecker, 1972). The more open discussion group format is very common in senior centers and the members appear to have a strong preference for it.

This is not to say that older persons do not want structure in their groups, but it has to come at their time and pace. Thus, the introduction of structure in integrative groups occurs in part as an outcome of group process. How this is done will be illustrated in Chapter 5.

CHAPTER FIVE

Integrative Counseling with a Group

THE GROUP PRESENTED here was selected to illustrate the points made in Chapter 4 about integrative practice with groups. It is a group I led and, although the outcomes were generally favorable, it represents a number of the vagaries, pitfalls, and "warts" of actual practice with integrative groups in a senior service setting.

Formation of the Group

As a result of my involvement in research and consultation activities for the Institute of Gerontology at the university at which I teach, a mutually beneficial arrangement was worked out with a rather large and active senior service center in a neighboring city. The executive director and program director were concerned about a number of persons attending the center whom they and their staff identified as having a clear need for counseling, particularly for a group therapy experience. Although there was a part-time counselor, she was inundated with clients needing help with financial, housing, and medical problems. In fact, she was a major source of referral to various outside services for the counseling group that was finally established.

The initial list of people identified by the center staff as in need of this group experience were seven women and three men. These were people who had either told a staff member that they were experiencing emotional problems or who had been observed by staff members in various center activities and were judged to be in need of a group therapy experience. When it was established that I would be available to work with the group, it was decided that the staff members who had identified the potential group members would approach them about the nature and purposes of the group and see whether they would be interested in participating in it. They were told that the group was being formed to help people who were experiencing problems like "loneliness, worries, the blues," and so on. I was described as a gerontology teacher and practitioner from a local university who works with people with problems in aging.

Not surprisingly, the ones who wished to participate when asked were those who had identified themselves as having problems. There were three people (two men and one woman) who had been identified by the staff rather than by themselves as having emotional problems. When they were approached by the staff members, they indicated that they did not want to participate in the group nor did they wish to talk to me at this time about the possibility of participating in it. The center director and staff felt that the problems and morale of some of the potential members needed to be dealt with soon and that it would not be wise or feasible to wait until a larger pool of potential members could be built up.

Thus, although it would have been preferable to select eight or nine members from a larger pool on the premise that approximately seven would remain with the group, it was actually necessary to begin with the seven who were willing to participate. I also bypassed the preferred individual interview because it would not be serving any screening purpose and the center staff had indicated the need to get the group helping process under way rather quickly. Consequently, my first meeting with the individuals was in the first group session. Six of the seven persons who said they wanted to be in the group actually showed up for the first session. Of these six persons five were women. It would have been preferable to have at least two men in the group but as indicated above the other two men did not wish to enter the group. Having one man in the group created a problem in the early stages, but it was overcome, as will be indicated. He was Fred Krauss, a 73-year-old retired engineer, who was married and regularly attended the center but whose wife never attended with him.

The other members of the group consisted of Agnes Morgan, a 66-year-old widow who was quite depressed and who had serious problems with her daughter, son-in-law, and grandson, all of whom lived with her in her small house. These difficulties were compounded by financial problems with which the Office for Aging counselor was helping her. It was the counselor who encouraged her to enter the group. Sylvia Rolfe, 71 years old, was referred because of interpersonal problems that had surfaced in other activities she had engaged in at the center. In a current affairs discussion group, for example, she talked so much and attempted to dominate discussion to such an extent that she was asked to leave the group. She confided in the program director of the center that she could not seem to help herself; she realized she talked too much and would like to do something about it. She admitted to feeling very lonely and wanted desperately to get into this group.

Two other women in the group were twin sisters, age 75, who were new to the center. Margaret Larson was a widow who had a mild heart attack about a year and a half earlier to which she had reacted with excessive anxiety, according to her doctor. She had been reassured by him that her heart had sustained no serious or permanent damage and that she was fully recovered, but she remained anxious about having another attack and about the possibility that she would be unable to care for her sister. The sister, Clovis Flynn, was a retired schoolteacher, never married, who complained of severe arthritis of the hips and lower extremities that she claimed kept her almost immobile. She admitted to feeling quite dependent on her sister and felt that she should enter the group with her sister to see what gains they could get from the experience.

Lily Silvano was the youngest member of the group, a 61-year-old married woman who, although she appeared to be quite vivacious and involved in a number of activities at the center, admitted to feeling troubled and "confused." She hoped the group experience would bring her more self-understanding. The program director indicated that there was some evidence of marital problems with which Lily needed help and therefore referred her to the group.

A more detailed description of the group members will be given later to indicate their situations before and after counseling, as well as their transactions and participation in the group. For the moment, it can be seen that all of them had a degree of motivation for counseling to achieve some personal change. There was also no indication of organic brain syndrome or manifestly severe emotional disturbance. Obviously, hallucinations or delusions indicative of cognitive dysfunctioning would preclude the cognitive approaches and techniques of the integrative approach. All members of the group were at least somewhat apprehensive about the nature of the experience and what it would entail, so much of the first session was spent in my explaining the intention of the group and the possible directions it might take.

The sessions were held once a week for an hour and a half, as agreed upon by the group at the first meeting. The room in which the sessions were held was relatively small, allowing for the arrangement of chairs in a fairly intimate circle without an intervening desk or table. I introduced myself as a teacher of gerontology at a local university and as a practitioner who was very much concerned with the problems and issues of aging. I indicated my personal interest by pointing to the increasing gray in my own hair and by noting that the middle-aged person is often more concerned with the "problems" of aging than are the so-called aged themselves, who might not see such things as problems. I indicated that the death of my father just three months before the session and the effect of his prolonged illness and physical dependency on my mother were problems I had not worked through for myself. I was aware that most if not all members of the group had experienced such losses and had worked them through and they could help others in the group and me by sharing their experiences and methods of coping. This approach goes back, of course, to the principle of androgogy—to identify the group members as teachers and helpers. It also reduces the distance and distinction between helper and helped and gives some authenticity to the helper's concern about them as persons like him/herself rather than as subjects or patients to be studied and cured.

I then told them that the group was intended to provide an opportunity to discuss some problems that are natural and common in the process of aging but that can create special difficulties for persons going through them— events such as retirement, declining health, geographic and emotional separation of families and generations, death of loved ones, loss of friends, and the feelings of depression that accompany them. Again I noted that each of the members had passed through some of these events and that their experiences could be helpful to others in working through or preparing for such events. I mentioned that the group could provide emotional support and recognition of one another in that its small size allowed for closer relationships than was true of the larger activity, crafts, and discussion groups in the center. I also indicated that there was an educational aspect to the group in that one member's special knowledge and experience could serve to stimulate another's thinking. I noted, too, that there would undoubtedly be differences of opinion since we may look upon or experience the same events or circumstances in quite different ways.

I finished by commenting that while these were the general purposes of the group, it was important to know what the group was *not*. It was not a group for the discussion of current affairs or impersonal topics of interest. Although occasionally discussion of such issues might occur, the group was intended for mutual support, help, and sharing of common *personal* problems and concerns.

I then asked the members to introduce themselves individually and to indicate a little something about their backgrounds and experience, about the concerns they had currently, and what they hoped to get out of the group. They were not only able but clearly pleased to tell something about their backgrounds, and each of them mentioned the personal problem or concern which had been identified by the center staff before the establishment of the group. This is not, of course, the invariable experience with such a group, but it does indicate that older persons can begin to identify and start to work on personal problems in the very first session.

The issue of how long the group would continue was not raised by anyone at the first session. However, when it did come up, in the third session, I said that it was up to the group and what the members wished to accomplish for themselves. As it turned out, the group continued for fifteen sessions by mutual agreement. The issue of time limits relative to objectives for this group will be discussed more fully later.

Toward the end of the first session I distributed the Life Satisfaction Index, the general morale question, and Semantic Differential Test forms and then discussed them. I indicated that the members did not have to fill out any or all of the items if they had any concerns about doing so. I also indicated that we would be discussing some of the issues raised in the instruments at the next session and that individuals who wished to discuss, clarify, or expand their responses, either in the group or privately with me, would have every chance to do so. As we discussed the types of questions on the forms, most of the members present expressed both interest and willingness to fill out the forms before the next meeting. I said that they would be given the same forms to fill out at the end of the group to provide us with some sense or measure of what kinds of changes had come about as a result of the group process. Thus, the instruments served to lend some structure and expectations about change, as well as some sense of evaluation of progress in the group process. These expectancies, of course, are important ingredients in promoting an atmosphere of hope and intentionality in the counseling process.

Description and Assessment of the Group Members

This section is intended to give a picture of the clients, their problems, their circumstances, and their characteristic ways of coping as these became evident through group process, interviewing, and testing in the early stages of counseling. Although some of the circumstances and details, as well as the names, of the individuals have been changed to provide greater anonymity, the salient problems, issues, and themes remain the same. What happened to the clients, the changes that occurred in the course of counseling, will be presented in the section on outcome. The focus here is on the clients as they were on entering the group, and what was learned about them through the process of study and assessment.

The reader is going to find that there is a great deal of information about the personal lives of the group members in this section. One question a reader might have is, "How is it possible to obtain so much information in a group situation?" First, older clients are not only naturally interested in reviewing their lives, past and present, but they are generally quite receptive to other persons' reminiscences in such groups. A great deal of this personal information comes out in the very first session, and it is amplified in detail and extent in later sessions. Further, individual sessions I had with some of the group members added even more information. Finally, the instruments they filled out and discussed provided fuller information from varied dimensions.

Another question that might be asked is, "Why is so much information collected for a short-term counseling situation?" The answer to that is that with an older client group like this we are working with past as well as present since the members are dealing with life review and integration even if it is in a short-term situation, because these are the natural tasks and concerns of that stage of life. Furthermore, reminiscence is a recognized element of the integrative counseling process, so that it serves treatment as well as assessment purposes. With these points in mind, let us turn now to the background information on each member of this group.

Sylvia Rolfe, 71, was referred to the group by the program director because of problems she had presented in various activity groups she attended in the senior center. She had been involved in a poetry group, a foreign language group, and a current affairs discussion group. In this last group she talked a great deal, often too loud, and appeared to try to dominate most of the discussions. When a two-minute time limit was put into effect in the discussion group, she invariably went over the limit. This caused a good deal of resentment among other members of that group, who then requested that the discussion leader ask her to leave the group. This is how the matter came to the attention of the program director, who learned that the same problem had occurred in all the other groups Sylvia had attended.

Mrs. Rolfe readily agreed that she did have this problem, that she seemed to alienate others in the process and that, as a result, she felt very lonely. She claimed she urgently wanted to work on the problem; so, although the addition of such a person to a group counseling situation often creates problems in terms of group process, she was admitted to the group on the basis of her apparently strong motivation and her loneliness. Since it was clear that she would need additional help to gain some insight into this particular interpersonal problem, she was also seen by me in individual counseling. It became evident early in the individual sessions that a problem of partial deafness aggravated the initial problem. She would tend to talk loudly, seeming thereby to be too aggressive, and she would inadvertently interrupt people who were talking, but who were not in her line of vision at the time. However, her awareness of this situation did not dissuade her from initially presenting the same problems for this group as she had for the others.

Sylvia Rolfe was born and reared in a small rural town in the northeastern United States. Her family was relatively poor, as her father was a carpenter and general handyman, although he later became a building contractor on a small scale. However, the family was one of the few in town of Anglo-Saxon background, as the area was a coal-mining region populated mostly by Poles, Germans, Hungarians, and other recent immigrant groups. Apparently, this "Old American" background gave her family, particularly in the eyes of her mother, a certain social status in the largely immigrant community. Sylvia often brought up the matter of "national stock" and lineage in the course of her participation in the group. Although both her parents were Methodist and considered themselves religious, they were not intense, fundamentalist practitioners. Sylvia herself retained an interest in religion, but claimed that she felt as much at home with Roman Catholicism as Methodism because of her childhood exposure to and involvement with other ethnic, largely Catholic groups.

She was the oldest of four children, and as a result she was given a heavy responsibility for the care of her younger brothers and sister. She claimed that her mother was a very demanding and domineering woman who was never satisfied with what Sylvia did in caring for the other children, for the home, and especially for the mother herself. She described her father as a kindly man, but somewhat distant, allowing her mother pretty much to run the family.

Sylvia married when she was quite young, only 16, to a man considerably older than she (31 years of age). He talked of finding new opportunities in the Southwest, and she was very much attracted to the idea and romance of carving out a new life there. She also very consciously wanted to get away from her family, particularly her mother, and all the burdens she felt she carried. However, she maintained contact with her family, and later, when her mother became a widow, Sylvia took her into her home.

Not long after she and her new husband settled into a small town in the Southwest, he injured his back and was unemployed for a long period of time. Sylvia had to take in laundry and sewing to try to keep things going financially. With the exception of a few odd jobs, her husband apparently spent a good deal of time with other men in the local tavern or around the courthouse. Mrs. Rolfe related this information about her husband in a factual, uncritical way, and claimed to hold him in high regard, speaking positively about his ideas and dreams about the future. He became involved in Republican Party politics on a small, local scale and as a result was given the position of deputy sheriff, the job he kept until he died of a heart attack at age 58.

Sylvia managed to raise three sons, all of whom she claimed turned out "all right." In relating her family background, she said at one point: "All my life I've never had any friends or associates of my own age. They have either been much older or much younger." Her mother had died about twenty years before at age 76 when the client was 50. Sylvia had cared for her for a number of years before having to admit her to a nursing home not long before her death. She claimed that none of her siblings was willing to put up with her mother's cantankerous behavior, so she ended up with full responsibility for her care and all decisions related to it. Throughout this, her mother remained dissatisfied and critical about the care Sylvia was giving her. When it was finally necessary to place her in the nursing home, the mother was particularly hateful and resentful toward Sylvia.

At the time Sylvia entered the group she was living alone in a small apartment. One of her sons, an engineer who did a good deal of foreign and domestic traveling for a large local corporation, lived nearby with his wife and five children. With the exception of weekly visits with her son and his family, she was quite alone and had no other close acquaintances.

In the first sessions of the group, Mrs. Rolfe exhibited the same behavior of talking too much and interrupting others that had brought her into counseling. She was, however, quite articulate and knowledgeable about a great many things. Although she had never completed grammar school, she had educated herself through reading and evening courses, so that she was able when she became a widow to get a job as typist and then secretary in various offices. Her last job involved not only clerical activities but also some interviewing of applicants and clients in a public assistance agency. She was actually quite pedantic in her early group participation, and the other group members were impressed as well as irritated by her apparent fund of knowledge.

On the Life Satisfaction Index form, Sylvia Rolfe had a low satisfaction score of 6 out of a possible 20. The score would have been even lower if it were not for the fact that she viewed her older years as better than her youth. Thus, for example, she agreed with the statement, "As I grow older, things seem better than I thought they would be," and she disagreed with the statement, "This is the dreariest time of my life." She also believed that some interesting and pleasant things were still going to happen in her life, so she displayed some degree of hopefulness, which was consistent with her strong motivation for group counseling. On the other hand, she felt that her "life could be happier than it is now" and that she did not get most of the important things she wanted out of life. This latter belief is, of course, indicative of the sense of regret Erikson refers to in describing the state of despair in old age.

Although these responses on the LSIA indicated a good deal of dissatisfaction about her life, it became clear in the course of counseling that Sylvia believed that she *should not* feel dissatisfied. In other words, although she had good reason to feel dissatisfied about some aspects of her life, she felt that it was not really right to express it or think it. Even though on the one hand she felt that she did not get most of the important things she wanted out of life, she agreed with the statement, "As I look back over my life, I am fairly well satisfied." This attitude that one should not think or express such negative thoughts also probably prompted her to check off on the general happiness scale that she was "pretty happy" rather than "not too happy," which would have been much more consistent with her low life satisfaction score. It also permeated her entire attitude about her mother. She had good reason for many negative feelings toward her mother, but she felt extremely guilty for having them. This became a focal point of concern in the plan for counseling in both individual and group sessions.

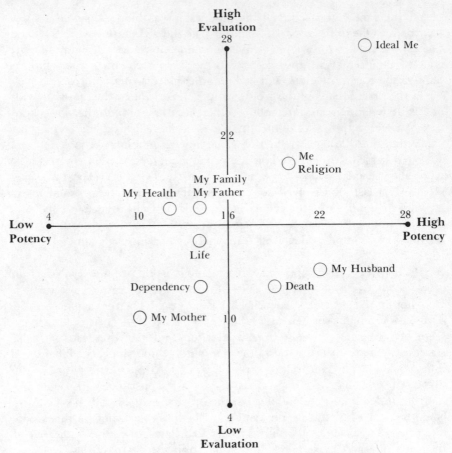

FIGURE 5-1.   *Sylvia Rolfe's First Semantic Differential Test*

Sylvia R.'s responses to the Semantic Differential Test (Figure 5-1) shed considerably more light on some of the problem areas and issues in her life. First, it should be noted that the lowest concept on both the evaluation and the potency dimension was "My Mother." Her mother was described as "extremely bad," "quite unfair," and "extremely weak." However, even though her mother had been dead for many years, she was seen as highly active on the activity dimension of the test. It was evident in the counseling process as well that her mother remained a dominant, obsessive theme in her life. When she discussed her mother's weakness, her controlling dependency, and her negative traits, it was with immediacy and affect, not with distance and perspective. She had not at all come to terms with the meaning of her mother in her life.

The second outstanding point in Figure 5-1 is the extremely high "Ideal Me." In fact, it could not have been any higher in terms of the scoring format of the test. Sylvia had extremely high aspirations and standards for herself, which led to a great many feelings of shame for not having attained them. It can be seen that there is a large discrepancy on the evaluative dimension between "Me" and "Ideal Me," between the self-concept and the self ideal, which is indicative of low self-esteem. Although her self-concept was slightly positive on the evaluation, potency, and activity dimension, the unrealistically high self ideal clearly created a problem in many aspects of her life, particularly in coming to terms with her past efforts, endeavors, and herself.

The reader might legitimately ask, "Why shouldn't the self ideal, the "Ideal Me," be extremely high? After all, isn't this what ideals are all about, to aim high, to achieve well?" It is true that ideals set standards for us to work toward and maintain, but if these are unrealistic, not cognizant of human fallibility, they serve the purpose of self-hate and self-denigration (Rubin, 1975). Rogers has noted that the process of achieving integrity involves the ever expanding recognition of acceptance of all aspects of ourselves, the negative as well as the positive (Rogers, 1965:510–517). Thus emotions of hatred, envy, jealousy, and so on are all human emotions that have to be recognized as such and as an aspect of one's self. Unfortunately, ego ideals are all too frequently *super*human and therefore *in*human. This can lead not only to denigration of one's self but to perfectionistic demands on others as well. Thus, one can be hypercritical of other's failings and shortcomings.

It should be noted that acceptance of negative aspects, impulses, and emotions in ourselves does not mean that we have to act on them. This was the critical issue in Sylvia Rolfe's case. She felt guilty about the thoughts she had about her mother, even though she had behaved extremely responsibly toward her and had rarely acted on those thoughts and impulses. She could not accept credit for this when it was first pointed out to her in the group and in individual counseling. In many respects, Sylvia Rolfe's self ideal fits Adler's description of the superiority complex (Adler, 1964:121–126). The self ideal is, after all, a part of the person's self system, and it is frequently grandiose. Sylvia was, in fact, often intolerant of the views, ideas, and knowledge of others in the group. Although she claimed that her hearing problem explained her tendency to interrupt others when they were talking, it became clear that in terms of her internalized standards (the criteria of her self ideal) the others were frequently not measuring up, did not know what they were talking about. Thus, she was pedantic with them, and this created problems in her interpersonal relationships.

In Sylvia's semantic differential chart, "Death" had the lowest evaluative content after "My Mother." Although it showed some potency in terms of her life space, it was not fraught with disabling anxiety or obsessive concern. "Dependency" was lower in potency and indeed was not very acceptable in light of her ideals. She had been a bulwark in caring for her mother, her children, and even her husband in their dependency, consistent with her self ideal, but in her idealized picture there was not much room for her own probable dependency in the not too distant future. However, this was not an overwhelming concern to her at the beginning of counseling. The primary emphasis in counseling was on the repetitive cycle of resentment and guilt about her mother and the toll of time and emotional energy this was taking, together with the problems inherent in the unrealistically high standards she had for herself. Ironically, it was in large part her mother who instilled these values and expectations, but it was of course the adult Sylvia Rolfe who continued to retain them as part of her self. These two issues of the mother and the self-defeating expectations were inextricably bound up with one another in the counseling plan and process.

Agnes Morgan, a 66-year-old widow, had been referred to the group by an Office for Aging counselor who felt that she could benefit from the emotional support a group could provide. She was described as quite depressed in general and distressed about her current family situation in particular. The counselor also noted that Agnes evidently had a very low sense of self-worth. Although she was involved in a number of activities in the senior center, she always took on the most menial tasks associated with these activities. She would volunteer for the dull heavy work of preparing and cooking meals, and especially cleaning up afterward, but she never became involved in planning or running the affairs. When she was encouraged to engage in dance groups, current affairs discussion groups, and in other activities, she would say that she was not interesting enough or smart enough to be in them.

Agnes Morgan came from a large, rather poor farm family of Scottish-Irish descent. She was the middle child in a family of nine children. She completed grammar school, but then went to work as a domestic rather than go on to high school. She was married when she was eighteen to a young machinist in a large electrical plant in a nearby city. She claimed that the first two years of her marriage, until her daughter was born, were fine. Then her husband began spending less and less time at home, drinking heavily, and gambling as well. Agnes found herself devoting most of her time and interest to her daughter and her church. She was born and reared a Baptist and remained an active churchgoer throughout her adulthood. Her husband's gambling got worse to such an extent that he was gambling away just about all of his earnings. When her daughter entered school, Agnes found it necessary to take a job as a waitress.

She later obtained a job as an assembly line operative in the same plant her husband worked in, and she remained there until her retirement at age 62. Her husband had died ten years earlier in an industrial accident, and the funds she received as a result of that enabled her to buy a small rural house within driving distance of her work. The house meant a great deal to her, one of the few things of worth she felt she had gotten out of life. There were no other children by her marriage. Her daughter remained with her until she married at age twenty-eight. Two years later the daughter had a child who was born with a spinal condition that left him paralyzed from the hips down.

The condition was somewhat correctible, but only through repeated, expensive surgery. Because of these expenses, Agnes's daughter and son-in-law asked if they could move in with her. The son-in-law said he would build an addition to the house for them to live in, thus allowing Agnes to remain in the part of the home that currently constituted the whole house. However, as the years passed her son-in-law never got around to putting up the addition, claiming lack of time and money. This meant that three adults and one child were living in cramped quarters with only two bedrooms and one bathroom.

Her relations with her son-in-law steadily deteriorated and became particularly stressful about two-and-a-half years before she entered the group. At that time, she claimed that he had taken about $130, which she had saved up for a major furnace repair, out of her bedroom dresser. She explored every possible explanation for the missing money, but could find no other. When she finally brought herself to raise the issue with him, taking care to make it clear that she was not condemning him for it, he heatedly denied it and became so incensed that he did not speak to her for months afterward. At the time she entered the group, their relationship was such that he would speak to her only when it was absolutely necessary. Consequently, her home life was extremely tense and stressful to her. Her daughter felt caught between her mother and her husband, and the only positive thing in Agnes's home life at that time was that her grandson, age 7 at the time, was slowly making progress after repeated surgery. He had progressed from a combination of crutches and leg braces to just leg braces, and she hoped the braces would become smaller and less burdensome as time went on.

Agnes found she had to get out of the house every day during good weather, and in this regard the senior center was a godsend to her. It was her refuge, and she wanted to do all she could to show her appreciation. However, the winter months often kept her from traveling into the city, and in the previous two winters she ended up in the hospital because of depression. The last depressive episode was so bad that she needed shock treatment, and she had doubted that she would ever come out of it. She was dreading the next winter, but she was in counseling on a weekly basis with the pastor of her church. She said that he had training in family counseling and that he planned to get her son-in-law and daughter involved in the counseling, since so many of her problems stemmed from the family situation.

From the beginning, Agnes was clear that the group was not going to be the primary therapeutic agent with regard to her personal problems. However, she welcomed the opportunity to share some of these problems with others who also had problems. She was encouraged in this by her minister and her Office for Aging counselor, who was helping her with financial and related problems. Given this arrangement, she never became involved in individual counseling with me.

As might be expected, Agnes Morgan had the lowest Life Satisfaction score in the entire group. She had only one positive item in that she agreed with the statement, "Compared to other people my age, I make a good appearance." In fact, she looked a good ten years younger than her 66 years. However, she agreed with the statement, "I feel old and somewhat tired." Also, she was emphatic in checking off the negative items in the LSIA, unlike Sylvia Rolfe, who checked off quite a few of the spaces indicating that she was not sure of her responses one way or the other. Again, as might be expected, Agnes indicated that she was "not too happy" on the general happiness scale.

She did not take the Semantic Differential Test either before or after treatment. She claimed that it looked complicated and that she was not "smart enough" to understand it or fill it out. I said that I could respect her decision not to do the test, but I could not accept her statement that she was not intelligent enough to do it. She left it this way, saying that she would rather not. This, of course, was consistent with her feeling that she could not do more than simple, menial tasks around the center. There was no question that she was a chronically depressed person, and she had the characteristic underestimation of her actual abilities and the concretistic ·hinking (the Semantic Differential called for some degree of symbolization) that depressed persons are usually found to have. However, it should be noted that there were some positive signs. She had a positive body image, which is an important element in the self-concept. She also showed considerable energy in getting herself out to the center, bowling with some women friends, and, especially, being involved in individual and family counseling. Furthermore, there were very realistic exogenous (family) factors involved in her depression. In fact, it would be hard to conceive of a clearer illustration of the social breakdown syndrome in operation than in Agnes Morgan's situation. If one begins with the precondition to psychological breakdown in terms of the depressive core and initial low self-esteem, then adds the social labeling as sick or incompetent involved in the mental hospitalizations and Agnes's inability to solve the family problem, the breakdown would continue via induction into a sick role. (She indicated she was "sicker" at the time of the last hospitalization than the first time.) And there was, of course, the self-identification as sick or inadequate which fed back into and exacerbated the initial precondition or susceptibility to breakdown.

Reversal of this process would involve helping Agnes to find a more positive evaluation of herself. The "functionalistic ethic" in her situation was expressed in her need to do menial tasks, to be self-effacing and unobtrusive, to be socially cooperative and compliant. Group counseling experiences could help her to see that she could be accepted in her own right, including the expression of her own concerns and frustrations, without the need to do menial tasks or to be continually helpful and functional. With group and counselor support to label herself as able and worthwhile, together with encouragement toward development of an internal locus of control, she could become less easily depressed by the external difficulties and problems in her life. While working on these problems through family counseling, she could be helped in the group to counteract her own self-denigrating thoughts and attitudes. This was, therefore, the focus of counseling in the group.

Fred Krauss was a 73-year-old retired, self-educated engineer. The program director referred him to the group because she felt he needed and seemed to be looking for a more intimate kind of relationship than he had as yet been able to find at the center. Although he came on an almost daily basis and was friendly and outgoing with a large number of people there, he had attached himself somewhat to the program director and confided in her that, although he was married and living with his wife, there was "not much at home for me." He enjoyed the current affairs discussion group but wanted badly to get into a smaller group. She told him about the counseling group, emphasizing that it was not a forum type of discussion group but one that dealt with personal problems. He said he understood and very much wanted to be included.

As was true of Sylvia Rolfe and Agnes Morgan, Fred Krauss came from a rural background. He was raised on a farm, the oldest of four children, including two girls and one other boy. He was not happy with the idea of farming as a lifetime occupation, even though his father had planned on his staying on the farm and eventually taking it over. When Fred was 19, he and his father had a bitter argument about this and Fred left home. As he described it, he "started drifting westward without much of a plan." He took odd jobs along the way, and, ironically, ended up on a farm, where he found a sort of second home. He was a bright and hard worker and became the farmer's "right-hand man and almost like a son" to him. He also became "good friends, real buddies" with the farmer's 16-year-old daughter. She, too, was unhappy with farm life and wanted to go to a city. They were married with the approval of their parents (Fred and his father were reconciled by this time) and moved to the Midwest, where he found a job on the assembly line of a Ford motor plant and she got a job in a hospital.

Fred spoke with bitterness about the inhuman pressures exerted on workers for productivity on the early assembly lines. The bitterness remained with him throughout his life, and he would speak of this experience in counseling with intense emotion, as though it were happening now. However, he was able to go to night school and take technical courses while he worked there, and his wife went into nurse's training and became a nurse before they moved back east where he took a job with a large electrical corporation. Through apprenticeship and a trainee program in the plant he became an electrical engineer, and over the years he was able to invent a number of technical devices that established his reputation and his value as a consultant to other electrical plants and companies. He would discuss some of these devices with a great deal of enthusiasm, and although the other members of the group, including me, were lost in the technicalities, his enthusiasm about them was infectious.

When he was established in his new job, he and his wife started raising a family. They had three children, two boys and a girl, who "turned out well," according to his description. All were married and apparently financially secure, although they all lived in distant parts of the country. Fred never spoke about his children unless asked, and he apparently had never been close enough to his grandchildren to enjoy the grandfather role.

About his wife he said "We get along, but she's still working. A head nurse, you know, one of those bossy types." He spoke of her appreciatively, but never affectionately, as his "partner" or "buddy." They had seen things through together in life from the time they left her father's home, but there was never any intimation of a romantic side to the marriage in his description.

Fred Krauss had the highest life satisfaction score (11) of any of the group members at the start of counseling, although it would not be considered high for the general population. On the positive side, he indicated that he had got more breaks in life than other people he knew, that his older years were the best years of his life, that he expected interesting and pleasant things to happen to him in the future, that he made a good appearance, and that he did not get down in the dumps too often. On the negative side, he indicated that he had made a lot of foolish decisions in his life, that he would change his past life if he could, that he hadn't gotten most of the important things in life he wanted, and that his "life could be happier than it is now."

It is interesting to note that Fred's responses were generally consistent with the fact that he had achieved quite a bit, had a degree of material comfort and security, and was generally enjoying his retirement. However, the responses also indicated some dissatisfaction that things were missing from his life and that his life could be happier. This impression was reinforced in his response to the happiness question; "not too happy." He added at the end of the LSIA form the statement, "Life is a thousand years too short."

His responses to the Semantic Differential Test (Figure 5-2) buttressed the impression of some dissatisfaction and added a few other insights which were helpful.

His self-concept ("Me") was quite adequate in the evaluative sense. He saw himself as "quite good" and "extremely valuable." However, it was the potency dimension that proved to be interesting in both a clinical and a developmental sense. He described himself as "quite soft" and only "slightly strong," which put the self-concept toward the low potency side of his semantic space. Discussion of this with him brought out the fact that while he saw himself ambitious, inventive, and productive in his professional career as an engineer, he felt he had not been ruthless and tough enough. Other men and the corporations he worked for took the credit as well as the financial gain for a number of the things he had invented. Thus, when he indicated on the LSIA form that he had not gotten "most of the important things" he wanted

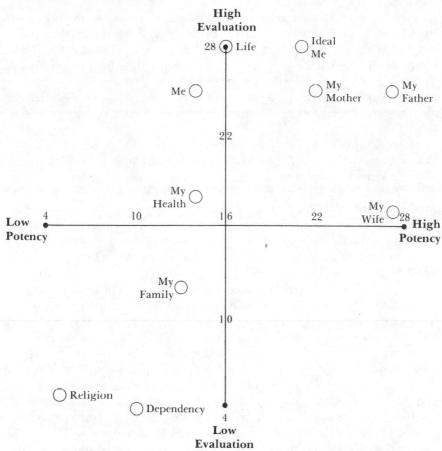

High Evaluation

28 ● Life   ○ Ideal Me

Me ○   ○ My Mother   ○ My Father

22

My Health ○

Low Potency   ●————4————10————16————22——My Wife ○28——● High Potency

My Family ○

10

○ Religion

○ Dependency
4

Low Evaluation

FIGURE 5-2. *Fred Krauss's First Semantic Differential Test*

out of life, he was speaking largely of the recognition and credit he deserved. He spoke with venom about these other men and the corporations. Yet, when checking the items on "Ideal Me," he checked off "extremely tough," a characteristic of these men he abhorred. Consequently, his self ideal was higher on the potency dimension, making for some discrepancy between the self-concept and the self ideal. This meant some lowering of self-esteem, but not as much as in the instances of Sylvia Rolfe and Agnes Morgan.

Mr. Krauss was obviously quite ambivalent about his feelings of softness, thinking that they meant a dilution of his strength. This became clear in regard to some other semantic differential items. He held the concept of "dependency" in extremely low regard and considered it "extremely weak." He even added the note "not me" to the word "dependency" on the Semantic Differential form. It is pertinent to note that he saw his wife as more potent than he. He described her as "extremely strong," "quite tough," and also "extremely cold." He was also not very accepting of some of the presumed "masculine" qualities in her makeup. In contrast, he saw his mother in a much more positive light. She is described as "extremely good," "fair," and "quite strong." His father is seen as even stronger than his mother though equally highly valued. However, some of his father's toughness (his stubborness in insisting that his son stay on the farm) was not viewed entirely positively by Fred, another indication of his ambivalence about this dimension.

Other features of Figure 5-2 worth commenting on include the place of "My Family," which was not high on the evaluative and potency dimensions or on the activity score. Although he was generally pleased with the fact that his children had turned out well, they were no longer close to him geographically or emotionally. He had no regrets about them, but they were not of primary concern to him at this stage of his life. It was clear that his career was a more important part of his identity than the role of father.

The concept "Religion" is also noteworthy here. He had an overt and active disdain for organized religion, and this came out in a rather conflictual way in group sessions. When he filled out the Semantic Differential form on the concept of "Religion," he half-jokingly wrote "Druid" on the top of it. He said that though he meant it in a somewhat sarcastic way, he was impressed with the fact that the Druids seemed to have a good scientific grasp of astronomy many years ago. In fact, Fred had an almost mystical reverence for science and technology. He claimed that the biggest regret in his life was that it was "too short," that he would not be able to witness all the marvelous discoveries that would be made in atomic research and space exploration. Much of his participation in the early stages of the group was concerned with these scientific and technical issues. It was clear that these had been the primary focus of his life, and that the affective, human relations aspect was not prominent. In terms of Jungian analytical psychology he would have been considered a "thinking extrovert" and a "feeling introvert" (Jung, 1928:60–61). Yet, there was evidence that this recessive, introverted aspect of his personality was seeking some expression.

Fred did not fill out the Semantic Differential form on the concept of "Death." Instead, he wrote in the statement, "can't explain—it's over your head." When the issue of death came up in group discussions he did not show signs of anxiety, but he did not participate. It was clear that he was at that time unable to deal with the issue of death.

In summary, it can be said that there was some degree of dissatisfaction and despair for Fred Krauss when he entered counseling. The sense of despair was not excessive and it could be worked with. It was expressed generally in his regret that he did not get all the recognition and credit he wanted out of his professional career, regret that he was "not tough enough" and had therefore made "foolish decisions" in his career. There was also an ambivalence about and lack of acceptance of certain affective, "feminine" aspects of himself, which detracted from integration of self, from ego integrity. These, then, became the focal points for counseling in his individual and group sessions.

Lily Silvano was the youngest member of the group at 61. She looked ten years younger than that, and she exuded an almost girlish enthusiasm about the group, the senior center, and the other activities she was engaged in. However, she claimed to be troubled and "confused" about a number of things, particularly her marriage. She said she needed to gain more self-understanding, because for all of her activities she was not feeling very good about herself at this point. She had spoken about this to the program director, and when she was told about the formation of the group she wanted very much to be included.

Lily came from a very religious French-Canadian family. She was the second of four children, with an older brother and two younger (twin) sisters. She said that her father had a lucrative lumber business, and she remembered her early childhood as happy and comfortable.

When she was about five years old, her father's financial fortunes began taking a turn for the worse. When she was about six her mother gave birth to twins and had a particularly difficult delivery that required the mother's hospitalization for a number of months afterward. Her father, with his declining business and the very heavy medical expenses of her mother, had to declare bankruptcy and go to work for low pay with another lumbering concern. He found it necessary to hire someone to care for the twins while his wife was in the hospital, and he placed Lily and her older brother in Catholic orphanages. She went to one for girls that seemed to be quite strict and rigid.

She recalled begging her father to let her stay home to take care of the twins. He tried to convince her of the impossibility of this, but she felt great resentment and expressed it in rebelliousness at the orphanage. She claimed that the nuns would regularly put her in a dark closet for hours at a time to make her promise to behave. Although she hated them for it at the time, she said that later in her life she appreciated what they had given her in the way of education, self-discipline, and faith. She remained a very strong believer in the Roman Catholic faith. There was nevertheless no evidence of strong moralistic and judgmental attitudes about others in her verbalizations and social interactions.

Her family reunited when Lily was thirteen years old. By that time her father was making a decent salary, and her mother had started a small millinery business. Lily helped her mother and became an expert seamstress while she continued in school. She left high school before graduation at age 17 to help her mother full-time, helping to build the business and later managing it as a fairly thriving enterprise, until she married at age 34. Her husband was fifteen years older than she, and although not French-Canadian he was also a strong Catholic (Italian-American background) and a friend of the family. She said that he was very much attracted to her liveliness and enthusiasm.

He tended to be on the quiet, retiring side, but he pursued her very avidly. She felt secure with him, and in most things it appeared that they complemented one another very well. She went to live with him in upstate New York, where he had a factory job as a skilled machinist.

There were no children by the marriage, and her husband's only living relative was a married sister who lived in a nearby state and with whom they exchanged visits a couple of times a year. Her husband had retired two years before, but had developed no interests outside of gardening and working on maintenance and additions to the house.

She began feeling hemmed in after his retirement and tried to get him interested in outside activities. He said he had no such desire, that he was content being at home. She started taking an interest in gardening also, but he contended that outside work was "man's work" and that she should busy herself inside with sewing, cooking, knitting, housekeeping, and so on. She found this stifling after a while and so joined the senior center. She became active in the dance class, the dramatics group, various crafts groups, and the choir. She also sang in her church choir, which gave performances in other churches and organizations in the area, and in which she was sometimes a soloist. Also, since she was an expert seamstress and designed her own dresses, she became active with a group of women who designed and modeled dresses in local department stores for charity.

Given her versatility, wide interests, and energy, her low score of 8 on the Life Satisfaction Index came as something of a surprise. However, self-report instruments like the LSIA can be affected by transient moods and factors, and that appears to be what happened to some extent in this instance.

Although the positive responses she checked off were few in number, Lily gave even fewer clearly negative responses: that things did not seem better as she got older, that this was the dreariest time of her life, that her life could be happier than it is now, and that these were not the best years of her life. The remaining eight items were either not answered (often with check marks scratched out) or checked off in the questionable or "not sure" category. She also reported in the happiness question that she was "not too happy."

The pattern in these responses indicated that she was unhappy with her current life situation, but could not indicate dissatisfaction with her past or her future. When I discussed the results with her, she agreed that this was the case. She was feeling particularly frustrated and almost hopeless about her marital situation, and it was affecting her general outlook. She said, for example, that she could not answer the LSIA statement, "Compared to other people, I get down in the dumps too often," because although she felt "in the dumps" when she took the test, the statement was not true of her in general.

This was borne out further by the results of the Semantic Differential Test (Figure 5-3) which picked up more of her positive, enduring attitudes and fewer of the negative, transient ones indicated on the LSIA.

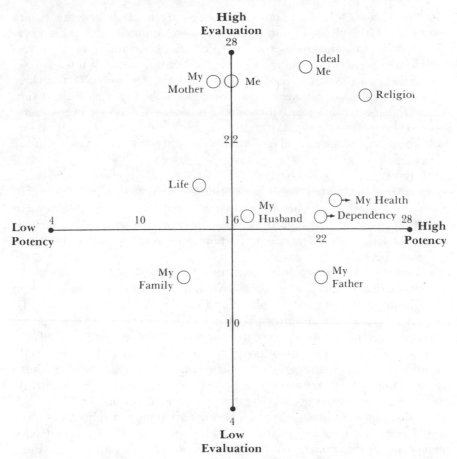

High
Evaluation
28

Ideal
Me

My   Me
Mother

Religion

22

Life

My Health

My
Husband   Dependency

Low   4   10   16   28   **High**
Potency   22   **Potency**

My   My
Family   Father

10

4
Low
Evaluation

FIGURE 5-3. *Lily Silvano's First Semantic Differential Test*

The most notable thing in Figure 5-3 was her good self-concept. "Me" was near the top of the evaluation dimension, and there was not much discrepancy between her self-concept and her self ideal, so her self-esteem was also quite good. What discrepancy there was occurred on the potency dimension. Although she saw herself (Me) as "extremely strong," she also saw herself as "extremely soft." According to her self ideal, she would like to be "quite tough." Discussion of this with her brought out the fact that this had a great deal to do with her marital relationship. She said she had recently taken a course in assertiveness training in the hope that it would help her deal with her husband's stubborn attitudes. She had gone into the course with high hopes and tried the various self-assertive techniques on him, but he remained adamant about not engaging in mutual outside activities or sharing the gardening with her. She felt that in part her lack of success was because she was not "tough enough." At any rate, she was clearly frustrated by this failure after her initial high hopes, and it was this that prompted most of her negative or noncommittal responses to the Life Satisfaction Index.

Her mother was held in very high regard but was seen as not too strong, which was probably reflective of the family history, her mother's hospitalization, and the subsequent events. Religion was also highly regarded and very potent in her life space. Her father, on the other hand, was held in considerably lower regard, but seen as stronger than her mother. There was probably still a good deal of unresolved rage about her father's placement of her in the orphanage.

Lily's response to the concept "My Family" was in terms of her former nuclear family of mother, father, and siblings, so the concept was not highly valued or potent in her life space. As far as her husband was concerned, despite the problems mentioned, he was still somewhat positively evaluated, unlike her father, and this was an important factor in assessment and counseling planning.

"Death" was very negatively evaluated by her, though not particularly potent. Basically, she saw herself as still very much involved in life, even though she claimed it gave her some "hard knocks," and death could only be seen as premature and negative in her life space. The concept of dependency was more salient. Her responses to this concept were interesting; dependency was "quite happy" and "quite good," although "quite tense." One could surmise that this was an area of some conflict. Lily's marriage to a man considerably older than she suggests some dependency needs on her part. At the same time, however, one could not readily describe her as passive-dependent, given her many activities and her attempts at assertiveness training. Certainly there was a good deal of tension along the dependency-independence dimension, which led her to describe the concept as "quite tense." She was aware that she did not want to risk her husband's disapproval, but did not as yet see its connection with her dependency needs. She wanted in one sense to remain his lively "little girl," but was struggling with the "good/bad" little girl theme that went back into her childhood in her family and the orphanage. Therefore, the focus in counseling was on helping her see that it was acceptable for her to lead her own life and pursue her own interests—in other words, to assert more independence—without feeling that to do so required her husband's approval. This meant dealing with the underlying fears related to dependency. Given her positive self-concept and other capabilities, she was able to make a great deal of progress in a short period of time. She had some individual counseling sessions in addition to the group, and as will be seen, these were sufficient to move her much further along the road to ego integrity.

Margaret Larson, age 75, was one of the twin sisters in the group. She had moved from the Midwest just eight months before entering the group. She had not had any prior involvement in other activities at the senior center, to which she went at the suggestion of her physician, who had advised her to get involved in some outside activities in order to divert her excessive concern about the mild heart attack she had suffered a year and a half before. When she came to the center, the program director recognized her need to deal with the unrealistic anxiety in a more direct manner than trying "to get her mind off it." Also, since Mrs. Larson had not made any friends in the local area since her arrival, the newly forming group appeared to be ideal for her.

Mrs. Larson was born and reared in the county seat of a midwestern agricultural area. From a middle class home, she completed high school, and then went on to normal school, a two-year college that prepared young women for elementary and high school teaching. She later taught for a number of years in the local elementary school and married a school principal who later became school superintendent of a large district. After marriage, she left teaching and devoted herself largely to rearing her six children. She did, however, remain active in community affairs related to her husband's position. She claimed to be very happy in her dual role as mother and helpmate/representative for her husband in his professional career.

All six children moved out of the local area to various distant parts of the United States. When Margaret's husband died in 1970, her twin sister, a retired schoolteacher from Chicago, came to live with her. The heart attack Margaret suffered a year and a half ago prompted her to move east with her sister to be near one of her sons and his large family, which consisted of him, his wife, and ten children. She found herself very much involved in baby sitting, sewing, and knitting things for the children and also in caring for her twin sister who by then was somewhat immobilized by arthritis. Rather than taking her mind off her heart ailment, these family activities only served to make her more anxious. She wondered, for example, what would happen to her sister when she died. She knew that she had completely recovered from the heart attack. Yet she could not accept this emotionally, and what started as an anxiety reaction to the attack became a more generalized, chronic anxiety.

Her Life Satisfaction Index was very low, a score of only five positive points out of a possible twenty. The positive points related to making plans for the future, expecting some pleasant things to happen in the future, and noting that she felt she had got more of the breaks in life than other people she knew. She also thought that she made a good appearance compared to other people her age, as in fact she did.

However, on the negative side she saw the present as the dreariest time of her life, was much less happy than she used to be, felt old and tired, and basically was not well-satisfied as she looked back over her life. As would be expected, she indicated on the happiness question that she was "not too happy."

Her responses to the Semantic Differential questions revealed some other important points about her frame of mind. Most striking was her lack of response to the concept of "death." She wrote in, "Do not want to think about it. Refuse to answer." She had willingly and thoroughly completed all items related to every other concept in the test, but this one indicated something of the depth of her concerns about her own mortality. Figure 5-4 gives the spatial representation of her Semantic Differential responses.

"Religion" was extremely highly valued and showed the most potency of all the concepts. The remarkable thing about this was the fact that Margaret Larson was a devout Roman Catholic who believed in an afterlife and felt that she had not led a sinful life and that she was not likely to die in a state of mortal sin. Yet, it is clear that she was very fearful of death. This underlines the point made earlier in the book in discussing Peck's concept of ego transcendence that religion is no guarantee in our secular society against despair and the dread of death. Something of the depth of her religiosity was revealed by the fact that she came from an area in the middle of the Bible Belt

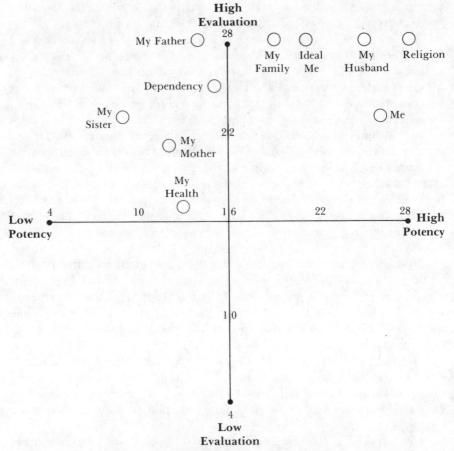

FIGURE 5-4.   *Margaret Larson's First Semantic Differential Test*

where fundamentalist Protestantism was predominant, yet she held to her faith stoutly throughout her childhood and her adulthood while there. She would become quite incensed when Fred Krauss would make jibes at organized religion in our group sessions.

Concepts of "Life" and "My Husband" were also extremely highly valued and very potent. The activity score on "Life" was also extremely high, and it was clear that she was quite actively trying to hang on to life. Her father, like her husband, was extremely highly valued, but not as potent a force in her life space. The concept "My Family" was also extremely highly valued and relatively potent, which was consistent with her current concerns and involvements.

"Ideal Me" was also extremely high on the evaluative dimension, "perfect" in the sense that she checked the highest scale positions on each of the evaluative objectives. Her responses to the concept "Me" indicated that she did not see herself as achieving these high ideals, even though her self-concept was not low or weak on the potency dimension. There was some discrepancy between self-concept and self ideal, indicating some problems with self-esteem, to which can be added the fact that she felt "extremely old." Although she felt she had not led a sinful life, she did not feel that she had led as exemplary a life as she should have.

Interestingly, the concept "My Mother" was not as highly valued as "My Father" and was also somewhat on the weak side of the potency dimensions. It was her father who was the strong one in the family (as was her husband) and who had the greatest influence on her adult ego ideal. The concept "My Sister" was low on the potency and activity dimensions. The sister was seen as somewhat weak, both physically and emotionally. This is interesting in light of the fact that "Dependency" was highly valued by Margaret on the Semantic Differential. The test has some projective value in that respondents often inadvertently give candid responses to items which, if put in the form of complete, direct questions would probably bring out defensive responses. In this instance she had inadvertently indicated that dependency was "extremely good," "extremely happy," "quite valuable," and "extremely fair." The irony was that she felt responsible for meeting the dependency needs of her sister and grandchildren whereas she would have liked to have some of her own dependency needs met, whether she could admit this to herself or not. She clearly saw her health as less than strong, and much of the anxiety she was feeling about it was probably related to her concern about who would take care of her. The anxiety was also related to her fear of death and probably to the traumatic effect her heart attack had on her self-concept, her very identity, as a strong, independent, responsible person.

With these considerations in mind, the focus of counseling Margaret was to be first on helping her cope with her immediate anxiety about her heart by identifying and dealing with some of her covert irrational ideas associated with the condition, and second, on the perfectionistic ideals and sense of responsibility she held. By confronting these rather grandiose ideas as illusions, and learning to allow for some of her own human frailties and failings she could reduce much of her distress and despair.

Clovis Flynn, Margaret's twin sister, joined the group because of her sister's involvement in it. She admitted to feeling quite dependent on her sister, and she thought that both of them might benefit from the group experience.

Clovis attended the same high school and normal school as her twin sister and she taught at the same school after her graduation. However, when her sister married she left the area to take a teaching position in Chicago. She never married, and when she retired she remained in the Chicago area until the death of her twin sister's husband, when she rejoined Margaret in the latter's house in their old childhood area. In the first few years of her retirement she busied herself socially with her acquaintances in the Chicago area, mostly other retired school teachers, and became heavily involved in taking courses at an art institute. She even won an award for a water color in a competition among students at the institute. She became progressively less mobile as a result of arthritis of the legs and hips, so she welcomed the opportunity to live with her sister. She did not need crutches or even a cane but she had to walk slowly and carefully. She also had difficulty sleeping because of the pain, lying awake most of the night and then sleeping late into the morning. She was painting a good deal less because she could not get outdoors as much to do her landscapes. She was feeling quite constricted and depressed in her life circumstances.

Clovis's Life Satisfaction Index was of course quite low, a score of only four positive items out of twenty. On the positive side, she did not agree that "this (was) the dreariest time of my life" and that most of the things she did were "boring or monotonous," and she agreed that she expected to have some interesting and pleasant things happen to her in the future and that she made a good appearance compared to other persons her own age. On the negative side, she felt that she was happier when she was younger, that she had not gotten the breaks in life, that her life could be happier, that she would change her life if she could, that she felt old and tired, that she "gets down in the dumps" too often, and so on. She also indicated on the general happiness question that she was "not too happy."

Her Semantic Differential responses (Figure 5-5) were somewhat at variance with her twin sister's (see Figure 5-4). This was a clear illustration of how the meanings associated with the same persons, objects, and environments can be unique to each person experiencing them.

Like her sister, she saw her mother as somewhat weak and "quite soft." But in some contrast to Margaret, she saw her mother as "extremely good," and evaluated her more highly than her father. The concept "My Family" was not valued anywhere nearly as highly as it was by her sister, probably because it was her family of origin. The concept "Religion" was not as highly

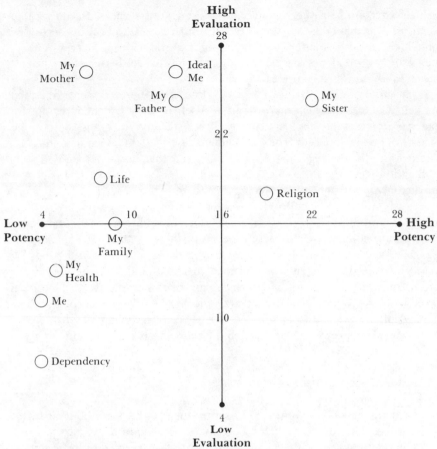

FIGURE 5-5. *Clovis Flynn's First Semantic Differential Test*

valued or as potent a factor in her semantic space as in her sister's. However, like Margaret, Clovis could not deal with the concept "Death." She wrote on the Semantic Differential form, "Very difficult to answer."

The most important feature of Clovis's Semantic Differential responses was the evidence it provided on her very low self-esteem. There was a great discrepancy between "Ideal Me" and "Me." Although her self ideal was not as high or perfectionistic as her sister's, it was still high while her self-concept was very low indeed. "My Health," "Me," and "Dependency" are all clustered at the low end of the evaluative and potency dimensions. Her health was seen as "quite bad" and "quite weak." She saw herself ("Me") as somewhat "worthless" and "quite sad," and also "extremely old." The concepts "Me" and "Dependency" are almost identical in the semantic space of Figure 5-5. She did, of course, see herself as quite dependent, and she did not like that, since she had a very poor opinion of the concept "Dependency." This is in marked contrast to her sister, whose test results indicated a rather high evaluation of that concept. Margaret might in fact like to be a bit dependent on Clovis, and if the latter could be brought to the point of meeting some of her sister's dependency needs, she might come to feel better about herself, less weak, and less incompetent.

The intervention plan for Clovis, in line with the integrative treatment model, was to build her coping skills and self-concept by encouraging supportive activities on her part toward her sister. By meeting some of her sister's dependency needs, she could view herself as less dependent and more competent. In this regard, it should be noted that her sister needed some "liberation from the functionalistic ethic." Clovis could serve as an agent or mediator in the process of freeing her sister from the need to perform faultlessly and selflessly for others (sister, children, and grandchildren) and becoming more accepting of her actual self. In addition, Clovis needed to incorporate some of her own past accomplishments as a part of her self-concept. She had, after all, supported herself throughout her adulthood, had performed responsibly as a professional teacher, and had the capacity to enjoy and gain a sense of accomplishment from her painting. The group would be the vehicle to support and encourage her to incorporate these aspects of her past into her self-concept, thereby reducing the discrepancy between self-concept and self ideal and enhancing her self-esteem.

Process and Evolvement of the Group

In the first session, after each of us introduced and spoke about ourselves, I indicated that my role would be that of a facilitator, that they would provide much of their own help and guidance. This seemed quite acceptable and understandable to them. In fact, the issue they were most concerned about and raised almost immediately was what the group should call itself. The members were all concerned that the group have some kind of identity in the senior center, but not one that would label them as a special problem group. The discussion brought out the fact that the group would be concerned about the problems of aging and that I was a teacher of gerontology. It was therefore decided to call it the "Gerontology Group," a name that they felt set them off somewhat and sounded "kind of scientific and impressive."

These matters took up the whole first session. In the second session and more emphatically in the third session, it became apparent that they were not comfortable or happy with the nondirective approach which I was purposely pursuing in line with the androgogy principle. They were exhibiting what Berne (1963) has called "structure hunger" (1963:159). They wanted more structure and more direction on my part, and they were feeling its absence acutely. Two members of the group (Fred Krauss immediately after the second session and Lily Silvano after the third session) strongly urged me to take a more active role, though for different reasons. The problem was exacerbated by Sylvia Rolfe's attempts to dominate the group discussion, largely in terms of her own experiences and knowledge rather than her problems. Although she was quite pedantic in this, Fred seemed for a while to respond to the more intellectual tone Sylvia would lend to the conversations and would interject his interests in science and technology. Agnes Morgan, the most depressed and distressed member of the group, observed in the middle of the third session that while she found much of the conversation interesting and planned to stay in the group because she liked the socializing, she did not think the group could offer her much help in dealing with her depression. At this point, I agreed with her interpretation that neither she nor anyone else in the group would gain much help with their problems if the discussion remained at the impersonal level it had assumed.

The objections Fred had raised with me individually about my nondirective approach was that I was "the teacher," regardless of my comment that each of them was a teacher. Therefore, I should actually instruct them in gerontology. Needless to say, he had misinterpreted the purposes of the group, and I reinterpreted what they were. However, it was not until the fourth session, which turned out to be pivotal, that the real purpose hit him with an impact that caused him some dismay and anxiety, as will be shown. Lily Silvano, on the other hand, was much more perceptive in noting that she and Agnes Morgan, who were particularly concerned with their own immediate family situations, would not gain much if I did not begin to help them directly with their problems. I made arrangements with her for individual counseling sessions, and I indicated that I would also guide group discussion much more directly toward each person's self-identified problems.

It should be mentioned here that the androgogy principle has to be tempered with the requirements of a cognitive approach. I knew that I would have to become somewhat more directive, because the cognitive approach is in large measure didactic and it often includes specific tasks and other goal-directed activities. There was already some empirical evidence that one cognitive approach, Rational-Emotive Therapy, could be used with older persons in groups (Keller, Croake, and Brooking, 1975), but it involves a more didactic, directive stance on the part of the group counselor than does the integrative approach. In integrative group practice, there is need first to establish the androgogy principle by identifying the members as teachers and healers in their own right. Then the counselor has to assume the role of facilitator for the first few sessions so that the members can establish their relationships and experience their impact on the group process. After this has taken place, usually in two or three sessions, they have no difficulty accepting some structure from the counselor. In fact, they welcome it, even if they do not specifically ask for it as in this group. It is important, however, that the counselor introduce this structure unobtrusively in the form of suggestions and with the flow of the group process. When the cognitive therapy framework is introduced in this way, it provides older clients with the tools and guidelines for helping one another and with the structure they frequently crave in groups and other ambiguous social situations.

The fourth session turned out to be the critical one in the development of the group. It was in that session that it became painfully clear to the members that they were there to work on their own individual problems as well as those of others, and that I was going to keep them at that task. I began the session by telling them that we were going to try an approach to identifying and handling their problems that had proved useful with other groups. I indicated that the crux of this approach was that thinking can affect emotions in a positive or negative way, that negative thinking can produce negative emotions. I mentioned that among older persons anxiety is often created by the idea that if something is potentially dangerous or detrimental, one should be terribly worried and upset about it. Often an exaggerated fear of not being able to care for oneself, of becoming dependent, can cause unnecessary and debilitating anxiety. I indicated that there were certain steps and techniques they could use to combat such common but irrational ideas and that the techniques would demonstrate that they could really determine how they would feel about an event or circumstance. Their behaviors too could be enhanced by the same techniques, because thinking, feeling, and acting were all intimately tied up with one another. If they could change certain irrational ideas, they could also change their emotions and behaviors.

I then outlined the "A-B-C" approach to Rational-Emotive Therapy (RET) as developed by Ellis (1974:55–66). Simply put, at point A there is an activity, action, or agent that disturbs the person. At point C the person experiences the negative consequence of the process initiated by A, usually a negative emotion or behavior. Most people assume that it is A, the activating event, that makes them sad, enraged, frustrated or whatever. However, according to RET and other cognitive therapies, it is what the person thinks or believes (B) about A that determines C. Thus, point B intervenes between the event or agent (A) and determines the kind of consequences (C) the person experiences. If the belief (B) is irrational (iB), it will lead to an irrational or inappropriate consequence (iC) and the person will experience A as extremely stressful or catastrophic. Ellis often talks about "catastrophic thinking" and notes that irrational beliefs tend to state or imply a should, ought, or must, an absolutistic demand or dictate that the individual must obtain what he or she wants (love, acceptance, respect) and if it is not received this is perceived as a catastrophe.

An example with which the group could readily identify was a situation in which an older person was turned down as a potential partner in a card game at a senior center because he had played rather poorly in a prior card game. Given that activating event (A), the person with an irrational belief (iB) about it might experience it as catastrophic (iC) through the following sequence of "self-talk": "It's awful to be turned down like that. It was really a rejection of *me* and I can't stand that, because I really do try hard to get along, to be nice and agreeable. I really should be able to play cards better. I wish I was more competent in things like that, and then I would be much more acceptable as a person." This type of self-talk or subvocal set of ideas, which expressed an irrational belief, thus led to an experience of the event as a very hurtful one and to further self-downing thoughts that eventuated in a feeling of depression. In short, the event was interpreted as a *personal* rejection.

In the RET system the person is taught to dispute (D) the irrational beliefs (iB's) and bring about a new evaluation (E) of the event. Thus, there is an A-B-C-D-E sequence involved in the change process. After bringing the irrational belief (iB) to awareness, it is openly disputed (D), first by the counselor, then by the client, and is then replaced by a rational belief (rB). In the example given, the client was asked what evidence there was that he was rejected as a person. The client readily recognized that it was his card-playing that was at issue. He further recognized that these same people were highly competitive card players who had been quite accepting and friendly toward him as an individual on other occasions. He therefore replaced his irrational belief with a rational one that was represented in the following sequence of self-talk: "It's not really pleasant to be turned down for a card game with them, but it's not awful. I do happen to be a poor card player, but then I really don't get much satisfaction out of the game. It's really the socializing that I like, but they don't do much socializing when they play." Thus, the inappropriate or irrational consequence (iC) of feelings of personal rejection and consequent depression could have been replaced by a rational consequence (rC) of feelings of mild but momentary displeasure. Of course, underlying this example there might have been a deeper and more pervasive belief on the part of the client that he should always be accepted by others under all circumstances, and such a belief would have to be disputed repeatedly over a longer period of time. However, the method was quickly picked up by members of the group. The method should be modeled first by the counselor in either group or individual counseling, but it takes very little time (usually one session) for the clients to learn it. Of course, the members of the group were more readily able to identify and dispute irrational beliefs in others than in themselves.

The clients were also given a "homework" assignment in the fourth session in which they were asked to study a section of the book *A New Guide to Rational Living* (Ellis and Harper, 1977:197–201) for discussion and work at the following session. The assigned section contained a list of the major irrational beliefs or ideas that have repeatedly cropped up in RET practice over the years. They are viewed as the basis for most emotional and behavioral problems, and they can be summed up as follows:

1. It is a dire necessity that you must be loved and accepted by others for almost everything you do.
2. You must always act with competence and adequacy or you are a failure.
3. Certain people are bad and evil and they should be severely blamed or punished for their wrongdoings.
4. It is terrible and horrible when things are not the way you would like them to be.
5. Human misery is caused by external circumstances and other persons, and you have no ability to control your own sense of misery.
6. You must get terribly upset and frightened because something *might* be dangerous or fearsome.
7. You must have immediate gratification and pleasure whenever possible, so it is best to avoid or put off unpleasant things that require attention.
8. Since something once strongly affected your life, it should do so indefinitely.
9. You should have certain and quick solutions to life's problems, or life will turn awful and horrible.
10. You should be able to achieve maximum human happiness by passively engaging in things that give you approval rather than by becoming committedly involved in what truly interests you.

Although we did not go over these points until the fifth session, I did point out when I distributed the copies that they would serve as guidelines for much of the work we would be undertaking as a group. I also indicated that some of the points would be more appropriate for some of the members than others. For example, point 6 in the guidelines spoke directly to the anxiety experienced by Margaret Larson ever since her heart attack, and it guided much of the work with her. Points 1 and 5 dealt very directly with development of an internal locus of control and thus were relevant to work with all members of the group. Point 2 set the tone for work with regrets, despair, and disgust over past events and circumstances with a view to greater acceptance of themselves and their lives.

After handing out the section for study, I recapitulated the A-B-C method and then asked them to think about and volunteer experiences or events that seemed to provoke anxiety or depression in them. Almost without hesitation, Sylvia Rolfe volunteered the fact that she was quite anxious at the beginning of each session of the group. Lily Silvano immediately noted that Sylvia talked a great deal in the group and seemed to be quite confident, not anxious, about her opinions and ideas. Sylvia responded that her apparent confidence was much more of a "front" than real. She admitted that she knew she talked too much in the group, and she did not understand it because she never did that with her own family. She recalled that as a child and right through her teens she had always been on the quiet, unassertive side in the context of the family, but not in the school or community.

Lily pursued the issue by asking Sylvia why she thought that was so, and without a moment's thought Sylvia replied that she was sure it was because of her mother. At this point tears came to Sylvia's eyes, and she went on to say that nothing she ever said or did seemed to satisfy her mother. She was criticized for how she cared for her younger siblings when they were so frequently left in her charge, and she was often criticized for any kind of self-expression in that her mother called her opinions and ideas foolish, headstrong, or childish.

By this time, Sylvia was sobbing uncontrollably, and Clovis Flynn who was sitting next to her, put her hand on Sylvia's arm to comfort her and remarked that it must have been awfully hard for her as a young girl to have all that responsibility and to receive criticism instead of recognition. At this point, Fred Krauss, who was becoming visibly uncomfortable as Sylvia cried, interjected, "Hey! We shouldn't be talking about this. There are a lot of happier, interesting things to talk about." He then mentioned an article he had read in the newspaper about some of the miraculous changes nuclear energy could bring to our lives in the future.

His efforts to change the subject were ignored by the women. Instead, Agnes Morgan, the most depressed member of the group, remarked that she was amazed that Sylvia had such doubts about herself because she seemed so intelligent and self-confident when she talked in the group. Agnes added that she could sympathize with Sylvia's unhappiness as a child because she knew how that felt. She also admitted to feeling "relieved" that others in the group were experiencing some of the same problems she had with sadness and dissatisfaction with herself.

It can be seen why this fourth session was so important for the group. Not only did we begin with the more structured cognitive approach, but Sylvia's openness about her anxiety, insecurities, and unhappy relationship with her mother brought about a number of changes in the group. As a result, Agnes came to feel more a part of the group, and Clovis, who was the apparently helpless, dependent one of the twin sisters, showed herself to be capable of very appropriate, empathic support for others. It was doubly significant that she displayed this support toward Sylvia, since Clovis had missed the second and third sessions probably because of Sylvia's near-monopolization of the discussion in the first session. (Margaret Larson had explained her sister's absence to the group on the basis of a flare-up of her arthritis, but at the close of the third session she had intimated to me that she and her sister were both bothered by the excessive talk of "one person" in the group.) Thus, Clovis and the other group members came to a new understanding and tolerance of Sylvia. Further, Sylvia's expression of vulnerability and emotional need dispelled the mixture of awe and irritation the group held toward her. She was considerably less dominant in the group thereafter.

On the other hand, Fred Krauss was clearly shaken up by the fourth session. He beat a very quick retreat from that meeting and did not show up for the next two. When he missed the fifth session the members of the group asked why, but none of them had seen or spoken to him in the interim. Just before the start of the sixth session I saw him look into the meeting but he moved quickly down the hall. It appeared as though he not only wanted to look in but also wanted to be seen. When the session started I raised the question of why he had not attended. Again, none of them had spoken to him in the interim. I then speculated about the possibility that something in the fourth session might have upset him. Sylvia Rolfe quickly noted that he might have been upset by her crying and display of emotions at that time. She went on to say that he might have been "scared off" and that she would like to talk to him and reassure him that it would not happen again. I said that the group was intended to work on personal problems and that would necessarily involve some very emotional things, so I did not see any way that we could reassure him in that respect. The others agreed with this by comment or gesture, and Sylvia observed that she, too, agreed with it after having thought about it. She suggested, instead, that she talk to Fred in terms of the group's wanting and needing him to participate, but with a clear understanding of the intent and orientation of the group. Since she was in fact closest to him (she had had a number of conversations with him following earlier sessions), the group felt it was appropriate for her to speak to him. He did come back for all the remaining group sessions, and also saw me in individual sessions in which we discussed the meaning of his departure and return to the group. I should note that all the other members of the group attended all the remaining eleven meetings from the fourth session on.

The fifth session began with a general discussion of the ten points for living rationally which had been distributed the week before. Each of the members of the group claimed to be in agreement with all the points without exception. I attempted to encourage any possible disagreement, and I was frankly surprised that some of the points, which argued strongly against highly moralistic attitudes, were not found objectionable by at least one or two of the group members. However, they all seemed to indicate that the points made a great deal of sense to them on the basis of their own experiences in life.

We then moved on to the homework assignment from the previous session, which was to bring in and discuss personal experiences that provoked anxiety or depression in them. The first to volunteer was Margaret Larson who said that she was becoming progressively more anxious about driving her car. When I asked her if she knew why she said she was sure it was a result of the heart attack. She admitted her fear that she would have another attack and that it could happen while she was driving under the stress of dealing with traffic. The doctor had said there were no restrictions on her driving, which was important to her for shopping and her almost daily visits to her children and grandchildren. But she still had the fear.

I then illustrated the A-B-C elements according to RET in Margaret's situation. The activating event (A) was driving her car, which appeared to lead to the consequence (C) of anxiety. However, it was her belief (B) that she might have a heart attack which led to her anxiety. She admitted that her belief was an irrational one (iB), given the medical evidence she had. However, the disputing of this irrational belief or thought was not easily accomplished. Her more general anxiety about having a heart attack was worked on during a number of sessions. One technique was to have her calculate the probabilities of her actually having an attack under various circumstances. She was asked to make notations after each trip with the car or some other anxiety-provoking event about the probabilities of an attack. Beck has recommended this technique in dealing with anxiety (1976:253–254). Margaret reduced the probability of having an attack while driving from 1 in 10 to 1 in 10,000. The technique of imagery (Ellis and Harper, 1977) was also used with her. She was asked to imagine the worst thing that could happen when she drove her car. She imagined having an attack and dying, and she imagined that as a result of this her twin sister, Clovis, would be left alone and uncared for. Actually, much of her sister's presumed dependency was a pseudo-dependency, and this became evident to everyone in the group as Clovis began to show her considerable emotional strengths. Thus, some of Margaret's anxieties were dispelled by the group process as well as by the cognitive techniques.

Although I would use various cognitive techniques, such as negative or positive imagery, with clients in the group or individually, the clients used the basic A-B-C approach and worked on identifying and disputing their own and others' irrational beliefs. They picked it up quite easily and used it in a supportive rather than attacking way when disputing the faulty beliefs in others. One interesting exception to this was when the technique of "vicariation" (Raimy, 1975) was used to help Agnes Morgan be more assertive in opening communications with her son-in-law. She was asked to observe Lily Silvano (who had received assertiveness training) confront me as I modeled the son-in-law using such stratagems as avoiding eye contact, lowering my head, and mumbling incomprehensibly. Lily persistently and politely insisted upon the fact that she wished to talk to me about certain matters, and it would be better if we looked at one another as we discussed them. Agnes later tried this with some success with her son-in-law, and she said Lily helped her the most by demonstrating that one can be gentle and polite and still be assertive.

Since they now had a method (A-B-C) for dealing with their own problems, as well as an understanding and a list of prevalent kinds of irrational beliefs (Ellis and Harper, 1977), the group members felt more secure about what they could do on their own, without the group and without me. Consequently, at the end of the fifth session the group agreed that it would continue for ten more sessions, or a total of fifteen. In addition to their feeling more secure as a result of the method they learned, they also noted that the fifteenth session would bring us to the beginning of summer, when group members would begin leaving town on trips, visits to relatives, and so on. As it turned out, these fifteen sessions provided some significant change in certain individuals and some promising beginnings for others.

The middle and later sessions included a good deal of reminiscing on the part of the group members, and since most of this was positive in nature it proved to be of real therapeutic value. Frequently, a client would relate some accomplishment or achievement from the past. This would be used by me or by other members of the group later on to enhance the self-image. Thus, when a client would display a self-denigrating belief (B), other members of the group would recall that client's prior positive reminiscence about achievement and competence as evidence to dispute the irrational, self-downing belief.

In the last few sessions, the group appeared to be spending more time discussing personal concerns and issues of a more philosophical nature. These concerns seemed very much akin to what Yalom (1975) has described as "existential factors," factors he found will emerge and become paramount for certain psychotherapy groups. In order to check out whether this was the same phenomenon he had observed and to follow the direction the group seemed to be taking, I shared with them the five existential factors Yalom had identified and delineated:

1. Recognizing that life is at times unfair and unjust.
2. Recognizing that ultimately there is no escape from some of life's pain and from death.
3. Recognizing that no matter how close I get to other people, I must still face life alone.
4. Facing the basic issues of my life and death, and thus living my life more honestly and being less caught up in trivialities.
5. Learning that I must take ultimate responsibility for the way I live my life no matter how much guidance and support I get from others (1975:84–85).

There was emphatic agreement by the group members with these points. They nodded their heads vigorously as I read the points off, and when we got to discussing them, several of the clients noted how long and hard it had been to come to terms with the ideas represented in the points. Some of them commented that it was still very, very hard to accept the points even though they knew they were true.

There were several remarkable aspects to the group's response to these existential factors. One was that the factors seemed to emerge from the group in its later sessions without prompting from me. Secondly, rather than being put off by the potentially grim nature of Yalom's five points, the clients accepted them and attested to their validity. The notion, for example, that a person must face life alone regardless of how close he or she gets to other people is rather hard to think about, much less accept. This suggests that older persons in a supportive context are willing and able to grapple with the problems and issues of meaning in their lives. For the most part, the members of this group did not give evidence of having a philosophical frame of mind in their earlier years. Yet, these philosophical, ontological concerns were on their minds and they were willing to talk about them in their later years.

Outcomes of the Group Process

In order to give some ideas of the kinds of gains one might expect in the type of group approach just described, each of the clients will now be assessed as they were at the end of the counseling process. There were, of course, important areas in which no significant gains were made, and these will be mentioned, too.

Sylvia Rolfe made some rather significant gains in the course of group counseling. The group experience helped to dissolve much of the intense loneliness and isolation she felt at the beginning. She had some friends (fellow members) as a result of the group, and for this she was highly appreciative. Much of the work with Sylvia in the group and in some individual sessions was combatting the feelings of guilt and worthlessness engendered by her mother. She began feeling less guilty about the hostile thoughts she had toward her mother as the group members kept pointing out to her that she had not acted on those thoughts, and that was what counted. They reiterated that she had in fact done a great deal for her mother, who had exploited her by playing on her guilt feelings.

In the several individual counseling sessions I had with her I tended to stress the unrealistically high expectations she had for herself, which were largely a function of the incorporation of demands made by her mother on her. I stressed that her feelings of worthlessness were not only a result of her acceptance of her mother's denigrating attitudes and actions from the past, but more immediately of the unrealistically high standards (self ideal) she had for herself. Even though these standards were largely engendered by her mother, it was she, Sylvia, who generated her own sense of shame for not meeting them. I also indicated the negative impressions she made when she applied these same critical standards to others, which resulted in her pedantry and her relative intolerance or sensitivity to their opinions. I further indicated that much of this one-upmanship was a result of her own feelings of low self-esteem. Given her good intelligence and desire to change, Sylvia could understand and accept these interpretations without a great deal of defensiveness.

Her score on the LSIA had been 6 at the beginning of counseling; it went up to 11 at the end of the fifteen sessions. Two of the items on which she now expressed positive responses were: "The things I do are as interesting to me as they ever were" and "As I look back on my life, I am fairly well satisfied." On three other items she had changed her response to a positive one from a no answer or doubtful one. On the general happiness scale, she indicated that she was "pretty happy." This was the same response she had given in the beginning of counseling, but she claimed that she was happier than she had been in the beginning. However, she did not feel that she could say that she was "very happy" in the general sense. Given the fact that the scale had only three levels (not too happy, pretty happy, and very happy) it was not picking up the gradation of change she felt she had experienced as a result of counseling.

Sylvia's responses on the Semantic Differential Test at the end of counseling showed some changes from those given at the beginning. The counseling plan called for a reduction in the discrepancy between the self-concept and the self ideal. As can be seen in Figure 5.6 (as compared to Figure 5-1), the "Ideal Me" is somewhat lower on the evaluative and potency dimensions. For example, Sylvia indicated that she would ideally like to be "quite good" rather than the more unrealistic and difficult "extremely good" she had checked off for her ideal self at the beginning of counseling. At the same time, her self-concept ("Me") improved in both evaluation and potency, thus indicating an enhancement of self-esteem.

The concept "Mother" showed some small change in a higher evaluation. This could be explained by the fact that in the counseling process Sylvia had worked through a good deal of the hostility she felt for her mother. She was less obsessed by thoughts of her mother and perhaps had a more mature, accepting attitude toward her at the end.

The concept that showed the most change in the course of counseling was "Life." It was much more highly valued and potent at the end of treatment than it had been at the start. This can probably be explained by the increased enjoyment and reduction in loneliness that she was experiencing at the center as a result of the friendships established with the members of the group.

Agnes Morgan had also been pleased with the group and the friendships she made in it, but she did not show the same positive change that Sylvia and others had shown. One will recall that Agnes had not thought that the group would be therapeutic for her, although she thought she would enjoy it from a social viewpoint. This in fact seems to be what happened. Her LSIA score went up only to a 2 from the score of 1 she had at the beginning of the group, still an extremely low score. The only response she changed in a positive direction on the index was to agree with the statement, "I would not change my past life even if I could." On the general happiness question she said that she was "not too happy," as she had at the start of the group. Since she had not filled out a Semantic Differential Test at the beginning of counseling, she was not asked to do so at the end.

Agnes Morgan did not have any individual counseling, largely because

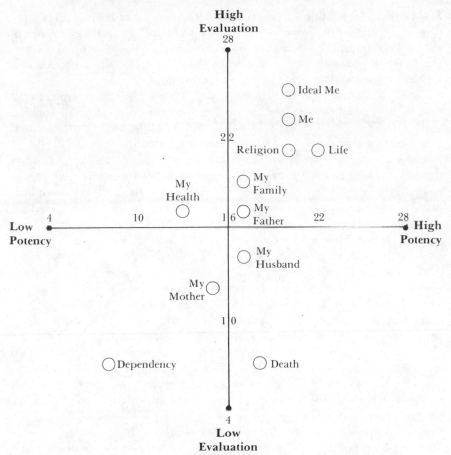

FIGURE 5-6. *Sylvia Rolfe's Final Semantic Differential Test*

she hoped that the family counseling that she, her son-in-law, and her daughter would undertake would change the stressful and depressing situation in their home. Unfortunately, her son-in-law was resisting the idea of participating in family counseling, and the disturbed family situation remained the same. Although Agnes could get some momentary relief and support when discussing the situation in the group she still had to go home to it.

On the other hand, Agnes claimed to be feeling somewhat better about herself, if not about her life situation. She now knew that she could participate in a group without having to excuse herself or ingratiate herself by doing menial tasks as she did in other activities at the center. She noted that others had problems and insecurities just as she did and that she was not unique in this respect. She seemed pleased that others would listen to her and heed her observations or advice, and she seemed in general to be less self-denigrating.

Fred Krauss, like Agnes Morgan, did not show much change on his Life

Satisfaction Index, but his score had not been very low to begin with (a score of 11 went up to 12). However, he claimed to be feeling better as a result of the counseling experience, and he responded to the general happiness question by stating that he was "pretty happy" at the end of counseling, whereas he had checked off "not too happy" at the beginning.

Fred made some clear gains in the group process when he returned to the group after he had dropped out for two sessions as a result of his discomfort with Sylvia's crying and the emotional tone of the whole fourth session. When he returned, he allowed some of his own nurturing feelings, the "soft" part of himself about which he had been somewhat disparaging, to come to the fore, which enabled him to be empathic with and supportive of the others. Although he was still a little uncomfortable about others' emotional displays in the group, he did not withdraw and he appropriately offered his support. As a result, he seemed to be experiencing closer relationships with other persons in the center as well as in the group.

Fred's relationship with his wife did not appear to be getting more intimate in the course of counseling, but he claimed to be satisfied with it since his social relations at the center were becoming more gratifying to him. Overall, Fred seemed to gain more from the group process than he did from individual counseling. Although he requested individual counseling, it amounted to only four sessions, and it consisted largely of reinforcing his first efforts at accepting the more emotional, nonintellectual aspects of the group and the "soft," nurturing side of himself. It was also clear that there were still some unresolved areas he was not yet prepared to get into. He still had some strong regrets about not getting due recognition for his past accomplishments and that there was not enough time for new ones. He did not fill out the Semantic Differential form on the concept "Death" at the beginning of counseling and he failed to fill it out at the end. His responses on the final Semantic Differential Test are given in Figure 5-7.

In addition to omitting responses to the death concept, Fred repeated some noteworthy responses in the aftermeasure from the initial measure. On both "Me" and "Ideal Me" he described himself as "extremely young." It was clear from his comments that he viewed old age as synonymous with being decrepit or sick. He talked constantly of the future and how he would like to be alive to witness all the new technological and scientific advances. Indeed, it was as though science and technology were his religion, a concept he still held in very low-esteem on the final Semantic Differential Test. The significant point was that he was so characteristically future-oriented that he had developed little capacity for appreciating and living in the present, a necessary skill for truly successful aging. Further, there was always the potential for despair because there would be so little time left in his life to see the wondrous future he envisaged.

Fred's last Semantic Differential Test does indicate some of the gains he made with respect to his self-esteem. It can be seen that there was less

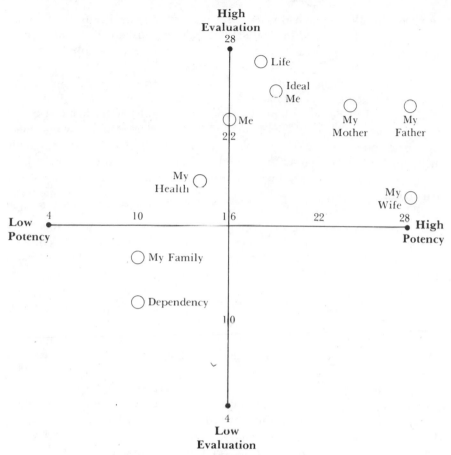

FIGURE 5-7.   *Fred Krauss's Final Semantic Differential Test*

discrepancy between the "Me" and the "Ideal Me" in the final measure than there had been in the first one (Figure 5-2). In both measures, his ideal was changed in line with his self-concept, about which he was more accepting. As a result of his acceptance of these nurturing aspects of himself he made some noteworthy gains in the interpersonal sphere, if not in the intrapersonal sphere of his life.

Lily Silvano in a sense had the most going for her. She was the youngest and most energetic, and she had a rather good self-concept and self-esteem, though she was clearly confused and distressed about her marital situation. There was a cultural expectation in Lily's background (French-Canadian) and her husband's (Italian) that the wife should perform certain functions in the home and that the central focus of her life should be in the home. Given the fact that Lily had no children plus a great deal of energy and interest in things outside the home, she was feeling guilty and constrained in her marital relationship. When she had taken assertiveness training before she entered the group she had hoped to be able to change her husband's attitudes. This was not working out as a strategy; she claimed he was too stubborn and she was feeling extremely frustrated in the process.

My focus with her in our several individual sessions and in her group sessions was to help her see that it was acceptable for her to pursue her own interests and to become more independent without her husband's explicit approval. I focused on the fact that she was creating most of her own feelings of frustration by insisting upon the belief that her husband *must* change his attitude. In terms of the A-B-C formula, the activating situation of her husband's intransigence (A) did not lead directly to the consequence (C) of her frustration and distress. It was her belief (B) that he should not be that way.

This strategy enabled Lily to maintain her high level of activity outside the home while reducing her feelings of stress and frustration about her husband's attitude. There was some residue of guilt about her acting so independently without his approval, but the other members of the group and I would identify and allay these feelings when they arose. Consequently, when Lily chose to work outside in the garden while her husband was there, even though he made it clear that he felt a woman's place was in the house and a man's was outside, he finally came to accept the fact that she was going to do it even if he disapproved. He made the best of the situation, and they began to develop mutual interests and topics of conversation as a result of their "outside" activities.

Acceptance of the fact that she was largely responsible for her own feelings through her beliefs or ideas (the crux of the cognitive approach) was an immensely liberating and enabling experience for Lily. Her Life Satisfaction Index went up sharply from 8 to 18. This indicated a very high level of morale, well above the norm for her age group. Her general happiness measure went up from "not too happy" to "very happy." It is most likely that the gain was not that dramatic, but that the first LSIA was uncharacteristically low due to circumstances at that time.

I must emphasize that Lily had a good self-concept to begin with, so that she was free to gain a great deal as a result of the cognitive approach in her group and individual counseling. Consequently, Lily's self-concept and self ideal did not change appreciably in the final Semantic Differential Test, but the concept "Life" was greatly enhanced, as shown in Figure 5-8.

In the before period (see Figure 5-3), "Life" was not very high in evaluation (19) and in potency (14). In the after period, it was more highly valued (23) and more potent (23). She was clearly enjoying her myriad activities and enthusiasms without the nagging guilt and frustration associated with her husband's attitudes.

Margaret Larson fared rather well as a result of group counseling alone. The initial focus in counseling was to help her deal with her unrealistic anxiety with respect to her heart condition. The use of imagery techniques in

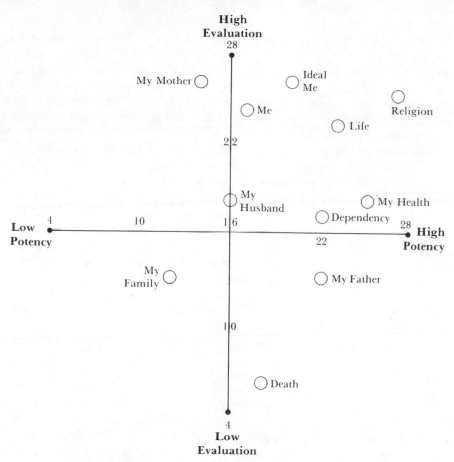

FIGURE 5-8. *Lily Silvano's Final Semantic Differential Test*

which she would try to imagine the worst that could happen has already been explained, as was the effort to have her calculate the realistic probabilities of a new attack. These seemed to help, but her greatest gains appeared to be related to her growing recognition of the emotional strength and independence of her sister, who provided her with a new source of emotional support. This was an apparent reversal of their roles in that Margaret was convinced at the beginning of counseling that her sister was an emotionally dependent person whose arthritis would make her a quasi-invalid. However, as Clovis became interested in and committed to the group, she managed to attend all of the meetings despite her arthritis, whereas she had earlier missed a couple of meetings ostensibly because of the arthritis. This demonstrated for Margaret that Clovis was not an invalid; Clovis's effective support of others in the group also showed that she was not such an emotionally dependent person. This served to allay Margaret's anxiety about what would happen to Clovis if Margaret were to get sick or die. Further, Margaret was able to indulge some of her own dependency needs with her sister's support. Clovis and the other members of the group also disputed her belief that she must do all of the things she was doing for the children and grandchildren, such as baby sitting, sewing, and knitting. This belief seemed to be related to the perfectionistic demands she put on herself to be a good grandmother, just as she had always striven to be a perfect wife and helpmate to her husband and mother to her children.

As Margaret began to realize that she was putting unrealistic demands on herself, she began to relax more and to become less anxious. She was encouraged by the group not to baby-sit for her grandchildren if she felt tired or indisposed. More than anything else, it was the reduction in her anxiety that made for positive change in her overall morale. Her Life Satisfaction Index score went up from 5 to 9. Thus, she was more in the normal range on the LSIA later, whereas she had been on the demoralized end earlier. Her response to the general happiness question at the end of counseling was "pretty happy" as contrasted with "not too happy" when she started.

Her responses on the Semantic Differential Test at the end of counseling also showed some changes. As Figure 5-9 shows, her "Ideal Me" was three points lower on the evaluation dimension (see Figure 5-4). She reduced her perfectionistic standard to "quite good" instead of "extremely good" and "quite fair" instead of "extremely fair." The discrepancy between her ideal self and her self-concept was thus reduced and her self-esteem was enhanced. As her anxiety about her heart lessened, her view of the concept "My Health" was scored higher on the potency dimensions. The concept "My Sister" was also higher on the potency dimension as a result of her recognition of Clovis's emotional strengths.

Margaret Larson was still fearful of the concept "Death" and again refused to fill out the Semantic Differential form on it. Had she expressed an interest in individual counseling, this issue might have been handled. However, it was not raised by the group members and I chose not to bring it up in our sessions since Margaret's anxiety about it would have been high and the group's ability to handle that anxiety was doubtful. However, it is clear that she made some gains on the basis of the group counseling alone. Her anxiety had abated a great deal and she seemed to be more relaxed and self-accepting.

Clovis Flynn fared even a little bit better than Margaret as a result of the group experience. Clovis's Life Satisfaction Index went up from 4 to 11. Thus, she was in the normal range on morale and life satisfaction. Among the positive items she checked off after counseling which had been negative before were: "I am just as happy as when I was younger," "The things I do are as interesting to me as they ever were," "I have made plans for things I will be doing a year or month from now" and she did not "get down in the dumps compared to other people." In addition, her general happiness measure went up from "not too happy" to "pretty happy."

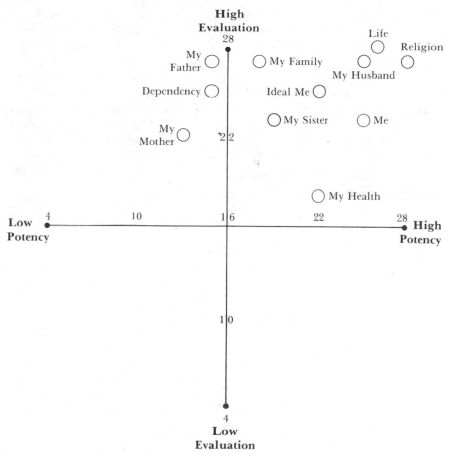

FIGURE 5-9. *Margaret Larson's Final Semantic Differential Test*

It has already been noted that Clovis was showing much greater emotional independence and supportiveness, both in her group interactions and in her relationships with her sister. In addition, she was becoming much more productive in her painting, which she had allowed to languish before her involvement in group counseling. She brought in some of her paintings for the group to see after very heavy efforts at persuasion by group members. She was quite modest about her work, but it genuinely impressed the group. They were very congratulatory about her work, especially Sylvia Rolfe who painted herself and whose work was displayed in local restaurants. Sylvia freely attested to the superiority, both aesthetically and technically, of Clovis's paintings. This proved to be a strong impetus to Clovis's productivity. As a result, she showed less concern and talked less about her arthritic condition. She ventured out more to paint landscapes, which she preferred over the still lifes she had resorted to when she kept herself more housebound. Her Semantic Differential Test responses after counseling reflected many of these changes. Figure 5-10 illustrates the changes when compared with her responses before counseling (see Figure 5-5). The most striking feature of the before and after comparison is the dramatic rise of the self-concept on both the evaluation and the potency dimension. It is also close to the "Ideal Me," which means a distinct rise in her self-esteem. The evaluation of the concept "Life" was also greatly enhanced. She was obviously enjoying herself more, as evidenced by her Life Satisfaction responses as well. She even responded to the concept "Death." Although it was naturally low in evaluation and somewhat potent in her psychological life space, she had apparently moved to a position in which she could face it. In the pretest, she had not responded to the concept "Death" but had noted instead that it was "very difficult to answer."

The concept "Health" was seen as somewhat stronger and more highly valued in the posttest, a reflection of her greater physical and artistic activity

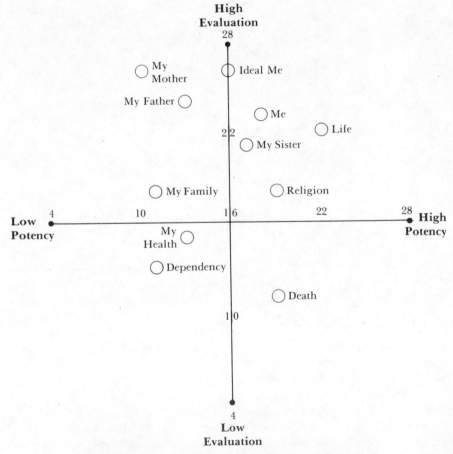

FIGURE 5-10.   *Clovis Flynn's Final Semantic Differential Test*

and her reduced rumination about her arthritic condition. Another concept that changed was "My Sister." Her sister was still highly valued in the after period, but she was seen as less potent than before. This, of course, was a reflection of Clovis's greater awareness of her sister's dependency needs and the realistic limits of her sister's emotional and physical strength.

All in all, Clovis, along with Lily Silvano, made the most dramatic progress in life satisfaction and ego integrity in the group, and this progress was accomplished entirely through the group process alone. The fact that such gains can be made in a relatively short period of time and without intensive, long-term, individual counseling for clients like these is noteworthy. Of course, there were major unresolved aspects of the integrity/despair issue remaining in all of the group members, but one gets the impression that the balance was tipped somewhat in the direction of ego integrity in several of the members.

One reason for this was that they did not attempt to deal with material and concrete environmental deficiencies in their lives via the group. Where these deficiencies existed, they were already being handled by the Office for Aging counselor or elsewhere. There are other possible ways of handling these deficiency needs so that groups can get on with the integrity/despair issue, and these will be explored in Chapter 7. However, another possible explanation for the gains is that the integrative approach, together with the supportive group experience, provided the group members with a method and some tools for dealing with the core issues of their lives.

CHAPTER SIX

Extended Counseling

Opportunities and Settings for Extended Counseling

Since we have defined extended counseling as lasting six months or longer, it is perhaps difficult to think of any opportunities for such psychotherapy in anything other than a private setting. Yet private therapy is not likely to be selected by most older persons, either because they are not motivated or knowledgeable about it or, more likely, because the cost is simply prohibitive for their limited incomes. There are now some older people who can obtain private psychotherapy through health insurance coverage, and there are a few affluent older persons who might be receiving such treatment.

Outside of private counseling, the setting most likely to be identified as appropriate for extended counseling is the outpatient mental health center or clinic. There has been relatively little use by older persons of outpatient mental health services. However, it is likely that there will be more use of such programs as communities develop mental health services involving outreach, day care, and related services. For example, there are currently mental health programs that provide not only outreach services to bring aged clients into the center but also regular visits by psychiatric nurses and social workers to homebound elderly persons suffering from depression or another diagnosed mental disorder. These visits may be continued for two or three years.

Other human service programs also offer opportunities for extended counseling for the elderly. Family service agencies have provided extended counseling for older adults and their families. Although this practice has not been extensive, it is clearly growing. In various cities throughout the country, Jewish Family Services, for example, has developed caseloads of older clients, many of them referred from Jewish community centers and other Jewish federation agencies.

Institutions such as nursing homes can certainly provide opportunities for extended counseling, both individual and group. There have been instances in nursing homes where mentally competent, though physically limited, older persons have benefited from extended counseling. On the basis of their own extensive experiences with this population, two practitioners have reported that "psychotherapy proper is a viable treatment modality with institutionalized elderly" (Ronch and Maizler, 1977:275).

I should like to stress again the abundant opportunities that are available for counseling the elderly in senior service centers. The group counseling described in Chapter 5 was of course in such a center. Although it lasted for only fifteen sessions, it should be clear that such groups could choose to continue for an extended period of time.

What is called for is adaptability on the part of the counselor to the norms and circumstances of the setting. In the case of senior centers group activity and programming are the norm, so extended group rather than extended individual counseling is the very first option the counselor should consider. In addition to the circumstances and norms of the setting, there are other advantages to the group approach. For one thing, just hearing the problems of other group members is often very helpful. The member finds that his or her own problems are not unique. Also, by acting as auxiliary counselors for others, members of the group learn how to combat their own self-defeating attitudes and behaviors. The fact that there are several persons in addition to the group leader who can reflect and provide feedback about such negative attitudes and behaviors makes it more likely that the individual member will take such information seriously and do something about it. The force of group approval can be an important incentive in this regard. The potential for greater emotional support than is possible through the single individual counselor is also a definite plus.

The use of a group may be the only way to get a troubled individual into counseling. It is highly unlikely that the three members of the group described in Chapter 5 would have gotten involved in individual counseling if they had not had the group experience first. Furthermore, it should be noted that the choice of group counseling over the individual approach, or vice versa, is frequently unnecessary. I have found that a combination of both methods is often best, at least in the short run. It might be best to start with a group, for the reasons just outlined, and then to have members become involved in individual counseling as the need and interest for such counseling becomes evident in the group process.

The case illustrations of extended integrative counseling in this chapter are all instances of individual rather than group counseling. It just so happens that I have counseled individuals for more extended periods of time, and it seems possible to achieve greater depth and thoroughness through individual counseling in dealing with issues of meaning in the lives of individuals.

Differential Objectives and Methods in Extended Counseling

One of the problems with short-term psychotherapy is that the clients are terminated from treatment before the intended changes are complete or can be observed by the counselor. Wolberg (1967) has noted that integrating changed self-concepts in behavior and the emotions is a long process, and it is only the long-term therapist or counselor who is apt to see these changes during the "working through" period. There is no question that there were some changed self-concepts in the group described in Chapter 5, and there was some indication that a few of the group members were on their way toward integrating these changed self-concepts into their behavior and their emotional lives. Frank (1974) has noted that long-term follow-up data seem to indicate that clients and patients continue to change and improve for years after short-term therapy. However, in the absence of a follow-up evaluation six months or a year later it is not possible to see the results in terms of changed behaviors and emotions. Most working counselors do not have the time and money to do such systematic follow-ups, so they have to be satisfied with what evidence is available at the termination of treatment.

The whole issue of changed self-concept is central to the integrative approach. If we look again at the treatment continuum of the integrative model (Table 4-1), we can see that stabilizing of self-esteem is an objective of short-term treatment, but we would hope that ultimately a changed self-concept would be integrated into the personality so as to lead to ego integrity. One of the differentiating objectives of extended integrative counseling is the achievement of "cognitive mastery." In short-term counseling, cognitive techniques tend to be used for coping purposes rather than mastery. In extended counseling significant cognitive restructuring has to take place.

Another objective of extended counseling is reduction in the functionalistic ethic (Objective 10), which means a reduction of unrealistic self-evaluations. This lays the groundwork for a significantly changed self-concept. Finally, the overriding goal of extended integrative counseling is significantly higher life satisfaction and ego integrity (Objective 12). How these objectives are met is dependent upon a range of cognitive and other methods.

In extended integrative counseling there is more emphasis on complex approaches to cognitive restructuring. I have already mentioned the cognitive techniques of distancing and decentering (Chapter 4). Distancing is "the process of regarding thoughts objectively" (Beck, 1976:243). A person who has the irrational automatic thought that another person is out to harm him or her and equates this thought with reality is showing an inability to "distance." If, on the other hand, the thought is regarded as a hypothesis or inference rather than a fact, the person is distancing well.

Decentering is a more pervasive and important technique in extended counseling. In fact, according to Piaget, decentering is a process begun in childhood in which the person abandons the egocentric position until gradually "the self is freed from itself and assigns itself a place as a thing among things, an event among events." Piaget sees this as a noble accomplishment, "the unacknowledged moral mainstream of his work" (Dinnage, 1978:24).

The ability to see oneself as an "event among events" in an almost cosmic sense is a necessity for any degree of tranquillity in the last years of life. It is the ego transcendence dimension of ego integrity (Peck, 1968). The person who continues to see him/herself as the center of the universe is destined for despair and dread of death. We can look at decentering as a technique or method as well as a process. It has been called "the technique of prying the patient loose from his pattern of regarding himself as the focal point of all events" (Beck, 1976:244). It can be used with various types of disorders such as depression, anxiety, and paranoid states in which a major distortion in thinking is the person's continuous attempt to personalize events that have no causal relation to him or her. An anxious man who hears an explosion thinks that his house has exploded. A depressed woman blames herself for having a handicapped child. A paranoid man hears someone curse and assumes that the person is cursing him.

Distortions of this type are commonly involved in the type of despair experienced by many older persons. They may feel that "luck was against them," which makes luck a personal thing rather than the random occurrence it is. Because persons in despair are depressed, they have a tendency to blame themselves and feel guilty for past events for which they had no personal or causal responsibility. Examples of decentering and distancing for this type of distortion will be provided in the case illustrations to follow.

Since short-term counseling concerns itself mostly with the "here-and-now," the current problems of clients, less use is made of reminiscence than in extended counseling. The reminiscences of positive accomplishment in the past were used to enhance the self-concept and self-esteem of clients in the present with the group in Chapter 5. The same use of reminiscence can be continued in extended counseling, but there will be ample opportunity to use reminiscence in greater depth because it will tend to increase over time.

Giambra (1977) found that there was no greater frequency of *thinking* about the past by older persons than by younger ones, but Cameron et al. (1977-1978) found that older persons *talked* more about past events in their lives. Butler and Lewis (1977) have taken this natural penchant of older persons to talk about their pasts and used it to develop what they call "life review therapy," that is, "putting memories to work in individual and group therapy." Butler (1963), however, warned that the life review process can have negative consequences leading to panic, guilt, and depression as well as positive consequences. With older persons who are already grappling with despair, many reminiscences are apt to be colored by distorted depressed thoughts in which they blame themselves for events in the past for which they were not really responsible. This is the depressogenic error of generalization (Beck, 1976) but is projected into the past rather than applied to the present. I call this "retrospective generalization." At any rate, it is clearly an example of personalizing from a depressed frame of mind, and it calls for decentering. One very helpful technique for dealing with this is "disattribution," which involves teaching the client to stop attributing all blame to himself by recognizing the role played by fate and others in the events (Rathjen, Rathjen, and Hiniker 1978). Another restructuring technique is the A-B-C disputation technique of Ellis, described earlier. The application of the restructuring techniques of distancing, decentering, disattribution, and the use of reminiscence and life review therapy will be specifically identified and illustrated in the two cases to follow.

There is an important caution regarding the use of certain techniques in life review therapy. Feelings of guilt and remorse may be reactivated in the life review process when the person has done some actual wrongs in the past to a loved one, friend, or relative. Often the loved one is dead, which makes it impossible to rectify the event or to be forgiven. In this instance, the client is not falsely attributing guilt on the basis of a distorted retrospective generalization and the counselor cannot appropriately use the technique of disattribution. To do this would tend to make matters worse by making the client attest to his or her guilt all the more, as well as reducing confidence in the counselor.

In this instance, what the counselor has to do is hear the client out, fully and completely, to provide the necessary catharsis. Then, the counselor has to work first with the intensity of the guilt and self-blame. In this regard, restructuring techniques such as Ellis's A-B-C or Beck's disputation of dysfunctional thoughts can be used to replace the client's belief that what was done was horrible, unforgiveable, and inhuman with the more rational and less self-denigrating belief that it was unfortunate and regrettable. This, however, is an interim approach, because ultimately the client is going to have to come up with an alternative way to evaluate his or her past. So, whether or not the reduction of intensity takes place by virtue of these techniques, the client will finally have to apply new standards of self-evaluation to old situations. What this calls for is a restructuring of the client's cognitions or beliefs about what was done in the past in light of a new frame of reference for viewing the self in the present, a new self-concept. This is an ultimate objective for all clients in extended integrative counseling.

Whether they are dealing with guilt and remorse from the past or with self-denigration in the present, a changed self-concept will be necessary.

What this means in practice is that the clients have to take a more realistic and compassionate view of themselves. They have to accept their limitations as human beings, accept the fact that they were and are fallible. This is quite different from the defense mechanism of denial. One would not, of course, attempt to expose the use of denial by an older person if it serves a purpose. But in instances where the individual is *aware* of his or her involvement in some transgression, the mechanism of denial is not working. In those cases, one works on exposing the futility and debilitating effects of guilt, showing how it creates self-hate, and also on helping the client to be more compassionate toward himself or herself by recognizing human fallibility.

In this regard, I have found Theodore I. Rubin's *Compassion and Self-Hate* (1975) to be very helpful in alleviating guilt and despair over the past and I often assign readings from his book to clients. The following excerpt spells out the essence of the kind of self-acceptance the clients will need:

> Whatever I do is an expression of me at any given time. Therefore, whatever I do *is* one of my signatures, that is, a particular signature of me, at a particular time. It is *my* best because it *is* me at the time that I do it. In terms of myself and in my nonjudgmental, self-accepting, compassionate frame of reference, my heart is my best heart, my head is my best head, my thought is my best thought, and this action in this now of mine is my best action.
>
> Indeed, best, good, bad are qualitative words that are applicable only in a judgmental frame of reference applied from the outside to me. I refuse to judge me. I am happier assuming that what I do expresses me the best way I can express me in the moment. If my energy and time are spent observing and examining my thoughts, feelings, choices and actions, I do so not in the service of judgment or to assign value to performance. It is for the purpose of better understanding me so as to better help myself to still further self-acceptance [Rubin, 1975:205].

Thus, in a situation in which a client believes that a past action was horrible, unforgivable and *inhuman*, that belief would be replaced by the belief that he or she was indeed human, and that this in fact accounted for the error or transgression in the first place. So, reminiscence is used therapeutically to apply new, more compassionate, and human self-evaluations to old regrets and self-disgust, which are at the heart of despair.

To recapitulate the uses of reminiscence in the integrative approach, the following three points should be made. First, reminiscense is used supportively by enabling the person to identify with past achievements and positive events so as to enhance self-esteem and fortify the self-concept. Second, it can be used to dispute retrospective generalizations, the negative distortions of the past which make for much of the despair. Rational disputation and disattribution are some of the cognitive techniques used to do this. Third, it is used for self-re-evaluation, by applying new standards of self-evaluation to old situations that are brought up in the life review process.

The re-evaluative use of reminiscence can be made to meet Objectives 10 and 11 of the integrative continuum: to reduce functionalistic self-evaluations and clarify alternate self-evaluations. The more the client applies functionalistic performance standards to his or her past, the more likely it is that those standards will continue to be applied in the present. Therefore, working through those evaluations retrospectively in reminiscence should serve the purposes of re-evaluation in the present. The new self-evaluation can of course be worked on in the here-and-now as well as in reminiscence, through bibliotherapy and various other cognitive procedures.

It should be recognized that the functionalistic ethic is difficult to deal with. Not only is it a deeply held value of most older persons in our society, but it also fuels much of the purposeful activity in the social roles people perform throughout most of their lives. This point is very important from both a theoretical and a philosophical point of view. There has been some concern expressed in the gerontological literature about the possible negative effects of alienation and uncertainity in the lives of older persons because of the lack of norms generally associated with the social roles of their younger years (Rosow, 1973). Although there is considerable explanatory power in this highly socialized view of old age, its pervasively negative view of loss of role should not be taken as the only interpretation.

Bengtson has offered the following alternative interpretation:

> Decrease in specific social requirements and expectations can also be interpreted as a gain in *freedom*. I would argue that the loss of norms (and roles with which they are associated) represents a potential *opportunity* to pick and choose among alternative behaviors—a degree of freedom from societal restraints that is perhaps greater than at any other period of the life cycle. One often hears about the negative consequences of normlessness in old age: what I am suggesting is that this decrease in normative specificity also implies freedom to those who choose (and have the capability) to exploit it [Bengtson, 1973].

I shall use the expression "alternative disputation" as a generic term for disputing the functionalistic ethic and self-evaluation and replacing it with an alternative view of self, essentially one based on compassionate self-acceptance regardless of performance, very much as stated by Rubin. Values clarification procedures can also be an important adjunct to the disputation process, as will be illustrated in the last case presented in this chapter.

One argument that can be used in alternative disputation is the argument of greater freedom, as posed by Bengtson above. In the beginning of counseling, freedom is usually the last thing on a client's mind. Clients are usually concerned with the lack of purposeful activities and with reclaiming a basic sense of competence. However, as counseling progresses, and especially in extended counseling, there is apt to be a growing appreciation that for the first time in their lives, or at least since early childhood, they do not have to be bound by social expectations and restraints. At this point, alternative disputation can be effective. The term "disputation" is not intended to imply that the self-re-evaluation phase of counseling is taken up entirely with formal, overt disputes and debates about the functionalistic ethic. In fact, much of the change comes about subtly through the client's identification with a different frame of reference as reflected by the counselor, so that the counseling relationship is a major vehicle for change in conjunction with the cognitive approaches. As the counselor reflects a more compassionate, humane, and equitable view of self, the client is able to incorporate this view into his or her self more and more over time.

These, then, are the objectives, major methods, and techniques in extended counseling according to the integrative approach. They will be illustrated in the cases to follow.

Illustrations of Extended Counseling

Several points should be made about the two cases selected to illustrate extended integrative counseling and the methods and techniques just described. They represent respectively a young-old (62) and an old-old (77) person. The younger woman illustrates a number of transitional problems from middle to old age that are becoming increasingly prevalent among the "new" young-old. This woman is still employed at age 62, although that is the age at which women are entitled to Social Security. However, like more and more women of that age today she neither desires nor can she afford to give up her employment. Also, her marriage is problematic in a way we traditionally associate with younger adults rather than older or even middle-age persons. Finally, she is developmentally beyond the "empty-nest" stage, but in reality she still has an older adolescent at home, as well as unmarried adult children who return home periodically for various lengths of time. Thus, her case would appear to represent some contemporary problems we would not associate with a person her age in more traditional circumstances. She also reflects some rather "modern" values in that she voluntarily sought out psychotherapy.

However, it is important to recognize that she, like Lily Silvano in Chapter 5, represents the imminent older client group coming into our community network of senior centers, mental health settings, and social agencies. Over the next few years more and more of them will be coming to us with these "modern" views and with expectations that are much more informed about the kinds and quality of service they seek. We have to be prepared for these "new old," and that is why the following case was selected for presentation here.

The first case of extended counseling represents a working through of the total continuum of the integrative model. Virgina Plummer, a 62-year-old woman, was seen at a center for psychotherapy over a period of twenty months, on a weekly basis for the first year and every other week for the last eight months. Mrs. Plummer had medical insurance from her employment in a large photography studio that provided coverage for outpatient psychotherapy. She was married, though currently separated, and the mother of four children.

She was referred to the center by her family physician because of depression. In her first session at the center she appeared to be somewhat anxious as well as depressed. She reported that her doctor had given her sleeping pills because she was waking up in the early hours of the morning and was unable to go back to sleep. She said that she was afraid of having the pills in the house in her current frame of mind. When questioned, she admitted that she was afraid she might take an overdose. She said she had not had suicidal thoughts at all in the past, but this feeling came on her a few days ago after the doctor had given her the pills. She had not made any plans nor even imagined how to go about taking the overdose. She asked me whether I would advise that she get rid of the pills, because she did not believe in principle in using medication if it was not needed for a physical condition. I replied that it would be quite consistent then for her to get rid of them, especially since their presence in the house was creating anxiety for her. She seemed quite relieved about this and said she would dispose of them when she got home.

I then said that she must have been feeling quite distraught and agitated to have the sleeping and other difficulties she described. Although she spoke slowly and deliberately (which turned out to be her characteristic way of speaking), she said she was both agitated and depressed as a result of her family situation. The most upsetting aspect was her marriage, but her children were also a source of great concern to her.

About two years earlier her husband, a high school English teacher, took a new teaching post in a midwestern city, which paid considerably more than his teaching job in the East. He accepted the job offer on short notice in the late summer and then went to the Midwest by himself just before Labor Day to start the job and find a place for them to live. However, Mrs. Plummer found out from a former colleague of her husband that Mr. Plummer had met a woman at a national teachers conference that summer with whom he had spent the whole conference, and that the woman, also an English teacher, and about twenty years younger than Mr. Plummer, taught in the same school in which he had just taken a job.

Mrs. Plummer confronted her husband with this information on the telephone when he called home to indicate his progress in locating a home for the family (which at that time included their 18-year-old daughter, Jill). Mr. Plummer did not deny the truth of the information but protested that the woman did not really mean anything to him. Mrs. P. then told him that she and Jill would not join him there. Either Mr. P. would have to leave the job and come back east or his wife would need to know that the "other person," as she always referred to her, had left the area. She said she did not want to speak to him again until he did something about the situation.

Mrs. P. said she was so hurt that she did not know whether she could ever reconcile with her husband, even if he did meet either one of her conditions. Mr. P. called back a few days later and said that he had been thinking over what she had said. He did not want their marriage to break up, but he could not give up his new job because his age would make it extremely difficult for him to get a different teaching post. He promised to break off his relationship with the other woman and try to convince her to move elsewhere. However, he was not sure he could do so, since she had quite a few years of seniority in that school system. In the meantime, Mrs. P. would have to take his word for it that the relationship with this woman was over. During that time he wanted to be able to stay in touch with Mrs. P. and their children. He wanted to be able to talk to Jill when he called and to come home when the whole family got together at Thanksgiving, Christmas, and other occasions. Mrs. P. said she did not trust him in terms of his relationship with the "other person," but she felt she could not deny the children the opportunity to talk or visit with him. So, for the past two years he had come east when the family got together several times a year on those special occasions. She said she had not mentioned the "other person" to the children, and they thought the reason for the separation was the difficulty presented by Mr. and Mrs. P's jobs and Jill's education back east.

Mrs. P., who had been a commercial photographer before her marriage, had found her current job shortly after the discovery about her husband and the other woman. She felt that she had to establish her financial independence, regardless of what would happen with her marriage. She felt fortunate to get even a part-time job in her field when she was just about to turn 60. She had, however, kept up with her photography, and examples of her work had sufficiently impressed her employer that he offered her all he could then, which was part-time at a rather modest pay. Her husband supplemented this with regular payments in an amount upon which they had agreed. Mrs. P. said that her husband had at least been trustworthy in this regard.

Another reason Mrs. P. would not consider leaving her home was that Jill, a freshman in a local college, was doing well in school, where she had a scholarship, and Mrs. P. did not want to jeopardize this. Also, her oldest child, a 34-year-old daughter, lived nearby with her husband and their two children.

Over the first few sessions, Mrs. P. told me that she was the youngest in a family of three girls and one boy. Her mother had died about two years earlier and her father about two years before that. She described her family as warm and loving.

She completed high school and two years of training in photography at a technical institute in her home city. She moved east in 1942 with a girlfriend to take a job as a technical photographer in a local war plant. It was toward the end of 1942 that she met Mr. P., who was home on leave from the Air Force. In 1943 they married, and in 1944 their first child, Carrie, was born.

Mr. P. was discharged toward the end of 1945, and began college on the

G.I. Bill. Their second child, Paul, was born in 1951, the year Mr. P. got his master's degree in English and his first teaching job in a local high school. Another child, Virginia, was born two years later. The last child, Jill, was unplanned, born in 1958 when Mrs. P. was 39.

Mrs. P. said she was feeling quite guilty about her children. She thought Jill suspected she had not been planned, because she was never a happy child. Although Jill had always done well at school, she did not do so well socially. She was quite a bit overweight and seemed to have few friends. Paul, 27, and Virginia, 25, were also causing Mrs. P. a lot of concern, because they seemed to be living a kind of "hippie" existence that their mother found rather alien and distressing. When Paul was 19, he had gone to college for a couple of years, but it was mainly to allow him to stay out of the Vietnam war. As soon as that danger had passed, he left college to live in a commune in the far west. Just before her first session, Paul had shown up at Mrs. P's house very depressed because he had just broken up with the young woman he had been living with in a communal arrangement for the previous two years. He was looking for a job in this area and wanted to stay with his mother until he could "find himself." Mrs. P. said that Paul was well-meaning and had promised to try to "straighten Jill out" in terms of her social life and weight problems. However, Mrs. P. felt that he was just one more burden under the present circumstances.

Another problem was Virginia, who was living with a young man in the East Village of New York City, where they were trying unsuccessfully to make a living by selling the jewelry he made and the paintings she made. This was apparently a pattern with Virginia; from time to time she would come drifting home from various parts of the country after trying out different artistic commercial enterprises, usually with a young man, but without any success.

Mrs. P. said she was feeling like a failure as a parent. The only child who did not seem to have any major problems was Carrie, who seemed to have a stable, happy marriage and two well-adjusted children. The others, however, were a source of considerable guilt. She felt responsible for the fact that Paul and Virginia had not yet settled down and resentful that they kept coming back to her for financial and emotional support. She said she was feeling tired and drained and simply wanted to think of herself for a change. It was these feelings of burden, resentment, and what she thought of as selfishness that made her feel guilty.

As upsetting as her problems with the children were, what really brought her into psychotherapy had to do with her husband. He had come home for a few days the previous week, when all the children got together at Mrs. P.'s house. Shortly after he had left a woman called and asked to speak with him. When Mrs. P., who had answered the phone, told the woman her husband had already left the woman asked to speak to Paul. Mrs. P. said Paul looked very sheepish as he tried to reassure the woman that Mr. P. had indeed left.

Mrs. P. was sure this woman was the "other person," and this infuriated her. The woman's "gall" to call Mrs. P.'s home when her family was together and then to ask to talk to Paul was too much. She felt betrayed again by her husband, who had assured her that his relationship with this woman had long before ended and that she would soon be taking a new job out west that same fall.

After some attempts at evasion, Paul admitted that the caller was the "other person," and that he had met her when he visited his father on his way back east. When Mrs. P. said she could never forgive his father for this and could not remain married to him under these circumstances, Paul said he was sure there was nothing serious between this other woman and Mr. P. She was a "nice enough lady," but not nice enough for Mr. P. to risk his marriage. When Mrs.P. said she did not care about that and would divorce Mr. P. regardless, Paul became agitated and told her that he and the other children would be very upset if there were a divorce and they were unable to see their parents together again, all over some "unimportant affair."

This lack of support and understanding from Paul further enraged and hurt her. She now felt that she had no one to turn to. Her sense of outrage at the "other person" and her betrayal by her husband worked on her mind and she was very agitated for the next few days. It was in this context that she became very depressed and was unable to sleep or eat adequately.

The first session provided Mrs. P. considerable relief because she was allowed the opportunity for some catharsis, which had been denied her because of Paul's reaction and because she did not want to share the problem with the other children until she was able to sort things out and come to some conclusions. In addition, she was relieved by my support of her desire to get rid of the sleeping pills. On subsequent visits, Mrs. P. said she had had no recurrence of concern that she might harm herself and that she had thrown out the sleeping pills immediately after her first counseling session. After the first few sessions, in which she was able to express her feelings of anger, frustration, and inadequacy, Mrs. P.'s appetite returned, although she still had problems sleeping. She expressed a desire to learn more about herself, her marriage, and how she should plan for the future.

She indicated an interest in taking the Semantic Differential Test and some other tests in the hope of understanding herself and her current circumstances. She responded to the tests very well and welcomed feedback from them. Her responses on the Semantic Differential Test are illustrated in spatial form in Figure 6-1.

The discrepancy between self and ideal is the most important aspect of Figure 6-1. Mrs. P.'s self-esteem was understandably low at this time, but there were several items in the ideal self measure that would have made for self-esteem problems under any circumstances. These items were on the following scales: worthless/valuable, happy/sad, strong/weak, and tense/relaxed.

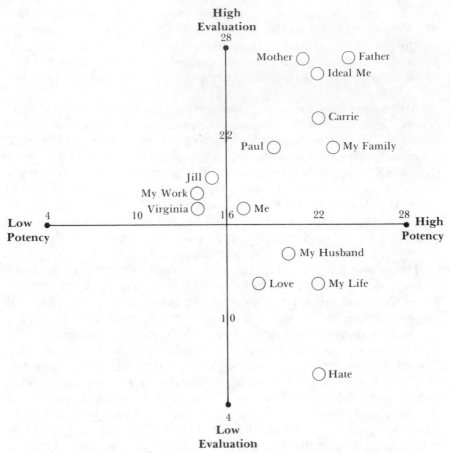

FIGURE 6-1. *Virginia Plummer's First Semantic Differential Test*

Mrs. P. wanted to be "extremely valuable" but saw herself as "quite worthless." This she explained in terms of her feelings as a wife; her husband had chosen another woman over her. She also felt worthless as a mother because of the problems her children were having. Thus, in terms of two major roles in her life, mother and wife, Mrs. P. found herself lacking. She also wanted to be "extremely happy" while she was "quite sad," and she wanted to be "quite strong," whereas she felt "quite weak." Her mental association with the strength issue was that she felt she should have been and should now be strong enough to handle her children's problems effectively without feeling burdened or overwhelmed. She also wanted to feel "extremely relaxed" rather than the way she did feel, "extremely tense." She said she had been feeling tense over her marital situation for so long that she was probably reacting in an exaggerated way in saying that she wanted to be "extremely relaxed."

Another item that provides some insight into her frame of mind was the hot/cold dimension. She marked "quite cold" in describing herself and "quite hot" for what she would like to be. When asked about this she said that she was feeling quite cold and unloving as a result of her husband's actions. She also had feelings of wanting to meet her own needs while it was clear that her children needed her attention and concern. This she saw as cold and selfish.

At the same time, she wanted to be "quite tough" but felt "slightly soft." She explained this by saying that she wanted to be tough with her husband and the "other person," even though she would ordinarily not value toughness. She felt, too, that she would need the quality of toughness to see her through the hard times ahead.

Another indicator of her current poor morale was her description of herself as "slightly old," whereas she wanted to be "quite young." She also wanted to be "quite light" but described herself as "quite heavy." This was due to the fact that she was overweight and quite dissatisfied with her body image. Although she had pretty hair and pleasant facial features she did look tired and drawn, as well as overweight.

Her responses to the concept "My Life" were clearly a function of her feelings of failure in her marital and family roles, and she was also quite bitter in her comments about love in light of her failed marriage, the only serious love relationship in her life. "My husband" was low on the evaluation dimension, as one would expect in this situation. The concept "Hate" was also very low in evaluation, which might seem natural. However, there could be no question that Mrs. P. was feeling a great deal of rage against her husband and the other woman. Other people who have felt the same rage might evaluate "Hate" somewhat more positively on the Semantic Differential Test because they accepted the anger they were feeling in the process of working it through rather than deny it. I was concerned that much of Mrs. P.'s depressed mood might be due to her inability to accept the rage she felt. This was an area I planned to explore in the counseling process.

She had put "Jill" and "Virginia" at the lower part of the potency scale, explaining that she did not see either of them as particularly strong emotionally. In fact, she was somewhat surprised to see that Virginia, her namesake, was so close to her in the semantic space diagram. After seeing it she said, "I guess we are more alike than I ever realized." When I asked how they were alike, she said, "We are both somewhat artistic by nature . . . and vulnerable."

The concept "My Work" was relatively low in potency and not at all highly valued on the evaluation dimension. Mrs. P. had mentioned to me in her first session that she very much wanted to find some time for herself so that she could do some creative photography. She wanted to put out a book of photographs with accompanying text on eighteenth-century houses that were located in the midst of commercial and industrial buildings built in the nineteenth and twentieth centuries. The contrasts in style and era as well as size could be emphasized by the proper use of shadow, and such photographs could vividly convey a sense of the sharp dislocations which took place in history, while still retaining the quality of durability in the houses themselves. Mrs. P. was much more articulate when she discussed her creative photography than ordinarily. Her characteristically slow and deliberate speech pattern turned out to be an important ingredient in her self-concept and in the dynamics of her relationship to her husband. At any rate, her response to the concept "My Work" came as a surprise to me in view of her enthusiasm for creative photography. When I indicated my surprise, she said that she was not thinking of her creative photography when she responded to that concept but to her job, which provided her with money she needed, but about which she was not really enthusiastic.

A final point of great importance in Figure 6-1 are the extremely high evaluations of "My Mother" and "My Father." They were both seen as "extremely valuable," "quite happy," "extremely good," and "extremely fair." Her father was seen as somewhat more potent than her mother because of Mrs. P.'s description of him as "quite tough" in contrast to her mother as "slightly tough." Mrs. P. said that her parents were warm and loving as well as strong and firm. She could not think of a better combination of qualities in a set of parents and considered herself quite lucky in this respect. But she felt badly about her own parenting when she thought of it in terms of her parents. The same thing was true of her parents' marriage, which she described as loving and "true." When I asked her what she meant by "true," she said that first, they remained true to each other (she was sure there was no hint of infidelity in their lives) and that she was sure they were truthful with each other. There were no big lies in their relationship, as there had been repeatedly in her marriage for the past two years. All in all, she felt very depressed about the way her life had gone when she compared it with the lives of her parents. She said at one point, "I want to be able to look back on my life and say I did a good job with my marriage and family, as my parents could when they were my age. But I can't and I don't foresee when I will ever be able to."

It was evident that Mrs. P.'s parents were central to her ego ideal. The extremely high standards they set as parents and marital partners would be very difficult to equal or even approach for most people, and Mrs. P. clearly felt that she was a failure in regard to both marriage and parenting. So, as major elements in her ideal self-concept and as standards for self-evaluation, her parents symbolically would be the source of considerable discrepancy between her ideal and her self-concept, and therefore of continued low self-esteem.

Dealing with this in counseling was a long and delicate process, and it was evident it would be so from the very beginning. Even if her image of her parents was a highly idealized one, it could not and should not be undermined in the counseling process. It was quite possible that she had not yet reached "filial maturity," as Blenkner (1965) described it, because there did not seem to be the identification or acceptance of any of the negatives about her parents which must have been there at least to some small degree. At any rate, the process and techniques used in dealing with her poor self-image vis-à-vis her parents took time and care.

Mrs. P. was found to have a very low internal locus of control score on ten items adapted from the Rotter Test, with three responses that were internal and seven that were external. In short, she felt she was very much determined by external forces and events, at least at this period in her life.

Her cognitive mastery score was as low as it could be, 3 out of a possible 12. Her responses indicated that she was very much bothered by the fact that there were things in her life over which she had no control. She also had a very high score on the functionalistic ethic scale, a total of 15 of a possible 16. She strongly agreed with the two following statements: "Unless I feel that I have accomplished or done something that other people value, I feel quite worthless," and "When you are no longer a contributing member of society by functioning in such roles as worker, parent, etc., you can't really feel that you have any value as a person." She strongly disagreed with the statement, "A person's worth does not depend on how good a citizen, parent, or worker he or she is, but simply that he or she is a human being." And, in her least extreme functionalistic response, she simply agreed with the statement, "A person isn't worth much when he or she is no longer able to carry on as a productive member of the community."

Mrs. P. had a very low score of 3 out of 20 on the Life Satisfaction Index. Her responses were consistent with her general mood and her locus of control measures, so that it would be safe to say that Mrs. P. was much closer to a state of despair than to ego integrity at the beginning of counseling.

During the first few counseling sessions the focus was initially on reducing Mrs. P.'s anxiety concerning the medication and possible suicidal impulses, then on having her vent her anger and her deep sense of hurt and disappointment. This was very much in line with the integrative treatment continuum in that the first efforts were aimed at reduction of stress.

Thereafter, Mrs. P. was more depressed than anxious and tended to talk mostly about her failure in marriage and parenting. At this point it was necessary to sustain her morale and buttress her self-esteem, for she was being very hard on herself. My efforts here were in the nature of reminding her of the fact that she had been functioning responsibly and with a good deal of competence over the past two years, while her marriage was in a state of limbo and uncertainty, in handling the house, her daughter Jill, and her job.

This pretty much followed the Input B part of the continuum, where the emphasis is on emotional support and sustaining coping strategies. But it soom became apparent that the locus of control factor required attention, for Mrs. P. had reached a state in which she felt any real change in her life circumstances were completely dependent upon her husband rather than herself. This became apparent after the first sessions in which she vented some of her outrage at her husband and the "other person." She did not again threaten divorce, as she did to Paul when the telephone incident occurred. In fact, things stabilized at a level similar to the period preceding that incident. Basically, that was an extended period of indecision on Mrs. P.'s part as she waited for some word from her husband that the other woman had left, or that he was coming home, or that he had made some other decision.

It became evident, then, that the issue of her marriage, which involved establishing some sense of control in Mrs. P., should be the first priority of counseling. She was also feeling some concern that she could not handle her additional burdens at home with Paul present in addition to Jill. Both the marriage and the children involved a locus of control issue, so it was possible to use similar techniques in dealing with them. The more distant issues of alternate self-evaluations, which involved work on her beliefs concerning the standards her parents set, as well as finding a more compassionate alternative view of herself, would have to come later. This was so not only because the treatment continuum indicates that kind of progression but also because the problems were actually presenting themselves in that sequence.

At this point I introduced her to the A-B-C approach and how to identify thoughts or beliefs that led to dysfunctional emotions and behaviors. This approach was focused on her current lassitude in awaiting some kind of decision from her husband.

In our fifth session I raised the question as to why she was waiting for a decision from her husband. She asked, "What else can I do? Doesn't it really depend on him, whether he wants to keep the marriage or the other woman?" I noted that it might depend on her as to whether she wanted the marriage, under the circumstances. She responded "How can I really decide that until I know how he feels about me?" I said that we seemed to to be back at the same place - waiting for something from Mr. P. She again asked, "What else can I do?" I replied that there were several options that we might explore. First, she could continue waiting for something decisive from him, but it had already gone on for two years. Second, she could try to force him to make a decision within a specified period of time or file for divorce. Third, she might simply begin divorce action without any time stipulation, as she had threatened in her interchange with Paul. She said, "Oh, I wouldn't do that!" I asked why not, and she replied, "I can't imagine breaking up the marriage on my own whim."

I pursued this line of discussion with her, indicating that I was not favoring divorce but that we needed to look for some possible irrational beliefs that might explain her unwillingness to consider divorce unilaterally in the face of the current untenable but interminable situation. It was clear that she had a number of "musts" and "shoulds" behind her behavior. She readily acknowledged that she harbored the belief that she *must* not break the marriage because she *should* be married. If her husband chose to break the marriage, that was one thing, but she must not. When we pursued this belief in terms of its origins, she said she believed in the sanctity of marriage, but it was more that she just couldn't imagine herself not married, especially through her own action in obtaining a divorce. We finally got to the point where she said, "I was not raised that way," and from there we discussed the kind of models her parents were and how disappointed they would have been if she terminated the marriage. I asked whether she thought they would have preferred that she be unhappily married, or divorced with the possibility of finding happiness. She was sure they would have chosen happiness for her, but she still said she would feel like a failure in the light of their example. We returned to this issue of presumed failure repeatedly in the course of counseling, and I kept underlining the fact that her parents would have felt better *as parents* if she were happy and divorced or separated rather than unhappily married.

Much of this phase of the counseling was taken up with working on Mrs. P.'s right to have and pursue "inner" concerns even if this sometimes conflicted with the demands her children were making on her. I indicated that her increased desire to be alone at times and to pursue her creative photography was a natural development at this point in her life (the increased interiority discussed in Chapter 2). At the same time, her children were all adults now, even if she felt they were not sufficiently settled or independent. This phase of the counseling entailed my encouraging her to give herself permission to consider her own inner desires and needs without guilt.

As counseling progressed she saw that her needs and their needs were not mutually exclusive. If she indicated that she would not always be available at their whim they would have to grow up, in effect. Pursuing her own interests was also a way of indicating that she would not always be available. She began spending more time on her creative photography and stated directly to Paul and Jill what she did and did not want for herself when they made demands on her. Jill seemed to take rather well to her mother's pursuing her own interests. She actually seemed relieved that she was no longer the center of her mother's concern and attention. She began a couple of new friendships in the process and seemed to be feeling better about herself.

Paul did not take the change in his mother so well. His plans for getting her more involved in family matters and gatherings kept running afoul. He was also asked to do a great deal more around the house, which made his stay there less pleasant. There were also a couple of sharp disagreements between him and his mother about Mr. P.'s current place in the family picture. These differences were mended, but in the process he came to see that he was no longer the little boy who could return home and have his needs taken care of with every change in fortune. He left to go back west about five months after Mrs. P. had gone into counseling.

Although there was still some concern for Virginia, Mrs. P. had a long talk with her at the time of her visit and they became much closer than they had been. As a result, Mrs. P. felt better about Virginia; she saw that the girl wasn't quite as vulnerable as she had seemed and that she had a certain resilience (not far removed from what she came to believe about herself!). She began to see some closure on her parental responsibilities, which were so much of a part of the Eriksonian generativity issue. In addition, she was countering the stagnation—that is, the negative outcome of the generativity/stagnation issue—by pursuing a creative interest in her photography and her planned book.

The marriage dilemma was considerably more difficult to resolve. Mrs. P. had so identified with her role of wife and had such strong conceptions about the relationship between husband and wife, based largely on the role models of her parents, that she had a great deal of difficulty seeing her husband as a person. The more we explored his own family background and their life together and apart, the more she came to understand him objectively.

She related that her husband's childhood had not been a happy one. His parents were rather old (father 41 and mother 38) when he was born and they were quite punitive, restrictive, and cold in their relationship with him. She said that she wanted very much to make up in their marriage for what he had lacked in his family background. When I asked whether he had shown any of the qualities of his parents in his behavior toward his own children, she said that he did seem quite restrictive, insisting that he had to "uphold standards" in the house. She often had to handle discipline problems by herself because of his tendency to be too punitive—not so much physically abusive as verbally cutting and demeaning.

She went on to relate that the precise use of language was a very important thing to him. He would often try to handle family dilemmas by analyzing each person's verbalizations in great detail. Over the course of counseling Mrs. P. had a chance to see this characteristic in a more objective light during her husband's visits, and she did not like what she saw. She came to realize that he had always made a point of showing her how inept she was in the use of language. She said she had always felt inarticulate, and he played into this feeling relentlessly. At the same time, he was unable to express his feelings in direct language. When he was angry, he became more precise and tight in his language rather than more expressive.

The more we discussed her husband, the clearer it became that he was a rather isolated man who had great difficulty expressing his feelings and relating to his family on more than a formal role basis. He would often simply pontificate from his position as father in a stereotyped, almost ritualistic way. The children saw these discussions or pronouncements as a bore, and this made Mrs. P. more and more aware of how little her husband had to do with the real upbringing of the children and how much she did.

Finally, it became evident that this same kind of disconnectedness and passivity characterized his relationship toward her and even toward the "other person." Mrs. P. became keenly aware of this when she decided to apply for a divorce, after she had been in counseling for about three months. She then began pressing him for a clarification of their financial situation, as she had been advised by her lawyer. He would agree to send her necessary documents and information and then not follow through. He seemed to acquiesce in her decision about the divorce but would manage to avoid discussing plans for it on the telephone or on his visits home. He never said he was against the divorce but seemed to engage in a kind of passive resistance to anthing that would lead to it. She persisted, however, with her new-found determination and assertiveness in which she creatively applied the techniques she was learning in counseling.

There were several approaches used in the course of Mrs. P.'s counseling which should be delineated here. Some of them represent known cognitive techniques and others represent new approaches to problems encountered in her case.

As far as cognitive techniques were concerned, I used disattribution to have Mrs. P. stop acccpting all the blame for the fact that some of her adult children were not yet settled. This was accomplished in part by noting that her oldest daughter was well settled and that this indicated that the children themselves had played a major role in determining their present life circumstances; she was not the only causal factor in the situation. I also assigned her certain homework in the form of bibliotherapy. She found Rubin (1975) particularly helpful with regard to her children because of his eloquent statement that one does the best under given circumstances, and she was able to be more accepting of her earlier handling of the children.

Another cognitive technique used was distancing, which was helpful in dealing with her feelings about her husband. This involved having her view her husband's behavior toward her objectively rather than subjectively. In this way she came to realize that he was not so much trying to hurt her as he was unable to help himself and to behave differently, because of the shortcomings in his own personality and background. Of course, the process and technique of decentering were used throughout the counseling. Mrs. P. became more and more able to separate herself from the impact and occurrence of external events.

As is often the case in counseling, some of the changes and insights brought about by these techniques seemed to create other problems. As Mrs. P. began to see her husband and her marriage more objectively, she began to feel that her whole married life had been a "lie and a failure." Perhaps the best term to characterize this kind of thinking might be "contamination." That is, the whole marriage is contaminated or tainted by certain negatives in it. It is as though nothing good, nothing redeeming, could be found in it. This type of thinking unfortunately leads to wholesale regret. However, it was possible to counter it by identifying it when it occurred and disputing it. Mrs. P. had engaged in a number of positive reminiscences about her earlier years of marriage which I was later able to use in countering the effects of the "contamination."

Two other approaches were used with Mrs. P., but they do not have any designation in the cognitive or related treatment literature. One of these was a kind of therapeutic "permission" for Mrs. P. to engage in the introspection or interiority she desired. This was done, as noted earlier, by my indicating that this was a natural and not a selfish development at her stage in life. Another related approach involved my disputing her tendency to evaluate herself only in terms of her performance in parenting and marriage, both of which she viewed as failures. I proposed alternative arguments to show that she did not have to evaluate her self in terms of any performances. This could be called "alternative disputation" because it involves the presentation of arguments against the functionalistic ethic and for alternative self-evaluations.

The cumulative effect of these techniques and approaches seemed to show most clearly in her locus of control and her self-concept. She gained considerable self-confidence and decisiveness in the process. As noted, she was pressing for a divorce, but in about the fourth month of counseling her husband developed serious symptoms of angina. He had undergone by-pass surgery on his heart five years earlier, and there was no assurance that he would have more than five years to live.

When she learned about the renewed symptoms she decided to back away for the time being from her divorce plans, which he finally admitted were a source of considerable stress to him. It was fortunate that she had made this decision, for he suffered a fatal heart attack two weeks after she had learned of his renewed heart problems. She might have had to work through considerable guilt if she had continued with her divorce plans in the face of the stress he said he was feeling. However, even under these circumstances Mrs. P. probably would have done reasonably well. The decentering and distancing techniques had become part of her own repertoire as a result of the cognitive restructuring that had already gone on, and these would have stood her in good stead in combating any guilt feelings.

Mr. P. was brought home for a funeral ceremony and burial, and Mrs. P. was able to handle these quite competently. However, Mr. P.'s income had of course stopped, and he left only a $10,000 life insurance policy. Mrs. P. had financial worries which she did not have before. She managed to weather this by selling her house and buying a new house with rental income. She was also given a full-time job by her employer. Although she was far from affluent or even financially secure, she was able to handle this situation with real equanimity.

She was soon pursuing her interest in creative photography and was at work on her book by the end of counseling. She had also developed a close relationship with another woman who had been widowed but who was having a more difficult time of it. This provided Mrs. P. with an outlet for her need to support and nurture, as well as a close friend and confidante.

In her twelfth month of treatment, Mrs. P. had a dream which at first frightened her but then affected her profoundly in a way she couldn't explain. She dreamed she was upstairs in her house when she heard a powerful howling sound, like a very strong wind. She went downstairs and found that the sound was coming from her kitchen, but the door was closed. When she opened it she was almost sucked into the dark, howling interior of her kitchen, which had been stripped of all funiture, dishes, food, and other items by a powerful vacuumlike wind pulling things outside through the back door.

As she tried to make sense of this dream, she said that it seemed to represent the loss of her cherished role as mother and wife. The kitchen and its contents seemed to be the various aspects of those roles, and she was fearful of being swept away herself. This she felt represented her very identity, because all she had known of herself as a person up to that time was her identity as a mother and wife.

It became clear that although she had survived the loss of these roles, she was feeling a distinct emptiness in her life. This became further evident in her responses to a Role Constructs Repertory Test (Kelly, 1955) I gave her shortly thereafter. It showed that the key issue in her life at that time was "loving" and "caring" versus "indifference." Thus, her relationship with her widowed friend came at a very critical time for her.

She also became involved as a volunteer with mentally retarded children at a local residential facility and continued this activity throughout her counseling and beyond with great personal satisfaction, even though she found it physically tiring from time to time in view of her full-time job. This was the sort of thing she was looking for, much more than her creative photography which had not been prominent in her Repertory Test and which took a back seat for the remainder of counseling to her caring, altruistic activities.

She was seen in counseling only every other week for the last several months. It was clear by then that she was very much "her own person." She had developed a different kind of relationship with her adult children, more detached and less possessive, yet positive and warm. She enjoyed seeing them and corresponding with them, and there was no further sense of burden or failure about her feelings toward them.

At the end of her counseling, twenty months after the initial session in which she was extremely anxious about vague suicidal impulses, Virgina Plummer showed a number of significant changes. Figure 6-2 shows the results of her Semantic Differential Test after counseling. It is markedly different in a number of respects from the Semantic Differential Test results given in Figure 6-1.

The most significant change from all points of view was the much decreased discrepancy between her self-concept and her ideal self. This meant, of course, that her self-esteem was quite high. The changes in her responses on the self-concept which made a difference were that she saw herself as "quite valuable" instead of "quite worthless," "quite happy" rather than

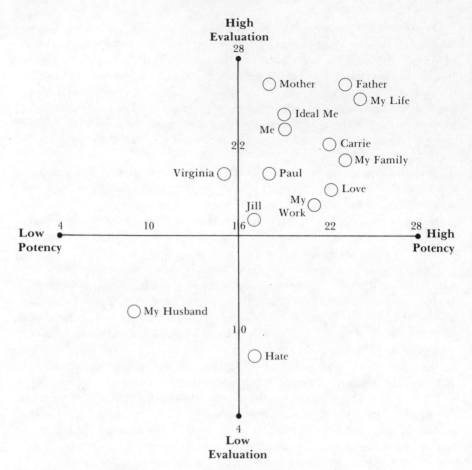

FIGURE 6-2. *Virginia Plummer's Final Semantic Differential Test*

"quite sad," and "quite strong" in contrast to "quite weak." She also noted that she was "quite young" as compared to her earlier response of "slightly old."

Some changes in her ideal self also served to reduce the discrepancy between self and ideal. She had dropped some old perfectionistic standards by responding to "I would like to be" in the following ways: "quite valuable" rather than "extremely valuable," "quite strong" as compared to "extremely strong," and "quite happy" in place of "extremely happy."

Another remarkable change in her "semantic space" after counseling was the position of "My Husband." He had not been highly valued in the initial test, but he was much lower on the potency dimension in the final test. This came about as a result of her recognition of some of his weaknesses and handicapping factors in his background. She had come to see him objectively rather than through her somewhat distorted earlier perceptions of him.

Her parents were still very highly valued, although they did not have the same degree of perfection in terms of her responses as they had had in the first test. She had indeed come to a more mature assessment of them, and she still found them to be quite good and fine, if not perfect. They undoubtedly did give her a great deal in the way of nurturing and preparation for later life, for she not only overcame the problems that brought her into counseling but emerged a very strong and secure person by any standards.

.Another item of importance in Figure 6-2 is the concept "Love." It will be recalled that at the time of her initial test "Love" had been rated very low. Mrs. P. was quite disillusioned and bitter about it. However, in the final test she had changed her whole conception of the meaning of the term. As she discussed it, in the initial test she had interpreted it largely in terms of her husband and her marriage, but in the final test she saw it more broadly in that it incorporated her current feelings about her children, her parents, her friend, and the children she worked with.

The other item of marked significance in Figure 6-2 is the concept "My Life." In the initial test it had been just about as low as "Love" in the spatial model. This simply reflected her heightened morale and enthusiasm for life.

Also, given the other test results, it is not surprising that Mrs. P.'s Life Satisfaction Index changed considerably, as well. Her final LSIA score was a very positive 17 out of a possible 20, almost a complete reversal of her initial score of 3 out of 20.

These results were consistent, then, with the overall positive outcome scores at the conclusion of counseling. There was much in Mrs. P.'s background before and even during her marriage that indicated basic strengths in her personality. What happened in the course of counseling, therefore, was that certain normal and healthy developmental changes of aging took place with the emotional support and certain cognitive tools provided by the integrative approach. All of the test results and just a few minutes of talking with and observing Mrs. P. would lead one to believe that she had certainly achieved a substantial degree of ego integrity.

The second case of extended individual counseling is one that began in a short-term (12-session) group at a senior service center. Marie Laughlin, a 77-year-old widow, was still recovering from the last remaining effects of a stroke she had suffered some months earlier. She still had a slight limp in her right leg and an almost imperceptible paralysis on the right side of her face. This caused some slurring of speech for which she was receiving outpatient speech therapy at a rehabilitation hospital. She indicated that she had joined the group in part as a way to make herself speak more often and practice the exercises she was being taught in speech therapy.

Since she lived alone, she did not get as much opportunity to talk as she wanted, but it was also clear that she joined the group for reasons other than her speech therapy. From the beginning of the group she was one of the more active and influential members. She had been the catalyst and organizer of a move to have the center procure a minibus for some members who needed transportation to and from the center. Although she was obviously intelligent, articulate, and respected by the other group members, she was also seen by them as sometimes "testy, moody, and superior." These were terms used at various times by other group members to describe her. She did at times appear to be impatient of others when they seemed to have difficulty comprehending some point or were doubtful about pursuing a course of action she thought would be fruitful. She also would have periods when she appeared glum or blue and distracted, in contrast to her usual crisp and alert manner.

When it came to discussing personal problems in the group, she focused mostly on her emotional reactions to the stroke. She said she had not yet gotten over the initial terrible fear that she would be terribly handicapped and dependent, which she saw as the worst possible event imaginable. She also admitted to being very irritated at herself for what she considered her slowness in getting her speech back in a perfectly clear and distinct manner. The speech therapist thought she was doing extremely well, but Mrs. Laughlin was sure she was not doing as well as she could.

Given her high achievement orientation, Mrs. L. had an intersting reaction to the rational-emotive A-B-C technique of disputing irrational ideas in group sessions. She liked its no-nonsense directness and rationality, but she disliked some of its implicit values. For example, she took exception to the following statement: "Give up the notion that you must act quite competently, adequately, and achievingly. Try to *do* or do *well* rather than to do *perfectly*" (Ellis and Harper, 1975:198). She felt that that idea could lead to mediocrity, but she was very much interested in discussing such ideas. She got very animated in discussing some of the items on the instruments in the pretest of the group, especially the questions about the functionalistic ethic. She strongly disagreed with the statement, "A person's worth does not depend on how good a citizen, parent, or worker he or she is, but simply that he or she is a human being." She said that she had lived her life according to the values of striving and achievement, so she could not see "settling for second best."

However, she was very much interested in pursuing the questions in the instruments beyond the confines of the group. After the third session she asked me if I would be willing to meet with her individually to go over her responses in detail, and it was as a result of that meeting that she requested individual counseling. At that meeting she said she had been "jolted" by the statement, "It is hard to feel good when there are certain things in life I can no longer influence." This statement was part of the cognitive mastery measure, and a response of "strongly disagree" would be indicative of high degree of cognitive mastery, whereas Mrs. Laughlin's response was "strongly agree."

She said that the statement seemed to get directly at something in her life she had been feeling more and more consciously over the years. It reached its worst point at the time of the stroke when she became acutely aware of the fact that she might not retain control of her body or even her mind, if the stroke caused too much brain damage. She was, of course, terribly anxious about that and this concern came out in the group sessions. Before that she had been very upset by her husband's stroke eight years earlier, which put him in a wheelchair and required that she care for him for the last five years of his life. She had felt very badly about those five years which were affected largely by events beyond her control. Also, she felt badly that she could not do much to influence or change what was happening currently with her children, particularly her 52-year-old daughter who was divorced and having trouble with her own children. These events had all upset her a great deal, and they were things she had no control over.

Her locus of control measure indicated a very high internal locus which allowed no room for any random or accidental happenings and in which success is always achieved by hard work, application, and individual determination. I commented that I could understand how upsetting these recent uncontrollable events in her life must be in light of her beliefs as expressed in the locus of control measure. However, the very fact that she was upset about these events *over which she had no control* indicated that she did feel that there are some important areas over which there is little or no individual control. This did not seem consistent with her responses on the locus of control measure. She said that she was aware of this, and it bothered her a great deal because she never thought of herself, at any time, as confused. However, she was definitely feeling that way currently, and she was very distraught over the frustration and anxiety she was experiencing as more and more events over which she had no control entered her life. Furthermore, she was becoming increasingly upset over what she thought were serious mistakes she had made in the past, particularly with regard to her family. These distressful feelings about the past were what led her to request individual counseling.

Mrs. L. was seen weekly in individual sessions for the first eight months and every other week for six more months. The early individual sessions involved considerable reminiscing on her part, but it was of a ruminating sort which reflected a lot of self-blame for past errors. She did not reminisce in the group sessions, where she continued to be more task-oriented about current issues and problems. She acknowledged to me that she had difficulty admitting any failures or mistakes in group situations, because she had always tended to assume leadership roles, and this meant projecting "a strong front" with others.

Mrs. L. provided the following personal background in the course of her reminiscence. She was born into a large Irish-Catholic family in a small industrial city in the East. She left high school in her second year and went to work in a local clothing mill. She married three years later and continued to work at the mill until she became pregnant with her first child, a son named John. Three years later her daughter, Helen, was born. After this she and her husband decided not to have any more children. She said that neither she nor her husband were devout Catholics so they had no problem over the issue of practicing birth control. Mrs. L. said that her family was quite devout, with one brother who studied for the priesthood. However, she more than any one of the eight children asserted herself against many of the religious involvements and practices of the family. She said, somewhat impishly and proudly, that religion was not the only area in which she asserted her independence in the family. She was very much a tomboy and tougher than a number of the boys in her class, as well as a couple of her brothers. She did not like school very much, not feeling challenged or stimulated, and resisting the kind of decorum demanded of young girls in those days. She indicated that her behavior did not involve sexual acting out, but she could be quite defiant and "fresh" when reprimanded by teachers. She said that she did not really appreciate the values of school and an education until much later in her life.

She said she basically led the life of a housewife until her children grew up and left home, although she could not say that she was content in that role. In retrospect she thought that all the ambition and organizational skills she demonstrated in her later vocational life were frustrated, yet applied inappropriately to her family. She was coming to realize that she had organized and run her family rather tightly and had attempted to realize her ambitions through her children, especially her son. She described her husband as an "easy-going man" who was quite willing to have her manage the household and finances single-handedly. He was a security guard in a large chain department store, and although he became head of the store's security staff before his retirement he was not at all as ambitious as she.

When her children left home she obtained a job as a file clerk in a state government office. It was only a temporary position offered to her by a friend of her husband's and could become permanent only if she took the civil service test for the position and placed high on the list. She took the test and placed very high on the list. It rapidly became evident to her that with her intelligence and ambition she could obtain better positions for herself within the state bureau but that she needed more formal schooling. She went to night school and obtained a high school equivalency diploma, and she continued taking civil service tests and obtained better positions as a result. She ended up by becoming the office manager in a fairly large and complex office of the state bureau in which she had started. This in itself was not enough of a challenge for her organizational skills and interests, so she became active in the civil service employees organization, which was the bargaining agent, in lieu of a union, for the state employees. After her retirement she remained active in the organization, frequently appearing at hearings in the state legislature lobbying for higher retirement and health benefits for retired state employees. She continued to engage in these activities with a good deal of personal satisfaction up to age 69, when her husband suffered his stroke and she had to stay home to care for him.

Mrs. L. was beginning to feel quite guilty about her children and the effect she thought she had had on their lives. She said that her 55-year-old son, John, was a successful accountant; however, he seemed to be a "workaholic," spending far too little time with his family while constantly working extra hours. She said she could see her own handiwork in this. She was ambitious for him and pushed him as a child, and he learned the lesson only too well. What distressed her most was the apparent unhappiness of his wife, although she did not overtly complain. Mrs. L. simply saw little joy or warmth in her son or his family life.

Her daughter's situation caused her even more distress. Helen's husband left her three years earlier, and she "completely fell apart" when the divorce became final a year later. She became quite depressed, began drinking heavily, and finally underwent outpatient psychotherapy and received antidepressant medication. This seemed to have stabilized her and ended the heavy drinking, but she was still having difficulty managing. Although two of her children were married and living away from home, there was still a 17-year-old in the home who was heavily involved in drug use and was in danger of being expelled from school. Mrs. L. said her daughter had always been a somewhat dependent girl, lacking in self-confidence, who had married a man who was quite dominant. When he left her, she did not seem able to cope on her own. However, there was never any question of Mrs. L. going to join Helen, who lived in the Southwest. Mrs. L. felt that she had alienated Helen to some extent by her impatience, her high expectations, and her implicit disapproval of her daughter's relative lack of social assertiveness and "management skills." Mrs. L. indicated that she thought her daughter's lack of self-confidence and low self-image was a result of Mrs. L. projecting a model of competence and assertiveness that Helen never felt able to attain and which therefore made her feel deficient and incompetent. Because of this Mrs. L. was reluctant to intervene in her daughter's life at this time. She felt that she had done too much of that in the past without her daughter having much to say about it.

Further, Mrs. L. was so concerned after her stroke about becoming physically dependent that she would not dream of wishing this dependency on her daughter.

Many of the above points about Mrs. L. and her family showed up in her Semantic Differential Test at the start of group counseling. As can be seen in Figure 6-3, Mrs. L. had a very high and demanding ideal self. She wished to be "extremely strong; extremely valuable," "quite happy," "quite good," and "extremely fair." Although there is some discrepancy between the ideal self and self-concept, it is not very great. However, it is the pattern of discrepancy that is significant. There is almost no difference between the ideal and

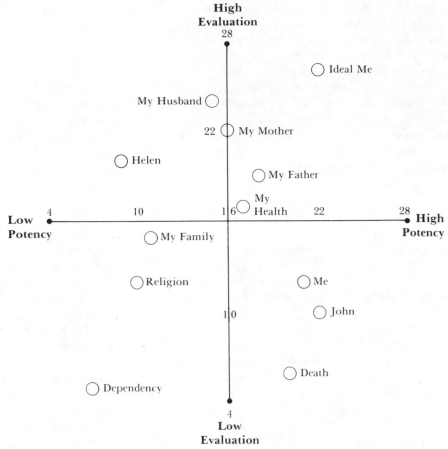

FIGURE 6-3. *Marie Laughlin's First Semantic Differential Test*

the actual self on the horizontal axis, the potency dimension, in Figure 6-3. The only difference was that while she would like to be "extremely strong" she felt she was actually "quite strong." The main discrepancy shows up on the vertical axis, or evaluation dimension. On that dimension she actually feels "quite sad" instead of her ideal of "quite happy," "somewhat bad" instead of "quite good," and "quite unfair" unstead of "quite fair."

Mrs. L. said she felt sad because of her feelings of failure and regret about her family. She felt bad in that she had been too impatient and demanding with her children and her husband, and she felt that this behavior was also unfair to them. As a result of what she saw as her failure with regard to her family, her responses to the concept of "My Family" indicated that it was "quite weak" and "quite sad." Her husband she viewed as "slightly weak" but "quite happy," "quite good," and "quite fair." Her son, John, on the other hand was viewed as "quite strong" and "quite tough" but "quite sad," "quite cold," and "extremely unfair." She explained this last response as meaning that he was unfair to his wife and children but not to her. Mrs. L. said that he was quite cool to her, and she had herself to blame for that, but it was unfair of him to treat his family that way.

Helen was viewed as "quite weak" and "extremely soft" but also as "extremely valuable" and "quite good," although "extremely sad." As far as her parents were concerned, Mrs. L. did not see either of them as dominant in their marriage as she had been in hers. They were not seen as particularly weak or strong but they were both seen as "good" and somewhat "happy."

The concept of health was important at this juncture in Mrs. L.'s life, and her responses to it on the Semantic Differential Test reflected some ambivalence. For example, she responded that it was "slightly weak" but "quite tough." When asked what this meant, she said that although she felt her health was somewhat vulnerable since she had experienced a stroke she felt she could be "tough" about it and work to overcome it—a clear indication of her motivation and determination to work on her problems. This was consistent with her internal locus of control, which was a positive factor in her prognosis from the beginning of counseling.

The concept of dependency had the lowest potency and evaluation scores of all of her responses. It was seen as "extremely small, weak, and soft," and also as "extremely bad, sad and unfair." Even the concept of death was not as negatively valued as dependency. However, death was seen as "extremely sad," "quite bad," and "extremely unfair." She explained these responses by saying that there was too much left to do in her life, by which she meant that she wanted somehow to accommodate or amend her past mistakes with her family before she died. It was not that she was fearful of death as much as it was her fear that it would occur too soon.

Finally, the concept of religion proved to have little valence in her life space. On the potency dimension she saw it as "quite small" and "quite weak," and on the evaluation dimension as "slightly worthless and sad" and "quite unfair." She felt that her religion of birth, Roman Catholicism, was unfair in its emphasis on mortal sin and eternal damnation for those who did not live by the precepts of the Church.

On the basis of those early sessions with Mrs. L. it was evident that she was rapidly becoming more regretful about her past behavior toward her family and was headed toward a state of despair. It was therefore essential that she have individual counseling with an emphasis on life review therapy if a clinical depression and more general despair was to be avoided (Butler, 1963). In fact, it was practically impossible to avoid life review therapy because Mrs. L.'s continuous ruminations and concerns in individual counseling were primarily those negative remembrances and regrets.

This general picture was exacerbated by Mrs. L.'s own excessively high standards and expectations for herself. She felt her performance as a mother was extremely poor, as evidenced by the unsatisfactory marital and family lives of her children. The fact that she tried hard as a mother did nothing to diminish her self-blame. The basic issue as far as she was concerned was that she had wrongly foisted her achievement aspirations on her children and attempted to "manage" them. The fact that she did what she knew how to do best and what she thought was right did not make any difference to her—she should have known better. It was a poor performance, even if it was out of ignorance. It was still incompetent by her standards. Furthermore, she was beginning to attribute some of this past behavior to malice or badness rather than just ignorance or incompetence on her part. There was in fact a decrease in her morale as reflected in the Life Satisfaction Index score of 5 at the end of group counseling (twelve weeks later) as compared to 7 at the pretest. This drop reflected the negative course of the life review process which had brought her to individual counseling at its outset. Although a score of 7 was low to begin with (much of it associated with the emotional trauma of her stroke), she had become more depressed, as indicated by her agreeing that she felt "old and somewhat tired" in the postgroup test but not in the pretest. She also felt that things she did were not as interesting to her as they ever were, which was a change from the pretest. Also, she responded with a question mark to the statement, "compared to other people, I get down in the dumps too often," in the pretest, but she emphatically agreed with it in the second administration of the test.

In effect, Mrs. L. got worse before she got better, but there is reason to believe that she would have become even more depressed in the absence of counseling. She was made aware of the tendency in depressogenic thinking to generalize negative evaluations to everything, even to the past as in retrospective generalization.

Although she faulted herself and lowered her self-esteem as far as her family functioning was concerned, she did not do this with her other adult functioning in the larger vocational and social areas. Therefore, Mrs. L. received counseling at a propitious time, which allowed her own innate strengths to resolve the integrity–despair struggle she was going through. Thus, the assessment in her case had to take into account her high motivation and willingness to work, an internal locus of control, a self-concept that still retained some positive aspects, and an intelligence that was both high and inquiring. This intelligence allowed her to use the cognitive techniques and to deal with the perplexing value issues effectively.

One of the intriguing aspects of Mrs. L.'s case was her own growing awareness of personal limitations and misplaced values in the past which she was beginning to question in the present, even without counseling. After all, she was a relatively self-assured person who seemed to be quite clear in her own mind about which values and way of life were correct, at least until she entered the group. When questioned about this change of mind, she said that she began having doubts about her whole approach to life and her values when she was recuperating from her stroke. She then felt first-hand how her husband must have felt when he suffered his stroke and was dependent upon her and her ministrations. She said that she was very appreciative of the patience and support offered to her by the staff at the rehabilitation center. As much as she wanted to do things for herself, she could not, and the staff seemed to understand this and offered support that was not intrusive or demeaning to her or her concept of herself as an independent person. She realized in the process that she had not been like that with her husband after his stroke. She felt that she had been impatient with him and that she resented him for keeping her homebound and away from her organizational activities. At the time she felt somewhat righteous about this, but she came to feel guilty and ashamed about it after her stroke. She said it took her own traumatic experience to open up the questions and doubts she came to experience in her life review process. The self-doubt that began with her thoughts about her care of her husband then quickly spread to the care of the children.

The technique of distancing was used to help her deal with her self-blame about the care of her husband. I suggested that she was taking it as a fact that she had treated her husband badly after his stroke but that we needed to look at it carefully. In short, she had to distance herself from the situation somewhat to look at possible pluses as well as negatives, because of the tendency toward retrospective generalization. One question I raised was how much she had *felt* impatience with her husband and how much she *acted* impatiently with him. I had the advantage of having seen her in group and individual sessions, so I was able to point out instances in which she had expressed in individual sessions feelings of impatience with a group member but in the group situation did not show any evidence of impatience to that person. I suggested that to some extent she might be mistaking her thoughts for actual behavior toward her husband. She was willing to entertain that as an idea or hypothesis as we worked on her remembrance of her care of her husband.

She also blamed herself for not being as sensitive as the rehabilitation staff had been to her in dealing with the terrible feeling of shame her husband must have experienced over being dependent. The distancing approach in this instance was for me to remind her that her husband was quite a different person than she. She had earlier described him as somewhat passive and dependent upon her in other matters, and yet he did not seem distressed by it but accepted it as a natural part of their relationship. Therefore, it was possible that he was nowhere near as sensitive about his dependency as she was about hers. She said that she had to admit that the more she thought about it the more she thought that was true. This also opened up the whole area of her intense distaste and fear of dependency which was very unrealistic and maladaptive under the circumstances. This was something we worked on repeatedly over time.

The techniques of decentering and disattribution were used to contend with her self-blame over her children. Beck's (1976) view of decentering as loosening the patient's pattern of regarding himself as the focal point of every occurrence was implemented by indicating that factors other than her care of the children in their childhood could explain her children's current family situations. She was asked to consider the possibility that they were at least partially and she therefore not totally responsible for the current state of affairs. In addition, disattribution was used in calling her attention to the fact that adults have a good deal more intellectual and problem-solving equipment, as well as freedom of choice, than do children. In this sense her children themselves, since they had spent more of their lives apart from her as adults, were in large part instrumental in creating their current life circumstances. Finally, by using some of her reminiscences in life review therapy I was able to discover and remind her that she had been very loving and nurturing toward her children before they entered school, which were their most important formative years. When they went to school, she "pushed and managed" them in terms of achievement and school performance, but she had not stopped loving them or even showing love to them.

All of this, of course, took a great deal of working and reworking, but her essential rationality would not allow her to continue distorting remembrances or current thinking. In many respects the most difficult technique to implement with Mrs. L. was alternative disputation of the functionalistic ethic, which was a strong component in her current self-evaluation. It was one thing to change her misperceptions of the past or present but it was another thing to dispute her lifelong values. She even used the term "performance" to describe her parenting as well as her vocational roles. Hers was very much a functional performance ethic, as evidenced by her high pretest score on the functionalistic ethic scale. Nevertheless, she was intrigued by alternative views because she saw their potential for perceiving her self and her life in a more compassionate way. However, her own tough standards and self-demands were such that she could not easily accept a more compassionate view precisely because it would seem "too easy." However, since she was beginning to change her mind on issues such as dependency she was open to entertaining new ideas.

Mrs. L. was given a values clarification exercise for homework in which she had to rank her values according to Rokeach's (1973) classification of instrumental and terminal values. Although she was highly motivated and interested, she had a great deal of difficulty with this assignment, and we spent quite a bit of time on it in several sessions. After she had ranked her values we looked at them in comparison to her past and how she would have ranked them then. We also looked for any apparent inconsistencies or incongruences between current values that might need clarification and work.

Mrs. L.'s ranked list of instrumental values surprised her considerably, even though she had spent many hours in ranking them. The first-ranked instrumental value of the eighteen was "intellectual (intelligent, reflective)." She said she was not pleased with the word "intellectual" but the clarifying words "intelligent" and "reflective" were more appropriate. She felt that she needed to be both intelligent and reflective at this stage of her life in order to deal with her current emotional and value dilemmas. She said that in the past (before her stroke) she would have ranked "intellectual" only about ninth among the eighteen values.

Her second-ranked current value was even more discrepant with the past. It was "broadminded (open-minded)," and in the past she would have ranked it near the bottom, about sixteenth. However, her current view of that value was that she had to have an open mind so as to find the perspectives and values to put her life into some kind of order and meaning.

Her third-ranked value was "capable (competent, effective)," and she noted that this would have been her first-ranked value in the past. Although she found herself to be lacking in competence and effectiveness as a mother, this was not how she viewed her performance in other social and vocational roles. This remained a high-priority value for her, although no longer first.

Mrs. L.'s fourth-ranked current value was highly discrepant with the past. It was "forgiving (willing to pardon others)." She said this one surprised her, because in the past it would have been quite low in ranking—about thirteenth. She now realized that her high standards for herself made her apply them equally remorselessly to others. She was therefore demanding of others in terms of their performances and was unwilling to forgive or pardon poor performances, incompetence, or lack of effort. She said she wanted to be more forgiving, really more accepting and compassionate, toward others. She felt that she could not be more compassionate toward herself until she could do the same for others. She was working quite consciously on this in her activities at the senior center. When she found herself becoming critical of certain persons who were also active in committee and organizational work at the center, she would take it up in individual sessions. Sometimes she would go through a cognitive rehearsal of how she would handle herself emotionally and behaviorally with these persons. Most of the time we would go over and dispute the dysfunctional automatic thoughts, the shoulds and oughts, behind her critical attitudes. These would then be replaced with more rational conceptions of human fallibility, allowing for more humane and accepting attitudes toward others.

The fifth-ranked of her current instrumental values was "independent (self-reliant, self-sufficient)." This would have been her third-ranked in the past, almost neck-and-neck with the other two top values—capable and ambitious. She saw them as all interrelated and central to her functioning in the past. She still held independence in high regard even though she was working on being more accepting of appropriate dependency. The shift in the independence value from past to present, although not great, probably represented a real shift in her whole value system.

Rokeach (1973) has shown that terminal values are more difficult to change. However, when they are changed they tend to bring about more significant and lasting change in instrumental values, attitudes, and behaviors. Terminal values are obviously much more important for the last stage of life and over these Mrs. L. agonized the most. There were some evident changes in her terminal values at the time value clarification was begun in individual counseling about five months after its inception. These changes were probably responsible for many of the shifts in instrumental values which were just discussed. At any rate, the most significant changes were in the top two terminal values. She identified the first-ranked as "inner harmony (freedom from inner conflict)," which would have been about sixth in the past. The second-ranked value was "wisdom (a mature understanding of life)", which would have been about eleventh in the past.

Mrs. L. said that she did not like the word "wisdom" and that she did not believe older persons had a monopoly on it. However, "a mature understanding of life" was very much what she wanted before she died. Interestingly, her third-ranked value, "happiness (contentedness)," would have been ranked third in the past. She said that was very misleading because what she meant by happiness in the past was not what it was in the present. In the past she would have identified happiness in terms of her first- and second-ranked values—"social recognition (respect, admiration)" and "self-respect (self-esteem)" respectively. Currently, however, she would identify happiness with the presence of inner harmony and wisdom, consistent with her new ranking. This type of identification of a terminal value as instrumental for another terminal value (for example, inner harmony and wisdom as instrumental for happiness) has been found in other applications and studies of Rokeach's values classification scheme (Robinson and Shaver, 1973). It shows how difficult it is to separate instrumental from terminal values in any mutually exclusive measurement sense, and it shows how complex value systems are. However, Rokeach's system certainly does lead to much greater clarity. Mrs. L. said that she had not realized how much her happiness was dependent on social recognition, the respect and admiration of others, in the past. Currently, she would rank social recognition very low as a terminal value—about fifteenth.

Mrs. L. became conscious of these clarified values as she had never been in the past, and she was prepared, characteristically, to work hard on them. She was aware that value changes are not implemented simply by identifying priorities but by acting on them until they indeed become second nature—a way of life. This process went on through the entire length of her counseling, but the most difficult part for Mrs. L. was her tendency to apply her old functionalistic, performance standards to the new value priorities. She had difficulty in being compassionate with herself in allowing for mistakes and slips, as she tried to live these new values.

This tendency on Mrs. L.'s part meant that a great deal of time and effort in counseling had to go into developing alternative evaluations of self. My first efforts were to show her the graphic discrepancy between her self-concept and her self ideal on the evaluative dimension (Figure 6-3) and to explain its effect on self-esteem. She had little difficulty understanding these formulations and found them helpful in focusing on the issue of self-esteem in her everyday activities. In addition, she used the Daily Record of Dysfunctional Thoughts (Appendix D) to monitor her self-downing thoughts resulting from irrational, perfectionistic standards concerning her behavior and values. It took quite a bit of work with this before I recommended Rubin's book (1975) as bibliotherapy to help Mrs. L. develop greater self-acceptance without performance standards. It was six months into individual counseling before I recommended it, because at any earlier point she would have rejected its precepts as "too easy." As it was, Rubin's direct approach to self-esteem was not sufficient, even in conjunction with the alternative disputation technique, to bring about a significantly more compassionate self-evaluation.

Most of the latter month of individual counseling involved the broader use of decentering on the client's part. By that I mean broader than the specific technique identified by Beck (1976) and more like the general process that Piaget identified as one in which the person abandons the egocentric position and the self is forced from itself by assigning itself a place as a thing or event among other events (Dinnage, 1978). The more Mrs. L. was moved away from evaluating (and thereby identifying) herself through performances and events, the more she was decentering. When a person identifies these performances and events as self, the egocentric position emerges and possessively maintains itself.

One technique in this decentering process that she found particularly helpful was the assignment for bibliotherapy of Alan W. Watts's *The Book* (1966) which clearly and simply dismantles the "myth of the self"—the idea that the self somehow resides within the person's body and directs all the person's activities and thoughts much like a driver in a car. Watt's book shows how the person is part of a complex panorama of life in which each element is related to every other and in which artificial boundaries such as between self and other are ultimately meaningless. According to Watts, the simple idea of linear cause and effect is also meaningless, so it is both senseless and invalid to ascribe total blame to one's self as the sole cause of another's unhappiness. Of course, this had clear implications for Mrs. L. and her guilt concerning her children.

The impact of the thoughts in the Watts book was particularly great in the context of Mrs. L.'s shifting value system. It was as though after all the disputation exercises, the Rubin book, and the other techniques of cognitive restructuring she had found the last piece in the puzzle. Given this decentered perception of herself, Mrs. L. rapidly started reinterpreting a number of things about herself and her life. She said that she now saw how very self-centered it was to focus on *her* guilt about her children and how grandiose it was of her to assume that it was she and only she who caused all her children's unhappiness.

It was in this new frame of mind that she visited both her children toward the end of her counseling. She spoke openly with Helen about her regrets over mistaken approaches in the past, and she shared with Helen her changed ideas. Helen was surprised and remarked upon her mother's uncharacteristic "mellowness." She did not deny that she had often felt pained and hurt in response to Mrs. L.'s high expectations and criticisms but said she still felt her mother's love very clearly from her early childhood. Helen did not hold her mother responsible for her present difficulties and said she was managing better.

John was not as accessible, emotionally or physically, to Mrs. L.'s gestures of openness and sharing of concerns about past and present. He spent little time at the house while Mrs. L. visited, claiming to have to meet some deadlines at the office. During the little time she was able to spend with him he was cool and distant, making it clear that he was not interested and saw no purpose in a discussion of the past. She took her son's attitude philosophically, saying that she was sorry that he did not see the unhappiness in his current life situation but that she was not as deeply regretful as she had been in the past when she felt so completely responsible for his current problems.

After fourteen months of individual counseling Mrs. L. showed a number of notable changes in her responses to the tests she had taken at the start and end of group counseling. On the Semantic Differential Test she showed less discrepancy between her self-concept and her ideal self on the evaluative dimension. There had not been much discrepancy on the potency dimension in the pretest. Figure 6-4 shows the results of Mrs. L.'s final test.

Most of the discrepancy between self and ideal self had been reduced in the final test by a slight lowering of the ideal self but mainly by a more positive evaluation of self. There was also a slightly more positive evaluation (from 15 to 17 points) of "My Family" in the posttest, and it was seen as less weak on the potency dimension (11 pretest, 16 posttest).

There was not much change in the concept of "My Husband," with a rather high evaluative score in both pretest and posttest situations. There were also practically no changes in the concepts of "My Mother" and "My Father," which were evaluated slightly more positively than in the pretest. On the other hand, there were some changes in her responses to "John," primarily in seeing him as less strong in the posttest (15 points) as compared to the pretest (22 points) on the potency dimension. For example, Mrs. L. changed her description of him from "quite strong" to "quite weak," and explained this by saying that she found out that "he did not have the flexibility for real strength." Such a comment would have been highly unlikely for Mrs. L. prior to counseling.

Helen, on the contrary, was seen in the posttest as less weak (13 points on potency dimension) than in the pretest (8 points). This change was made on the basis of their visit and the recognition that Helen had more resilience than Mrs. L. realized at the time of the pretest. She was obviously less worried

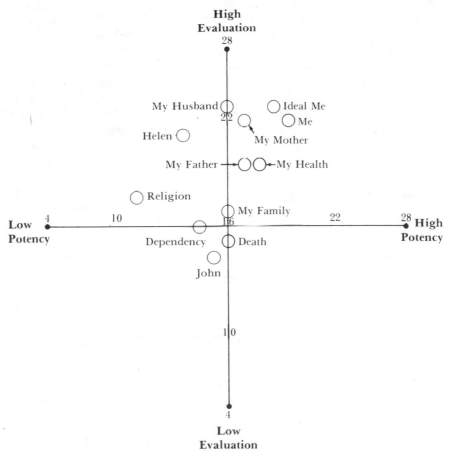

FIGURE 6-4. *Marie Laughlin's Final Semantic Differential Test*

about her daughter and more sure that Helen would weather the worst of her problems.

Other concepts that showed some change were "Dependency" and "Death." Mrs. L. did not see dependency as indicative of weakness to anywhere near the extent she did in the pretest (from 7 to 14 points on the potency scale) nor did she see it as denegrating as she did (from 5 to 16 points on the evaluation scale). "Death" was less potent at posttest (down to 16 from 20 points) and not as negatively evaluated (up to 15 from 6 points). In the pretest, Mrs. L. had seen death as "extremely unfair" and "extremely sad" because she had too many things to do before her death but in the posttest Mrs. L. felt she had put things in order and perspective in her life; she thought death was neither "happy" nor "sad" "fair" nor "unfair."

The concept "My Health" remained about the same on the potency dimension, but it was somewhat higher on the evaluation dimension because it

was no longer seen as "quite sad" in the posttest. "Religion" did not change at
all from pretest to posttest. Mrs. L. said she responded to the concept in
terms of formal religion, namely the Roman Catholic faith she was born into.
In this sense she saw little value in it for herself, although she could see it
providing solace to others. She did say that she was experiencing herself as
part of something much larger, more universal, and perhaps this was a kind
of religious experience. It was not only a reassuring feeling but she found
herself enjoying a new awareness of everything from simple daily activities
and pleasures without having to feel that somehow she had to make her mark
or make every moment count as she did in the old days. Each moment now
counted in its own right.

Other tests at the end of counseling showed changes, notably her morale
measures. She described herself as "very happy" in the posttest as compared
to "not too happy" in the pretest, and her Life Satisfaction Index score went
up to 17 from 7 at the pretest and 5 at the end of group counseling. She had
no completely negative responses on her posttest LSIA. She was not sure
whether she agreed or disagreed with three statements: "In spite of what
people say, the lot of the average man is getting worse, not better"; "My life
could be happier than it is now"; and "I am just as happy as when I was
younger." Mrs. L. said that she was very happy when her children were
preschoolers and her family was intact, so she was not sure whether she was
currently as happy as then.

Some of the most notable changes in the test scores came on Mrs. L.'s
responses to the functionalistic ethic and cognitive mastery items. Her locus
of control, on the other hand, changed very little. That measure remained
highly internal in locus, but less intensely so. For example, she changed her
response to the following alternative statements:

A. In the long run the bad things that happen to us are balanced by the good
   ones.
B. Most misfortunes are the result of lack of ability, ignorance, laziness, or
   all three.

In the pretest she was very sure she agreed with statement B. In the
posttest she was very clear that she disagreed with it. She said she was not so
sure about how true statement A was but she felt that statement B was much
further from the truth. Although her high internal locus of control was a
distinct asset in her treatment, it will be recalled that she was very upset
about perceived lack of control in certain areas as a result of her stroke. Her
cognitive mastery score was therefore quite low in the pretest. It had shifted
markedly by the end of extended counseling. For example, she dramatically
changed her response to the statement: "It is hard to feel good when there are
certain things in life I can no longer influence or change." In the pretest she
strongly agreed with this statement but in the posttest she strongly disagreed
with it. The same type of shift occurred in response to the statement: "I find

that I am not bothered by the fact that there are now many things in my life over which I have no control." Her pretest response to this statement was "strongly disagree" but in the posttest it was "agree." It was clear that she could view the reality of lesser control in certain areas of her life, particularly the physical, with greater equanimity at the end of extended counseling.

Because of her high achievement and performance orientation, alternative disputation of the functionalistic ethic was perhaps the most difficult area of counseling. Yet, even that value gave way, as it had to if she was going to accept more compassionate alternatives. Consequently, she made several sharp changes in her responses to certain functionalistic ethic statements. The most notable change was in response to the statement: "A person's worth does not depend on how good a citizen, parent, or worker he or she is, but simply that he or she is a human being." Mrs. L.'s response to this in the pretest was "strongly disagree," but in the posttest it was diametrically changed to "strongly agree."

The statement represents the essence of a value position which amounts to a basic goal in integrative counseling — the acceptance by the client as well as the counselor that the person has innate value as a human being without respect to performance. Acceptance of this position by Marie Laughlin meant that she could now be compassionate with herself as well as with others.

The quality of Mrs. L.'s relationships at the senior center were quite different at the end of extended counseling. Her approach to others was softer and she became more of a facilitator and enabler than an organizer and director in committee and other organizational work. She was also becoming well-liked as well as respected, and she was being sought out by others for advice and support with personal problems. At the same time, her relationships with others were becoming more mutual in nature. She no longer found it necessary to be the independent and dominant one in the relationship, and she found she could lean on others as she had not been able to in the past. However, she continued to be seen in the center as primarily a strong person who could be counted on for help and support when necessary. Thus, by the end of extended counseling there was no evidence of the impending despair she feared at the start of counseling, and the balance appeared to be tipped clearly in the direction of ego integrity.

CHAPTER SEVEN

Conclusions
and New Directions

Conclusions from Theory, Research, and Practice

The design of this book and the development of the integrative approach which it describes followed from certain salient points and findings in gerontological theory and research, outlined in Chapter 3. First is the developmental veiw of aging, which stresses the value of seeing developmental changes as adaptive to the needs and tasks of people in the last stage of life. Thus, concepts and findings from research about "increased interiority," "passive mastery," reminiscence, changes in covert aspects of personality, and continuity in overt aspects of personality were all incorporated into the principles and practices of the integrative approach.

A major contribution from gerontological theory are the social breakdown and social reconstruction syndromes of Kuypers and Bengtson (1973). The reconstruction syndrome is particularly valuable because it incorporates some concepts and elements central to the integrative approach: the self-concept, the locus of control concept, social system inputs (positive supports as well as negative labeling), and the importance of alternative values (in place of the functionalistic ethic) in aging.

Even the emphasis on cognitive approaches and techniques is consistent with much gerontological theory and research. First, because cognitive approaches deal with conscious content, they do not threaten certain unconscious defense mechanisms which serve an important adaptive function in many elderly persons (Busse and Pfeiffer, 1969). Second, there is evidence that of all the capacities of the individual (physical, social, behavioral; and so on) the cognitive capacities tend to remain intact longest (Troll, 1971). Also, there is considerable empirical evidence of the efficacy of cognitive approaches in the types of functional psychological problems the aged most often faced—namely, depression and anxiety (Beck, 1976).

In addition, the cognitive approach is insight-oriented, and since it emphasizes conscious processes in gaining insight it is well-adapted to the life review process and reminiscence. Because of this potential for insight, cognitive approaches have a distinct advantage over the purely behavioral approaches to treatment of the elderly. Finally, cognitive approaches are much better suited to questions of meaning, which are so central to the last stage of life.

All of these findings concerning human development in the later years of life and the efficacy of cognitive approaches in counseling and psychotherapy were adapted from existing theory and research and applied to the integrative approach. However, a number of new findings have emerged in the actual application of the integrative practice model over the past five years. One of these was the finding that a counselor can give "permission for increased interiority." This is clear in the case of Virginia Plummer (Chapter 6). She readily accepted and acted upon the idea that a person naturally becomes concerned with inner matters at a later time in life and that this is not at all abnormal or selfish. Obviously, there has to be a relationship of trust and respect between the client and the counselor for this permission to work. Nevertheless, it is an important idea to keep in mind in cases in which the client continues in a state of some distress as a result of resisting the inclination toward greater inner concern.

A second useful finding or concept is what I have called "retrospective generalization." As noted before, Beck (1976) has written about the cognitive error of generalization in depressogenic thinking, whereby the person generalizes from one negative event or behavior to many other unrelated events or behaviors. I found that when elderly persons are depressed in the present, they tend to generalize into the past. Thus, many or most relationships and events in their pasts are viewed negatively because of present depressogenic thinking, when in fact those things in the past were not really negative. The counselor should deal with this by demonstrating for the client the negative effects of generalizing in the present and then having the client apply this insight to the past. Then, as the present depression lets up, the client should be encouraged to reappraise events of the past from his/her present, more positive frame of mind.

Another finding or concept that is somewhat related to "retrospective generalization" is what I have called "contamination." One of the differences between this and retrospective generalization is that contamination can take place in the present as well as in the past. It is a misconception based on an all-or-nothing principle which is exemplified by Virginia Plummer's idea that *all* of her marriage had to be good or else *none* of it was any good. This particular error can cause a great deal of distress to those older persons who believe they have made a wrong or weak or cowardly decision in the past and therefore think everything related to that decision is bad or wrong or cowardly. This error overlooks the fact that much of life involves mistakes and moments of weakness, thoughtlessness, and so on, but that people frequently overcome these. To taint everything related to that mistake (in generalization even unrelated things are "tainted") is to make the error of contamination.

The counselor should handle the problem of contamination by identifying it as an irrational belief (iB) and disputing it in accordance with cognitive treatment techniques.

The fourth area in which some new findings and ideas emerged was in differential use of reminiscence. I have found that there are several ways of using reminiscence for the purposes of cognitive restructuring. One use, which is not totally new, is in reminding the client about past achievements and positive events in order to enhance self-concept and self-esteem. A second and quite different approach is to dispute retrospective generalizations as these occur in reminiscence. I have already mentioned retrospective generalization as a straightforward error of attribution about the past. In the context of the life review process, reminiscence may provide the material and evidence of that error, which can be disputed as it occurs.

A fifth idea, called "alternative disputation," is a form of disputation directed specifically at the functionalistic ethic, the evaluation of self by social role performances. This disputation is carried out by a number of techniques, including disidentification with the roles (Assagioli, 1965), bibliotherapy (Rubin, 1975), and disputation favoring the value of intrinsic worth of the person or of indicating accomplishment of the past as sufficient for positive self-evaluation.

These were some of the concepts and techniques developed directly from practice using the integrative approach. The process of operationalizing the integrative treatment model also led to some new ideas or concepts. One was the concept of "cognitive mastery," which augments the locus of control factor in that it represents the capacity to redefine cognitively one's relationship to the environment so that one can accept the *real* limitations of control over the environment. This concept was operationalized by the Cognitive Mastery Assessment Questionnaire in Appendix B.

At the same time, the functionalistic ethic and its nonfunctionalistic opposite were operationalized by the Functionalistic Ethic Assessment Questionnaire in Appendix C. The functionalistic ethic had not been spelled out by Kuypers and Bengtson when they included it in their model, so it had to be operationalized for the purposes of integrative practice. It is too early to tell how this measure of the ethic will correlate with other variables in the model, but it appears to be making sense to individual respondents, as was evident in the cases of Virginia Plummer and Marie Laughlin in Chapter 6.

Proposals for Further Development

A number of promising leads for future work in the aged were suggested by practice experiences with the integrative model. Some of the more promising ones were in the use of the group modality. Some rather dramatic changes occurred in the course of short-term group counseling using the integrative approach. This experience indicates that older persons can pick up the A-B-C and other structured cognitive approaches quite quickly and apply them quite accurately and successfully. I am convinced that the rather dramatic changes made in a short period of time were due to *peer* help, guided by the cognitive/integrative approaches. This suggests to me that an even shorter-term program—perhaps only four or five sessions for exposure and training—could enable the members to continue on alone as a mutual support and peer counseling group.

Little systematic work has been done with the peer group approach, but Waters, Fink, and White (1976) developed a peer group program that offered time-limited group counseling in seven two-hour sessions which involved a series of structured communication skills, values clarification exercises, and other activities that enhance the self-esteem of the participants. After the seven sessions the participants were encouraged to continue in less structured personal counseling and to enroll in a paraprofessional training program. About a third chose to continue in small group counseling. Those who took the training program then went on to be real assets in their senior center programs (Marie Laughlin illustrated this potential in the last chapter). They also got a great deal out of helping others, because such altruism certainly lends much meaning to an older person's life.

The relative success of this peer counseling approach is of course due to the fact that the older counselors frequently share the same life experiences as their clients, which speaks again to the viability of the androgogy principle. There is need for the elderly to be their own teachers and helpers, if only to counteract "a dangerous trend . . . toward . . . *gerontologocracy:* a situation in which their alleged knowledge would give power to the gerontologists: . . . a power to reduce the aged, once honored and listened to, to material for investigation" (Philibert, 1979:383).

It will be recalled that the desire for structure by the members of the integrative group described in Chapter 5 seemed to run counter to the androgogy idea. It seems that a structured, verbal, and active group technique is most successful in assisting aged individuals to find an interest in life and to focus on the present and future (Burnside, 1978). However, the desire for and use of structure does not preclude the self-help potential inherent in the androgogy principle. As Waters, Fink, and White (1976) found with their peer counseling groups in Detroit and as I have found with groups of older persons, the clients themselves are very capable of using the techniques and skills they learn in the earlier orientation sessions.

In developing an integrative peer counseling group, it would be best to find as group leaders older individuals who have already attained and clearly represent the ego integrity at which the integrative approach is aimed. They would not only make the most able and emotionally mature leaders but would provide the added dimension of a role model.

There is also a need for the demonstration of extended group counseling using the integrative approach, regardless of whether the group is led by a peer or a professional. The group described in Chapter 5 was short-term, but the gains made in the fifteen-week period suggest that extended group counseling would get further into questions concerning the meaning of the members' lives and related issues. The gains achieved were probably made because the members of that group had met many of their deficiency (D) needs in the course of group counseling and were beginning to wish to meet their being (B) needs (Maslow, 1968). According to Egan (1976), a group whose members are primarily interested in B needs is best called a "life-style group," because the questions they raise and discuss have to do with how one lives one's life and what gives life meaning. It would seem that an extended integrative group counseling experience with older persons would very much parallel Egan's lifestyle groups, but with some attention to the past as well as the present and the future.

One further point should be made about the group modality from the integrative perspective. I have found after trying it both ways that it is advisable to have one leader rather than co-leaders. The most cogent reasons for this have already been expressed by Haley (1976:16): "The use of a co-therapist is usually for the security of the clinician and not for the value to the client. Outcome studies do not indicate that cotherapy does better, and the cost is twice as much. A therapist working alone can develop and carry out ideas without having to delay to consult with a colleague." Single group leaders are preferred to co-leaders in certain cognitive therapies (Ellis, 1962), and I would add that the co-leader approach is somewhat at odds with the androgogy idea: the elderly clients will face two professional leaders or "experts."

A final proposal concerning the group modality with aging persons has to do with the potential value of combining the self-help with the mutual support function of groups. The clients in such a group engage in social action to remedy common social problems they face and at the same time provide emotional support for one another.

Implications for Aging in General

It is difficult if not impossible to observe and work with older persons who are struggling with the issue of integrity versus despair and the meaning of their lives and not wonder what all of this implies to those of us who are younger. There has to be something of value here beyond the purely professional, technical, and practice concerns of "applied gerontology," because the issues involved are so much larger. Gerontology, after all, is a branch of knowledge dealing with aging in general and not just the problems of the aged.

What, then, can the experience of integrative practice with older persons tell us about aging in general? It is my belief that older persons who have achieved ego integrity can show us a great deal not only about aging but about living in general. It is hard not to believe that those persons have adopted an approach to their lives, at least in their later years, which is somewhat different from the majority of us who are still heavily engaged in the socioeconomic system.

The issue of the functionalistic ethic posed by Kuypers and Bengtson in their social reconstruction syndrome is a crucial one, as is the value orientation toward living which Kluckhohn and Strodtbeck (1961) have called the "doing" orientation, which has the functionalistic ethic at its core. They contrasted this with a "being" orientation and a "being-in-becoming" orientation on the basis of their cross-cultural studies. Kluckhohn and Strodtbeck describe the "doing" orientation as follows:

> Its most distinctive feature is a demand for the kind of activity which results in accomplishments that are measurable by standards conceived to be external to the individual. That aspect of self-judgment or judgment of others which relates to the nature of activity is based mainly upon a measurable accomplishment achieved by acting upon persons, things, or situations. What does the individual do? What can he or will he accomplish? These are almost always the primary questions in the American's scale of appraisal of persons. "Getting things done" and "let's *do* something about it" are stock American phrases [1961].

The being orientation is characterized by the spontaneous expression in activity of impulses and desires within accepted cultural limitations. It is an emphasis on the "is-ness" of the personality. The being-in-becoming orientation shares with the being orientation an emphasis on what a person *is* rather than on what he can accomplish, but it also includes the concept of self-development. "The Being-in Becoming orientation emphasizes that kind of activity which has as its goal the development of all aspects of the self as an integrated whole" (Kluckhohn and Strodtbeck, 1961). This orientation is very much in line with Erikson's (1963) concept of "integrity" in old age, and it therefore represents a viable alternative to the functionalistic ethic within the social reconstruction model.

Spiegel (1971) did some further work with these value orientations by incorporating them into a somewhat larger conceptual scheme which is very instructive in terms of viewing the developmental changes in aging during the later years of life. He identified some crucial questions common to all human groups, along with the orientations relating to those questions (Spiegel, 1971:163). Three of them have particular bearing on developmental issues in aging, and they can be paraphrased as follows:

1. What is the preferred relation of man to nature (*man-nature* orientation)?
2. What is the preferred temporal focus of human life (*time* orientation)?
3. What is the preferred mode of human activity (*activity* orientation)?

It can be seen that the value orientations (being, being-becoming, and doing) which were identified by Kluckhohn and Strodtbeck are related to the third question concerning the preferred mode of human activity. Three alternative value orientations were identified by Spiegel for the first two questions, as well.

The alternative man-nature orientations to question 1 are: (1) subjugation to nature; (2) harmony with nature; and (3) mastery over nature. Spiegel notes that in the recent past Spanish-American culture in the American Southwest served as an example of subjugation to nature. The typical Spanish-American shepherd believed that there was little or nothing a man could do to save either his land or flocks when damaging storms occurred. He accepted the losses as inevitable. The same kind of fatalism was seen in Spanish-American attitudes toward death and illness.

The harmony-with-nature alternative, on the other hand, sees no real separation between man and nature. One is simply an extension of the other and they are both necessary parts of a whole. Spiegel notes that this would have been the dominant orientation in certain of the past centuries in Chinese society.

The mastery-over-nature alternative is characteristic of Americans who view natural forces as something to be subjugated and put to human use by blasting through mountains, building bridges, creating lakes, and so on. This makes for an orientation toward life that is one of overcoming obstacles.

The three alternative time orientations to question 2 are: (1) past; (2) present; and (3) future. The past time orientation was exemplified by traditional Chinese society, according to Spiegel. There is a primary emphasis on past time expressed in such practices as ancestor worship and the strong family tradition, and there is the attitude that nothing new happens in the present nor will it happen in the future.

For the present time orientation Spiegel again uses the Spanish-American example. He notes that the attitude in this orientation is one which emphasizes the value of the present because the future is vague and unpredictable and the past is just that—over and done with.

Finally, Spiegel notes that Americans more than most of the other peoples of the world place an emphasis on future time, which we tend to anticipate and plan for. We are seldom content with the present and do not value the ways of the past as good just because they are past. Consequently, we are a people who place a high value on change. In sum, then, modern American society demonstrates rather clear preferences for the value orientations of doing, mastery over nature, and future.

It should be informative to look at the appropriateness of each of these orientations for the older individual in American society. The fit between individual and culture is, after all, an important one for anyone, young or old. The dominant value orientations of American society do not make for a very good fit for the older person, as we have noted in different ways throughout this book. First, given the findings on locus of control measures, it is unlikely that older Americans feel that they have a great deal of control over nature or that they are totally masters of their own social fates. Their man-nature orientation has probably mellowed somewhat over time, and the harmony-with-nature orientation is probably more descriptive as well as more appropriate for them than is mastery over nature.

The time dimension presents some unique problems. Although the larger society is future-oriented in terms of planning for change in the future, the older individual does not have the luxury of time in which to plan. On the other hand, it is not good for an older person to live predominantly in the past. As Buhler (1968) has noted, the best psychological adjustments at any age seem to be associated with a present time orientation. Many of the gerontologists who have studied successful aging have noted that there is a great interest in the immediate and moment-to-moment experiences, a quality of "presentness" among those who age successfully.

The "doing" orientation has already been defined by Kuypers and Bengtson as problematic, and the being-in-becoming orientation seems to come closest to Erikson's conception of ego integrity. The being orientation, geared as it is to more impulsive and spontaneous activity, is generally associated with a present orientation, but it is usually also associated with fatalism and little conscious concern with meaning in life. Overall, then, the dominant values and orientations of American society do not provide a very good fit with those of the elderly. As Bellah (1976) has stated, "If Erik Erikson found that the mature personality expresses itself in both action and contemplation, then we might ask whether a culture that exclusively emphasizes action (or contemplation either, for that matter) can be a very healthy environment for human growth" (1976:71-72).

On the basis of my experience with persons who appear to have ego integrity, it seems that they do have a contemplative side to them. There does appear to be a certain introspection or interiority which is contemplative in nature and not simply self-absorbed.

Spiegel noted that the being-in-becoming type of orientation is very close to Fromm's (1941) "total integrated personality." Fromm recently developed some ideas about the functioning of the integrated personality in contemporary society which bear directly on the lifestyle of older persons who seem to possess ego integrity (Fromm, 1976). Fromm talks about two modes of existence, one of which is the "having" mode: "In the having mode of existence my relationship to the world is one of possessing and owning, one in which I want to make everybody and everything, including myself, my property" (1976:24).

The other mode he calls the "being" mode, but it is clearly based on his conception of the totally integrated personality, which represents the being-in-becoming orientation. This is clear when he equates the "being" mode with "the concept of *process, activity, and movement as an element in being* . . . the idea that being implies change, i.e., that being is *becoming*" (Fromm, 1976:25). Basically, what he is saying is that one mode (being) views life as a process while the other (having) views life as a substance, something that can be possessed.

It would seem to me that those older persons who view life as a process are in a better position to handle the various decrements and vicissitudes of old age than those who see life as a substance or a possession. From the perspective of patterns of aging discussed in Chapter 2, it is possible to see the being mode represented in the integrated personality, regardless of whether the person's pattern of aging was "reorganizer," "focused," or "disengaged." On the other hand, the "holding-on" pattern of aging, even though it was associated with high activity and life satisfaction levels, would be destined for considerable distress and despair when physical decrements take too great a toll. This pattern, of course, is characterized by a "having" orientation.

Now, many of these points about value orientations in old age verge on philosophy. The more I work with older persons the more I am convinced that what is most called for in this work is a *psychophilosophy*. Rubin (1975), who introduced this term, defines it as "a philosophy which has the power to change a person's psychology, or way of feeling and thinking about himself" (1975:181). Further, Rubin notes that we need a "psychophilosophy which strengthens us so as to be better able to both enjoy life here and now and to face the inevitable adversity we all meet from time to'time and must be ready to handle" (1975:134).

The integrative approach is intended to be such a psychophilosophy, and the key to the whole approach is *compassionate acceptance of self*—past, present, and future. This is quite the opposite of the doing orientation, whose "most distinguishing feature is a demand for the kind of activity which results in accomplishments that are measurable by standards conceived to be external to the acting individual. The aspect of self-judgment or judgment of others which relates to the nature of activity is based mainly upon a measurable accomplishment achieved by acting upon persons, things, or situations" (Spiegel, 1971:166).

There is one further step as far as the self is concerned in the last stage of life. Paradoxically, that is the loss of self in the process of what Peck (1968) described as ego transcendence. It is the highest value perspective in the hierarchy identified by Kohlberg (1973) in his research on moral development, and it is the outcome of the lifelong process of decentering which Piaget so valued. It is the perspective achieved by Marie Laughlin (Chapter 6) after her reading of *The Book* (Watts, 1966), and it includes the view or orientation which Spiegel describes as "the harmonious oneness of man and nature" (1973:164).

This paradox of the self was noted by Brandt (1980) in an article on recent developments in conceptions of the self in the field of psychology. He says, " 'The fact is,' Alan Watts wrote, 'that because no one thing or feature of this universe is separable from the whole, the only real You, or Self, is the whole.' The experience of wholeness, must therefore be the final goal of any attempt to understand the self" (Brandt, 1980:101).

It is essential that older persons be prepared for further, inevitable loss and adversity. However, this does not mean preparation in the sense of girding oneself for adversity, but in the sense of not hanging on to what they have, that is, of being in the present rather than trying to have or possess the present. The lesson to be learned from the aged with ego integrity is that the adversity and losses they have sustained have served to move them toward a more mellow and compassionate view of themselves and others. It is not that they have benefited from the pain of the losses they have suffered, but that they have learned that they cannot have what they cherish in a possessive sense, not even their egocentric self. They have moved closer to the being and away from the having orientation.

The ultimate goal, then, is essentially acceptance—acceptance of life as a process, rather than as a possession, in a larger scheme of things. However, self-acceptance comes before acceptance of one's life, and this is the underlying theme of the integrative approach.

Appendix A

Life Satisfaction Index –
Form A

Here are some statements about life in general that people feel differently about. Would you read each statement on the list, and if you agree with it, put a check mark in the space under "AGREE." If you do not agree with a statement, put a check mark in the space under "DISAGREE." If you are not sure one way or the other, put a check mark in the space under "?".
PLEASE BE SURE TO ANSWER EVERY QUESTION ON THE LIST.

	AGREE	DISAGREE	?
1. As I grow older, things seem better than I thought they would be.			
2. I have gotten more of the breaks in life than most of the people I know.			
3. This is the dreariest time of my life.			
4. I am just as happy as when I was younger.			
5. My life could be happier than it is now.			
6. These are the best years of my life.			
7. Most of the things I do are boring or monotonous.			
8. I expect some interesting and pleasant things to happen to me in the future.			
9. The things I do are as interesting to me as they ever were.			
10. I feel old and somewhat tired.			
11. I feel my age, but it does not bother me.			
12. As I look back on my life, I am fairly well satisfied.			
13. I would not change my past life even if I could.			

14. Compared to other people my age, I've made a lot of foolish decisions in my life. ___ ___ ___

15. Compared to other people my age, I make a good appearance. ___ ___ ___

16. I have made plans for things I'll be doing a month or a year from now. ___ ___ ___

17. When I think back over my life, I didn't get most of the important things I wanted. ___ ___ ___

18. Compared to other people, I get down in the dumps too often. ___ ___ ___

19. I've gotten pretty much what I expected out of life. ___ ___ ___

20. In spite of what people say, the lot of the average man is getting worse, not better. ___ ___ ___

Appendix B

The Cognitive Mastery Assessment Questionnaire

Instructions: Please circle the response (strongly agree, agree, disagree, etcetera) that comes closest to your opinion.

1. I find that I am not much bothered by the fact that there are now many things in my life over which I have no control.

    strongly agree   agree   disagree   strongly disagree

2. It is hard to feel good when there are certain things in life I can no longer influence or change.

    strongly agree   agree   disagree   strongly disagree

3. I feel very bad when there are things I want to have or want to change and am not able to do so.

    strongly agree   agree   disagree   strongly disagree

Scoring instructions: (SA = strongly agree, A = agree, D = disagree, SD = strongly disagree):
Question 1: SA = 4, A = 3, D = 2, SD = 1
Question 2: SA = 1, A = 2, D = 3, SD = 4
Question 3: SA = 1, A = 2, D = 3, SD = 4
Highest cognitive mastery score = 12
Lowest cognitive mastery score = 3

Appendix C

The Functionalistic Ethic Assessment Questionnaire

Instructions: Please circle the response (strongly agree, agree, disagree, etcetera) that comes closest to your opinion.

1. Unless I feel that I have accomplished or done something that other people value, I feel quite worthless.

    strongly agree   agree   disagree   strongly disagree

2. A person's worth does not depend on how good a citizen, parent, or worker he or she is, but simply that he or she is a human being.

    strongly agree   agree   disagree   strongly disagree

3. When you are no longer a contributing member of society by functioning in such roles as worker, parent, and so on, you can't really feel that you have any value as a person.

    strongly agree   agree   disagree   strongly disagree

4. A person isn't worth much when he or she is no longer able to carry on as a productive member of the community.

    strongly agree   agree   disagree   strongly disagree

Scoring instructions: (SA = strongly agree, A = agree, D = disagree, SD = strongly disagree):
Question 1: SA = 4, A = 3, D = 2, SD = 1
Question 2: SA = 1, A = 2, D = 3, SD = 4
Question 3: SA = 4, A = 3, D = 2, SD = 1
Question 4: SA = 4, A = 3, D = 2, SD = 1
Highest functionalistic ethic score = 16
Lowest functionalistic ethic score = 4

Appendix D

Daily Record of Dysfunctional Thoughts

Date	Situation Describe: 1. Actual event leading to unpleasant emotion, or 2. Stream of thoughts, day-dream, or recollection, leading to unpleasant emotion.	Emotion(s) 1. Specify sad/anxious/angry, etc. 2. Rate degree of emotion, 1–100.	Automatic Thought(s) 1. Write automatic thought(s) that preceded emotion(s). 2. Rate belief in automatic thought(s), 0–100%.	Rational Response 1. Write rational response to automatic thought(s). 2. Rate belief in rational response, 0–100.	Outcome 1. Re-rate belief in automatic thought(s), 0–100. 2. Specify and rate subsequent emotions, 1–100.

Explanation: When you experience an unpleasant emotion, note the situation that seemed to stimulate the emotion. (If the emotion occurred while you were thinking, daydreaming, etc., please note this.) Then note the automatic thought associated with the emotion. Record the degree to which you believe this thought: 0 = not at all; 100 = completely. In rating degree of emotion: 1 = a trace; 100 = the most intense possible.

References

ADAMS, B. Isolation, function, and beyond: American kinship in the 1960's. *Journal of Marriage and the Family*, 1970, 32, 575-597.

ADLER, A. *The practice and theory of individual psychology*. New York: Harcourt, 1927.

ADLER, A. *Social interest: A challenge to mankind*. New York: Capricon Books, 1964.

AMERICAN PSYCHIATRIC ASSOCIATION. *Diagnostic and statistical manual of mental disorders* (3rd ed). Washington, D.C.: American Psychiatric Association, 1980.

ASSAGIOLI, R. *Psychosynthesis: A manual of principles and techniques*. New York: Viking Press, 1965.

BATESON, G. *Steps to an ecology of mind*. New York: Ballantine, 1972.

BECK, A. T. *Cognitive therapy and the emotional disorders*. New York: International Universities Press, 1976.

BECK, A. T., and EMERY, G. *Cognitive therapy of anxiety and phobic disorders*. Philadelphia: Center for Cognitive Therapy, 1979.

BECK, A. T., and GREENBERG, R. L. *Coping with depression*. New York: Institute for Rational Living, 1974.

BECK, A. T., RUSH, A. J., SHAW, G. F., and EMERY, G. *Cognitive therapy of depression*. New York: Guilford Press, 1979.

BELLAH, R. N. The active life and the contemplative life. *Daedalus*, 1976, 105, 57-76.

BENGTSON, V. L. *The social psychology of aging*. Indianapolis: Bobbs-Merrill, 1973.

BERGIN, A. E., and LAMBERT, M. J. The evaluation of therapeutic outcomes. In S. L. Garfield and A. E. Bergin (eds.), *Handbook of psychotherapy and behavioral change* (2nd ed.). New York: Wiley, 1978.

BERNE, E. *The structure and dynamics of organizations and groups.* New York: Grove Press, 1963.

BERTSCHER, H. J., and MAPLE, F. F. *Creating groups.* Beverly Hills, CA: Sage Publications, 1977.

BINSWANGER, L. *Being-in-the-world: Selected papers of Ludwig Binswanger.* New York: Basic Books, 1963.

BIRREN, J. E. *The psychology of aging.* Englewood Cliffs, NJ: Prentice-Hall, 1964.

BLAU, Z. S. *Aging in a changing society* (2nd ed). New York: Franklin Watts, 1981.

BLENKNER, M. Social work and family relationships in later life with some thoughts on filial maturity. In E. Shanas and G. F. Streib (eds.), *Social structure and the family: Generational relations.* Englewood Cliffs, NJ: Prentice-Hall, 1965.

BLENKNER, M., BLOOM, M., and NIELSEN, M. A. A research and demonstration project of protective services. *Social Casework*, 1971, 52, 483-499.

BOSS, M. *Psychoanalysis and Daseinsanalysis.* New York: Basic Books, 1963.

BOWLBY, J. Process of mourning. *International Journal of Psychoanalysis*, 1961, 42, 317-340.

BRADLEY, R. H., and WEBB, R. Age-related differences in locus of control orientation in three behavior domains. *Human Development*, 1976, 19, 49-55.

BRANDT, A. Self-confrontations. *Psychology Today*, 1980, 14, 78-101.

BREARLEY, C. P. *Social work, aging and society.* London: Routledge and Kegan Paul, 1975.

BRUNER, J. On perceptual readiness. *Psychological Review*, 1957, 64, 123-52.

BUHLER, C. The course of human life as a psychological problem. *Human Development*, 1968, 11, 184-200.

BURNSIDE, I. M. *Working with the elderly: Group process and techniques.* Belmont, CA: Duxbury Press, 1978.

BUSSE, E. W., and PFEIFFER, E. (eds.). *Behavior and adaptation in late life.* Boston: Little, Brown, 1969.

BUTCHER, J. N., and KOSS, M. P. Research on brief and crisis-oriented therapies. In S. Garfield and A. Bergin (eds.), *Handbook of psychotherapy and behavior change: An empirical analysis* (2nd ed.). New York: Wiley, 1978.

BUTLER, J. M., and HAIGH, G. H. Changes in the relation between self-concepts and ideal concepts consequent upon client-centered counseling. In C. R. Rogers and R. F. Dymond (eds.), *Psychotherapy and personality change.* Chicago: University of Chicago Press, 1954.

BUTLER, R. N. The life review: An interpretation of reminiscence in the aged, *Psychiatry*, 1963, 26, 65-75.

BUTLER, R. N. Mental health and aging. *Geriatrics*, 1974, 29, 141-148.

BUTLER, R. N. Psychiatry and the elderly: An overview. *American Journal of Psychiatry*, 1975a, 132, 893-900.

BUTLER, R. N. *Why survive? Being old in america.* New York: Harper & Row, 1975b.

BUTLER, R. N., and LEWIS, M. I. *Aging and mental health.* St. Louis: C. V. Mosby Co., 1977.

CAMERON, B., DESAI, K. G., BAHADOR, D., and DREMEL, G. Temporality across the life span, *Journal of Aging and Human Development*, 1977-1978, 8, 229-259.

CANTRIL, H. Perception and interpersonal relations. *American Journal of Psychiatry*, 1957, 114, 119-126.

CAPLAN, G., and KILLILEA, M. (eds.). *Support systems and mutual help: Multidisciplinary explorations*. New York: Grune & Stratton, 1976.

CHOWN, S. M. Age and the rigidities. *Journal of Gerontology*, 1961, 16, 353-362.

CLARK, M., and ANDERSON, G. *Culture and aging*. Springfield, IL: Charles C. Thomas, 1967.

CLAYTON, V. Erikson's theory of human development as it applies to the aged: Wisdom as contradictive cognition. *Human Development*, 1975, 18, 119–128.

COMBS, A. W. A phenomenological approach to adjustment theory. *Journal of Abnormal and Social Psychology*, 1949, 44, 29-35.

COMBS, A. W., RICHARDS, A. C., and RICHARDS, F. *Perceptual psychology: A humanistic approach to the study of persons*. New York: Harper & Row, 1976.

COMBS, A. W., and SNYGG, D. *Individual behavior: A perceptual approach to behavior*. New York: Harper & Row, 1959.

CORMICAN, E. Task centered model for work with the aged. *Social Casework* 1977, 58, 490-494.

CRANDALL, R. L. *Gerontology: A behavioral science approach*. Reading, MA: Addison-Wesley, 1980.

CUMMING, E., and HENRY, W. *Growing old: The process of disengagement*, New York: Basic Books, 1961.

CUMMING, E. Further thoughts on the theory of disengagement, *International Social Science Journal*, 1963, 15, 377-393.

de BEAUVOIR, S. *The coming of age*. New York: Warner, 1973.

DINNAGE, R. The Piaget way. *The New York Review of Books*, 1978, 25, 18-25.

D'ZURILLA, T., and GOLDFRIED, M. Problem-soving and behavior modification. *Journal of Abnormal Psychology*, 1971, 78, 107-126.

EDWARDS, N., and KLEMMACK, L. Correlates of life satisfaction: A re-examination, *Journal of Gerontology*, 1973, 28, 497-502.

EGAN, G. *The skilled helper*. Monterey, CA: Brooks/Cole, 1975a.

EGAN, G. *Exercises in helping skills: A training manual to accompany "The skilled helper."* Monterey, CA: Brooks/Cole, 1975b.

EGAN, G. *Interpersonal living: A skills/contract approach to human relations training in groups*. Monterey, CA: Brooks/Cole, 1976.

ELLIS, A. *Reason and emotion in psychotherapy*. Secaucus, NJ: Citadel Press, 1962.

ELLIS, A. *Humanistic psychotherapy: The rational-emotive approach*. New York: McGraw-Hill, 1974.

ELLIS, A., and HARPER, R. A. *A new guide to rational living*. New York: Prentice-Hall, 1977.

EPSTEIN, L. *Helping people: The task-centered approach*. St. Louis: C. V. Mosby Co., 1980.

ERIKSON, E. *Childhood and society* (2nd ed.). New York: Norton, 1963.

ERIKSON, E. Dr. Borg's life cycle. *Daedalus*, 1976, 105, 1976.

FAIRWEATHER, G. W. *Social psychology in treating mental illness: An experimental approach*. New York: Wiley, 1964.

FRANK, J. *Persuasion and healing: A comparative study of psychotherapy*. New York: Schocken Books, 1974.

FRANKL, V. E. *Man's search for meaning: An introduction to logotherapy*. Boston: Beacon Press, 1959.

FRANKL, V. E. *The doctor and the soul*. New York: Knopf, 1965.

FRENKEL-BRUNSWICK, E. Adjustments and reorientation in the course of the life span. In R. G. Kuhlen and G. G. Thompson (eds.), *Psychological studies of human development*. New York: Appleton-Century-Crofts, 1963.

FRENKEL-BRUNSWICK, E. Personality theory and perception. In R. R. Blake and G. V. Ramsey (eds.), *Perception: An approach to personality*. New York: Ronald Press, 1951.

FRIEDMAN, I. Phenomenal, ideal, and projected conceptions of self. *Journal of Abnormal and Social Psychology*, 1955, 51, 611-615.

FROMM, E. *Escape from freedom*. New York: Holt, Rinehart, and Winston, 1941.

FROMM, E. *To have or to be?* New York: Harper & Row, 1976.

GAITZ, C. M., and SCOTT, J. Age and the measurement of mental health. *Journal of Health and Social Behavior*, 1972, 13, 55-67.

GAMBRILL, E. D. *Behavior modification: Handbook of assessment intervention and evaluation*. San Francisco: Jossey-Bass, 1977.

GARTNER, A. and RIESMANN, F. *Self-help in the human services*. San Francisco: Jossey-Bass, 1977.

GIAMBRA, L., Daydreaming about the past: The time setting of spontaneous thought intrusions. *The Gerontologist*, 1977, 17, 35-38.

GIORGI, A. *Psychology as a human science: A phenomenologically based approach*. New York: Harper & Row, 1970.

GOLDBERG, E. M., MORTIMER, A., and WILLIAMS, B. T. *Helping the aged*. London: Allen and Unwin, 1970.

GOLDFARB, A. I. Minor adjustments of the aged. In S. Arieti and E. B. Brody (eds.), *American Handbook of Psychiatry*, vol. 3. New York: Basic Books, 1974.

GOLDFRIED, M. R., DECENTECO, E. T., and WEINBERG, L. Systematic rational restructuring as a self-control technique. *Behavior Therapy*, 1974, 5, 247-254.

GOLDSTEIN, A. P. *Structured learning therapy*. New York: Academic Press, 1973.

GOLDSTEIN, A. P., HELLER, K., and SECHREST, L. B. *Psychotherapy and the psychology of behavioral change*. New York: Wiley, 1969.

GREENBERG, L., FATULA, B., HAMEISTER, D. R., and HICKEY, T. *Communication skills for the gerontological practitioner*. University Park, PA: Pennsylvania State University, 1976.

GREENWALD, H. *Direct decision therapy*. San Diego, CA: EdITS, 1973.

GURIN, G., VEROFF, J., and FELD, S. *Americans view their mental health*. New York: Basic Books, 1960.

HALEY, J. *Problem-solving therapy*. New York: Harper & Row, 1976.

HARTMAN, A. Diagrammatic assessment of family relationships. *Social Casework*, 1978, 59, 465-476.

HARTMANN, H. *Essays on ego psychology*. New York: International Universities Press, 1964.

HAVIGHURST, R. J. Personality and patterns of aging. *The Gerontologist*, 1968, 8, 20-23.

HAVIGHURST, R. J., and GLASSER, R. An exploratory study of reminiscence. *Journal of Gerontology*, 1972, 27, 245-253.

HENDRICKS, J. (ed.). *Being and becoming old*. New York: Baywood Publishing Co., 1980.

HENDRICKS, J. and HENDRICKS, C. T. *Dimensions of aging: Readings*. Cambridge, MA: Winthrop Publishers, 1979.

HEPWORTH, D. H. Early removal of resistance in task-centered casework. *Social work*, 1979, 24, 317-324.

HESS, B. B. Self-help among the aged. *Social Policy*, 1976, 7, 55-62.

HILGARD, E. R. Human motives and the concept of self. *American Psychologist*, 1949, 4, 374-382.

HOLON, S. D., and SHAW, B. F. Group cognitive therapy for depressed patients. In A. T. Beck et al. (eds.), *Cognitive therapy of depression*. New York: Guilford Press, 1979.

HUSSERL, E. [*Ideas*]. London: Allen & Unwin, 1958. (Originally published, 1913.)

HUSSERL, E. [*Cartesian mediatations*]. The Hague: Nyhoff, 1968. (Originally published, 1931.)

HUSSERL, E. (*The crisis of the European sciences and transcendental phenomenology*). Evanston: Northwestern University Press, 1970. (Originally published, 1936.)

INGALLS, JOHN D. *A trainer's guide to androgogy*, Washington, D.C.: U.S. Department of Health, Education, and Welfare: Social and Rehabilitation Service, May, 1973.

JUNG, C. G. *Two essays on analytical psychology*. New York: Dodd, Mead, 1928.

KEEN, E. A. *A primer in phenomenological psychology*. New York: Holt, Rinehart & Winston, 1975.

KELLER, J. F., CROAKE, J. W., and BROOKING, J. Y. Effects of a program in rational thinking on anxieties in older persons. *Journal of Counseling Psychology*, 1975, 22, 54-57.

KELLY, G. A. *The theory of personal constructs: A theory of personality* (2 vols). New York: Norton, 1955.

KERLINGER, F. N. *Foundations of behavioral research* (2nd ed.). New York: Holt, Rinehart & Winston, 1973.

KERLINGER, F. N. *Behavioral research: A conceptual approach*. New York: Holt, Rinehart & Winston, 1979.

KIVETT, V. R., WATSON, J., and BUSCH, J. The relative importance of physical, psychological and social variables to locus of control orientation in middle age. *Journal of Gerontology*, 1977, 32, 203-210.

KLUCKHOHN, F. R., and STRODTBECK, F. L. *Variations in value orientations*. Evanston IL: Row Peterson, 1961.

KOHLBERG, L. Continuities in childhood and adult moral development revisited. In P. Boltes and W. K. Schaie (eds.), *Life span developmental psychology: Personality and socialization*. New York: Academic Press, 1973.

KUYPERS, J. A. Internal locus of control, ego functioning, and personality characteristics in old age. *Gerontologist*, 1972, 27, 168-173.

KUYPERS, J. A., and BENGTSON, V. L. Competence and social breakdown: A social-psychological view of aging. *Human Development*, 1973, 16, 37-49.

LAING, R. D. *The divided self: An existential study in sanity and madness*. New York: Tavistock, 1960.

LAWTON, M. P. Morale: What are we measuring? In C. N. Nydegger (ed.), *Measuring morale: A guide to effective assessment*. Washington, D.C.: Gerontological Society, 1977.

LAZARUS, A. A. *Behavior therapy and beyond*. New York: McGraw-Hill, 1971.

LECKY, P. *Self-consistency: A theory of personality*, 1945. Edited and interpreted by F. C. Thorne. Hamden, Conn.: Shoe String, 1961.

LEMON, B., BENGTSON, V., and PETERSON, J. An exploration of the activity theory of aging: Activity types and life satisfaction among in-movers to a retirement community. *Journal of Gerontology*, 1972, 27, 511-523.

LEMON, E. C., and GOLDSTEIN, S. The use of time limits in planned brief casework. *Social Casework*, 1978, 59, 588-596.

LEWIN, K. *Field theory in social science: Selected theoretical papers*, D. Cartwright (ed.). New York: Harper, 1951.

LEWIS, C. N. Reminiscing and self-concept in old age. *Journal of Gerontology*, 1971, 26, 240-243.

LEWIS, M. I., and BUTLER, R. N. Life review therapy: Putting memories to work in individual and group psychotherapy. *Geriatrics*, 1974, 29, 165–169, 172–173.

LIEBERMAN, M. A. Social and psychological determinants of adaptation. In J. Hendricks, ed., *Being and becoming old*. Farmingdale, NY: Baywood Publishing Co., 1980.

LINN, M., and HUNTER, K. Perception of age in the elderly. *Journal of Gerontology*, 1979, 34, 46-52.

LITWAK, E. Geographic mobility and extended family cohesion. *American Sociological Review*, 1960, 25, 383-394.

LOPATA, H. Support systems of elderly urbanites: Chicago of the 1970's. *The Gerontologist*, 1975, 15, 35-41.

LOWENTHAL, M. F. Intentionality: Toward a framework for the study of adaptation in adulthood. In J. Hendricks, ed., *Being and becoming old*. Farmingdale, NY: Baywood Publishing Co., 1980.

LOWY, L. The group in social work with the aged. *Social Work*, 1962, 7, 43-50.

LOWY, L. *Social work with the aging: The challenge and promise of the later years*. New York: Harper & Row, 1979.

MAAS, H., and KUYPERS, J. *From 30 to 70*. San Francisco: Jossey-Bass, 1974.

MADDOX, G. L. Some correlates of differences in self-assessment of health status among the elderly. *Journal of Gerontology*, 1962, 17, 180-185.

MADDOX, G. L. Persistence of life style among the elderly: A longitudinal study of patterns of social activity in relation to life satisfaction. In B. L. Neugarten (ed.), *Middle age and aging: A reader in social psychology*. Chicago: University of Chicago Press, 1968.

MADDOX, G. L. Fact and artifact: Evidence bearing on disengagement theory. In E. Palmore (ed.)., *Normal aging*. Durham, NC: Duke University Press, 1970.

MADDOX, G. L., and DOUGLASS, E. B. Self-assessment of health: A longitudinal study of elderly subjects. *Journal of Health and Social Behavior*, 1973, 14, 87-93.

MAHONEY, M. J. *Cognition and behavior modification*. Cambridge, MA: Ballinger, 1974.

MAHONEY, M. J., and ARNKOFF, D. Cognitive and self-control therapies. In S. L. Garfield and A. E. Bergin (eds.), *Handbook of psychotherapy and behavior change* (2nd ed.). New York: Wiley, 1978.

MARKUS, H. The self in thought and memory. In D. M. Wegner and R. R. Vallacher (eds.), *The self in social psychology*. New York: Oxford University Press, 1980.

MASLOW, A. H. *Toward a psychology of being* (2nd ed.). New York: Van Nostrand-Reinhold, 1968.

MASLOW, A. *Motivation and personality*. New York: Harper & Row, 1970.

MAY, R. *Man's search for himself*. New York: Norton, 1953.

MAYER, J. E., and Timms, N. *The client speaks: Working class impressions of casework*. New York: Atherton Press, 1970.

MEICHENBAUM, D. *Cognitive behavior modification: An integrative approach*. New York: Plenum Press, 1977.

MERLEAU-PONTY, M. *The phenomenology of perception*. London: Routledge and Kegan Paul, 1962.

MERLEAU-PONTY, M. [*The structure of behavior*]. Boston: Beacon Press, 1963. (Originally published, 1942.)

MERLEAU-PONTY, M. *The primacy of perception*. Evanston: Northwestern University Press, 1964.

MIDDLEMAN, R. R. Returning group process to group work. *Social Work with Groups*, 1978, 1, 15-26.

MILLER, S. J. The dilemma of the aging leisure participants. In A. Rose and W. Peterson (eds.), *Older people and their social worlds*. Philadelphia: F. A. Davis, 1965.

MISCHEL, W. *Introduction to personality* (2nd ed.). New York: Holt, Rinehart & Winston, 1976.

MISCHEL, W. On the future of personality measurement. *American Psychologist*, 1977, 32, 246-254.

NEISSER, U. *Cognition and reality: Principles and implications of cognitive psychology*. San Francisco: Freeman, 1976.

NEUGARTEN, B. L. *Personality in middle and late life*. New York: Atherton, 1964.

NEUGARTEN, B. L. Personality changes in the aged. *Catholic Psychological Record*, 1965, 3, 9-17.

NEUGARTEN, B. L. Continuities and discontinuities of psychological issues into adult life, *Human Development*, 1969, 12, 121-130.

NEUGARTEN, B. L. The future and the young-old. *Gerontologist*, 1975, 15, 4-9.

NEUGARTEN, B. L., HAVIGHURST, R. J., and TOBIN, S. S. The measurement of life satisfaction. *Journal of Gerontology*, 1961, 16, 134-143.

NAUGARTEN, B. L., HAVIGHURST, R. J., and TOBIN, S. S. Personality and patterns of aging. In B. L. Neugarten (ed)., *Middle age and aging*. Chicago: University of Chicago Press, 1968.

NEWMAN, B. M., and NEWMAN, P. R. Later adulthood: A developmental stage. In J. Hendricks and C. D. Hendricks (eds.), *Dimensions of aging: A reader*. Cambridge, MA: Winthrop Publishers, 1979.

NORTHEN, H. *Social work with groups*. New York: Columbia University Press, 1969.

NOUWEN, H. J. M., and GAFFNEY, W. J. *Aging: The fulfillment of life*. Garden City, NY: Image Books, 1976.

OSGOOD, C. E., SUCI, G. J., and TANNENBAUM, P. H. *The measurement of meaning*. Urbana, IL: University of Illinois Press, 1957.

PALMORE, E., and LUIKART, C. Health and social factors related to life satisfaction. *Journal of Health and Social Behavior*, 1972, 13, 68-80.

PECK, R. C. Psychological developments in the second half of life. In B. L. Neugarten (ed.), *Middle age and aging: A reader in social psychology*. Chicago: University of Chicago Press, 1968.

PENKE, W. E. Age changes and correlations of internal–external locus of control. *Psychological Reports*, 1969, 25, 859.

PETTY, B., MOELLER, T., and CAMPBELL, R. Support groups for elderly persons in the community. *The Gerontologist*, 1976, 16, 522-528.

PFEIFFER, E. *Multidimensional functional assessment: The OARS methodology*. Durham, NC: Center for the Study of Aging and Human Development, 1975.

PFEIFFER, E. Psychopathology and social pathology. In J. Birren and K. W. Schiae (eds.), *Handbook of the psychology of aging*. New York: Litton Educ. Pub. 1977.

PHILIBERT, M. Philosophical approach to gerontology. In J. Hendricks and C. D. Hendricks (eds.), *Dimensions of aging: Readings*. Cambridge, MA: Winthrop Publishers, 1979.

PHILLIPS, B. A role theory approach to adjustment in old age. *American Sociological Review*, 1957, 22, 212-217.

PHILLIPS, E. L., and WIENER, D. N. *Short-term psychotherapy and structured behavior change*. New York: McGraw-Hill, 1966.

PIAGET, J. *The construction of reality in the child*. New York: Basic Books, 1954.

PINKUS, A. Toward a developmental view of aging for social work. *Social Work*, 1967, 3, 33-41.

PRELINGER, E., and ZIMET, C. N. *An ego-psychological approach to character assessment*. New York: Free Press, 1964.

RABKIN, R. *Strategic psychotherapy: Brief and symptomatic treatment*. New York: Basic Books, 1977.

RAIMY, V. *Misunderstandings of the self*. San Francisco: Jossey-Bass, 1975.

RATHJEN, D. P., RATHJEN, E. D., and HINIKER, A. A cognitive analysis of social performance. In J. P. Foreyt and D. P. Rathjen (eds.), *Cognitive behavior therapy: Research and application*. New York: Plenum Press, 1978.

REICHARD, S., LIVSON, F., and PETERSON, P. G. *Aging and personality*. New York: Wiley, 1962.

REID, W. J. *The task-centered system*. New York: Columbia University Press, 1978.

REID, W. J., and EPSTEIN, L. *Task-centered casework*. New York: Columbia University Press, 1972.

REID, W. J., and EPSTEIN, L. (eds.). *Task centered practice*. New York: Columbia University Press, 1977.

REID, W. J., and SHYNE, A. *Brief and extended casework*. New York: Columbia University Press, 1969.

RIEGEL, K. *Personality theory and aging*. In J. E. Birren (ed.), *Handbook of aging and the individual*. Chicago: University of Chicago Press, 1958.

RILEY, M., and FONER, A. *Aging and Society*, vol. 1, New York: Russell Sage Foundation, 1968.

ROBINSON, J. P., and SHAVER, P. R. *Measures of social psychological attitudes* (rev. ed.). Ann Arbor, MI: Institute for Social Research, 1973.

ROGERS, C. R. *Client-centered therapy*. Boston: Houghton Mifflin, 1965.

ROGERS, C. R. The necessary and sufficient conditions of therapeutic personality change. *Journal of Consulting Psychology*, 1957, 21, 95-103.

ROKEACH, M. *The nature of human values.* New York: Free Press, 1973.

RONCH, J., and MAIZLER, J. Individual psychotherapy with the institutionalized aged. *American Journal of Orthopsychiatry*, 1977, 47, 275-283.

ROSE, A. The subculture of the aging: A topic for sociological research, *The Gerontologist*, 1962, 2, 123-127.

ROSE, S. D. (ed.). *A casebook in group therapy: A behavioral-cognitive approach.* Englewood Cliffs, NJ: Prentice-Hall, 1980.

ROSE, S. D. *Group therapy: A behavioral approach.* Englewood Cliffs, NJ: Prentice-Hall, 1977.

ROSENBERG, M. *Conceiving the self.* New York: Basic Books, 1979.

Rosow, I. *Socialization to old age.* Berkeley: University of California, 1973.

ROTTER, J. B. Generalized expectancies for internal versus external control of reinforcement. *Psychological Monographs*, 1966, 80, all of issue #609.

RUBIN, T. I. *Compassion and self-hate.* New York: McKay, 1975.

RYFF, C. D. and BALTES, P. B. Value transition and adult development in women: the instrumentality-terminality sequence hypothesis. *Developmental Psychology*, 1976, 12, 567-568.

SALZMAN, C., and SHADER, R. Clinical evaluation of depression in the elderly. In A. Raskin and L. Jarvik (eds.), *Psychiatric symptoms and cognitive loss in the elderly.* Washington, D.C.: Hemisphere Publishing, 1979.

SCHAIE, K. W., and LABOUVIE-VIEF, G. Generational versus ontogenetic components of change in adult cognitive behavior: A fourteen-year cross-sequential study. *Developmental Psychology*, 1974, 34, 146-158.

SHANAS, E., TOWNSEND, P., WEDDERBURN, D., FRIIS, H., MIHOJ, P., and STEHOUWER, J. *Old people in three industrial societies.* New York: Atherton Press, 1968.

SHAW, M. *Group dynamics: The psychology of small group behavior.* New York: McGraw-Hill, 1976.

SHERMAN, E. A cognitive approach to direct practice with the aging. *Journal of Gerontological Social Work* 1979, 2, 43-53.

SHERMAN, E., and NEWMAN, E. The meaning of cherished personal possessions for the elderly. *Journal of Aging and Human Development*, 1977, 8, 181-192.

SHERMAN, E., NEWMAN, E., and NELSON, A. Patterns of age integration in public housing and the incidence and fears of crime among elderly tenants. In J. Goldsmith and S. S. Goldsmith (eds.), *Crime and the elderly.* Lexington, MA: Lexington Books, 1976.

SILL, J. S. Disengagement reconsidered: Awareness of finitude. *The Gerontologist*, 1980, 20, 457-462.

SIMOS, B. C. Adult children and their aging parents. *Social Work*, 1973, 18, 78-85.

SIPORIN, M. Situational assessment and intervention, *Social Casework*, 1972, 53, 91-109.

SMITH, S. A. Natural systems and the elderly: An unrecognized resource. Model Project Grant through the Older Americans Act (Title III) under the auspices of the Oregon State Program on Aging and the School of Social Work, Portland State University, Portland, Oregon, 1975.

SNYGG, D. The need for a phenomenological system of psychology. *Psychological Review*, 141, 48, 404-424.

SPIEGEL, J. *Transactions: The interplay between individual, family and society*, John

Papajohn (ed.). New York: Science House, 1971.

STREIB, G. J. Are the aged a minority group? In A. W. Gouldner and S. M. Miller (eds.), *Applied sociology*. New York: Free Press, 1965.

SZASZ, T. S. *The ethics of psychoanalysis*. New York: Dell Publishing, 1965.

TISSUE, T. Another look at self-rated health among the elderly. *Journal of Gerontology*, 1972, 27, 91-94.

TOSELAND, R. Group problem solving with the elderly. In S. D. Rose (ed.), *A casebook in group therapy*. Englewood Cliffs, NJ: Prentice-Hall, 1980.

TOSELAND, R., and ROSE, S. D. Evaluating social skills training for older adults in groups. *Social Work Research and Abstracts*, 1978, 14, 25-33.

TOSELAND, R., SHERMAN, E., and BLIVEN, S. *The comparative effectiveness of two group work approaches to the development of mutual support groups among the elderly*. In press.

TRECKER, H. B. *Social group work: Principles and practices*. New York: Association Press, 1972.

TROLL, L. The family of later life: A decade of review. *Journal of Marriage and the Family*, 1971, 33, 263-290.

TRUAX, C. B., and CARKHUFF, R. R. *Toward effective counseling and psychotherapy*. Chicago: Aldine, 1967.

U. S. Department of Health, Education, and Welfare, *Facts about older Americans*, Washington, D.C.: U.S. Government Printing Office, 1976.

VALECHA, G. K. Construct validation of internal–external locus of control as measured by an abbreviated 11-item I-E Scale. Unpublished doctoral dissertation, Ohio State University, 1972.

WATERS, E., FINK, S., and WHITE, B. Peer group counseling for older people. *Educational Gerontology*, 1976, 1, 157-170.

WATTS, A. W. *The book: On the taboo against knowing who you are*. New York: Collier Books, 1966.

WEGNER, D. M., and VALLACHER, R. R. (eds.). *The self in social psychology*. New York: Oxford University Press, 1980.

WEINER, M. B., BROK, A. J., and SNADOWSKY, A. M. *Working with the aged: Practical approaches in the institution and community*. Englewood Cliffs, NJ: Prentice-Hall, 1978.

WILLIAMS, R. H. Styles of life and successful aging. In R. H. Williams, C. Tibbitts, and W. Donahue (eds.), *Processes of aging*. New York: Atherton, 1963.

WILLIAMS, R. H., and WIRTHS, C. *Lives through the years*. New York: Atherton, 1965.

WOLBERG, L. R. *The techniques of psychotherapy* (2nd ed.). New York: Greene and Stratton, 1967.

WYLIE, R. C. *The self-concept: A review of methodological considerations and measuring instruments*. (rev. ed.), vol. 1. Lincoln, NB: University of Nebraska Press, 1974.

YALOM, I. D. *The theory and practice of group psychotherapy* (2nd ed.). New York: Basic Books, 1975.

ZARIT, S. H. *Aging and mental disorders: Psychological approaches to assessment and treatment*. New York: Free Press, 1980.

ZUSMAN, J. Some explanations of the changing appearance of psychotic patients: Antecedents of the social breakdown syndrome concept. *The Milbank Memorial Fund Quarterly*, 1966, 64, 363-394.

Index